VIKING VOYAGER

AN ICELANDIC MEMOIR

SVERRIR SIGURDSSON WITH VERONICA LI

W0006833

TABLE OF CONTENTS

PART ONE

ICELANDIC ROOTS

CHAPTER 1

THE SEA

My maternal grandfather, Þorkell Magnússon, was the captain of a fishing vessel called *Gyða*. In early April 1910, he and his seven-man crew, including his eldest son, set sail from Bíldudalur, a small town in northwest Iceland. Their destination was the rich fishing grounds beyond the fjord. April was the beginning of the fishing season, which lasted until September. These were the "mild" months. In

Gyða at Bíldudalur

reality, the weather was often stormy and below freezing, pushing both the boat and men to the limit of their endurance. Three weeks later, on April 23, *Gyða* headed for home, her hull laden with cod, the valuable cash fish many fishermen had died for. Nearing their home fjord, the men's hearts must have lifted. A hot meal, a warm bed, and the family's embrace were within a day's reach.

That night, a furious northerly gale pounded the region with snow and sleet, whipping the sea into a deadly cauldron of crashing waves. All hands would have scrambled on deck to wrestle with the wind, jibing and tacking to keep the gusts from capsizing the boat. The battle went on all night. The next morning, *Gyða* was still upright and staggering closer to home. Einar, my grandfather's neighbor and a former crew member, attested to seeing her from shore during a visit to his parents' farm on the outer reaches of Arnarfjörður (Eagle Fjord). The wind was still howling, pummeling the boat from left and right. But Einar was confident the boat could hold herself together. After all, *Gyða* was a sturdy oceangoing vessel, one of the first to be built in Iceland with state-of-the art technology. In just a few more hours, she would reach the safety of the harbor.

The next day, Einar found berth on a vessel that took him home to Bíldudalur. As his ship sailed into the harbor, he looked out for *Gyða*. He knew she was no longer out in the fjord, for he had sailed the length of it and hadn't seen another ship. The only place *Gyða* could be was home, at Bíldudalur. He scanned the half-dozen ships docked in the harbor. To his dismay, *Gyða* wasn't among them. With a sinking feeling, he knew what must have happened. The fjord had swallowed *Gyð*a and her crew.

In the spring of 1954, I sailed from Reykjavík on the coastal vessel *Esja* to Bíldurdalur, my grandfather's hometown. The sea was mirror calm as the ship's powerful twin diesel engines propelled her into Arnarfjörður, the scene of *Gyð*a's disappearance. This fjord was notorious for squalls that could come up without warning. But that day, it welcomed me and the other 170 passengers with a gentle embrace. The water was a sparkling blue satin cut from the same fabric as the sky. My fifteen-year-old self stood near her bow, marveling at the panorama of steep, snow-flecked mountains that rose abruptly out of the sea. Looking down, I was mesmerized by the thousands of jellyfish pulsating out of the way of *Esja*'s knife-like bow.

A year earlier, a shrimp trawler combing the bottom of the outer reaches of Arnarfjördur had hauled in a huge pole. Forensic analysis determined that this had been the mast of *Gyða*. The town decided to erect a monument, using the mast as the centerpiece. I was one of the relatives of those who perished on *Gyða* to attend the unveiling of the memorial. My mother and I, together with other family members, went to pay respects to *Gyða*'s skipper and her crew.

I tell this story sixty years later from my home in Virginia, across the Potomac River from the U.S. capital. I am now in my eighties, retired and carefree, with nothing better to do than pamper my grandchildren and tell them stories of my life. But they are too young to fully appreciate them, so I write them down for the time when they reach my age, when they are retired and carefree and want to record their own stories. As they search their memory, an eerie feeling that their lives aren't just the sum of their own experiences will haunt them. Strands of other people's memory will swirl in their heads, speaking in voices some of which they recognize and others not. They will find out life is a relay, every leg a continuation of the previous one. To understand themselves, they have to understand those who have gone before them.

I was born on February 5, 1939, in Reykjavík, in the hallway of Landspítalinn (the National Hospital) because of an overflow that night. I arrived at that time and place because of the confluence of the voyages my parents, grandparents, and all the previous generations had taken. My parents named me Þórólfur Sverrir Sigurðsson. The last is my patronymic surname, which identifies me as the son of Sigurður, my father's given name. Þórólfur (Þ is pronounced "th," as in thunder), means "Thor's wolf," and Sverrir means "swordsman," both names of the Viking era. For some reason, my parents always addressed me as Sverrir, perhaps because it rolls off the tongue more easily. In any case, the Viking brand is forever stamped on my forehead.

From an early age, I knew I would go on a voyage of my own, but I had never dreamed of reaching such distant shores as the Middle East, Africa, the Asia-Pacific region, and America. These travels have given me a great sense of fulfillment, but they are insignificant compared with the miraculous progress my people have made within my lifetime. I have the satisfaction of seeing my country thrive during the renaissance born of the most destructive war in human history, and rise from being one of the poorest nations in Europe to one of the most prosperous. There were many occasions in our thousand-year history when volcanic eruption, disease, and prolonged winters drove our tiny nation to the verge of extinction. We survived, though barely. Thanks to the new postwar order, we made a quantum leap, joining the ranks of the world's advanced nations in a matter of decades. During this time, our population swelled from 120,000 to 350,000, and many a survey named us one of the happiest people in the world.

But I don't want to forget the hardships. My ancestors' endurance is my strength, in the same way Icelandic winters have seeped into my veins and inoculated me from the cold. My American friends poke fun at me for running around in shorts when they're shivering in jackets. So, I start my story by dwelling on the hardships—the sinking of *Gyða* and the loss of two family members that fateful day. My grandfather was forty-five at the time. His oldest son, Magnús, eighteen, was the mate. A merciful turn of fate spared his second son, Ólafur (Óli), who was fourteen. He had been fishing alongside the men since the age of ten, but that spring, he had to stay behind to complete his school-leaving certificate; otherwise he would have been on board *Gyða* too.

My grandmother, Ingibjörg Sigurðardóttir, became a widow at forty-two. She had four surviving children, ranging from sixteen to an eighteen-month-old, my mother. *Gyða*'s disappearance shattered my grandmother's life. In one fell swoop, she was transformed from managing a relatively well-off household in a prosperous town to a destitute widow

with four children to feed. The two breadwinners were gone, and there was no insurance or other source of income to ensure the family's future.

To put the tragedy in a broader perspective, the loss of eight men out of a total of 270 residents in the town of Bíldudalur represented almost 3 percent of the population. And this wasn't all. A couple of months later, the fishing boat *Industri*, from the adjacent town, disappeared in a gale. The crew of ten included Einar, the last man to see *Gyða,* and his thirteen-year-old son. The ship had left the nearby town of Ísafjörður and was headed for Patreksfjörður, immediately south of Bíldudalur. She never arrived. The families mourned, the town mourned, and life limped on until the next tragedy.

Today it is hard to imagine an Icelandic fisherman's life at the turn of the twentieth century. Crammed into a boat with eight or nine other men, he suffered backbreaking work in the face of wind, rain, snow and ice for weeks on end. My grandfather didn't live long enough to write his memoirs, but in this day and age, the world's archives are at my fingertips through the Internet. Two websites proved to be most useful: one contains the Icelandic censuses of 1703 through 1920, and the other stores every newspaper and magazine article published in the Icelandic language, including those published in Canada in the 1800s. I went online for information on *Gyða*. One link led to another, and it came to my attention that the Icelandic National Library had interviewed my uncle Óli for a cultural heritage project. I emailed the librarian, who promptly replied that Óli's granddaughter had digitized the cassette tapes. I clicked on one of the attached files, and there was my late uncle Óli speaking to me in his gravelly voice.

I could almost see him—a garrulous man with a big nose red from sniffing snuff—sitting in my childhood home, gesturing and regaling me with his seafaring stories. My poor Uncle Óli, who lost his father and brother at an early age, knew he should have gone down with them. What survivor's guilt he must have suffered. As if one tragedy wasn't enough, fate dealt him another blow when his wife died prematurely of illness, leaving him a widower at forty-nine with a teenage daughter to raise. Once in a while, when life became unbearable, he would hide somewhere and drink himself into oblivion. My mother would fret until he reappeared a week or so later. Despite all his hardships, he lived to ninety-one.

In the interviews, conducted over three days, he describes life on board a fishing vessel. Having spent three seasons aboard *Gyða* as a child sailor from 1907 to 1909, and later as crew on several other ships, he has plenty to tell. His material fills five hours of tapes.

For obvious reasons, I was most interested in Uncle Óli's accounts of *Gyða*. She was a sturdy vessel designed to sail the turbulent and fish-abundant currents of the North Atlantic. Óli estimates her to be twelve to fourteen tons. Knowledgeable sources in Iceland call her a Gaff Cutter and estimate that she would have been forty feet in length, about the size of a modern city bus. As we can see in the photo, there wasn't a whole lot of elbow space for eight men to live and work in. Indeed, Óli describes the cramped living conditions on board *Gyða* in the interviews. The forecastle, the forward part of the ship below the deck, was used as living quarters and could accommodate only four beds. The eight men took turns to sleep. As a child, and a "half-earner," Óli was last in line for everything. One night, he was so tired he didn't care that all the bunks were occupied. He crawled into bed with someone already in it and folded himself into a sliver of space. The next morning, he woke up bleary-eyed after a restless night of contorting his body. The cook, noticing his yawning, put something under his nose and told him to sniff it. He did, and his eyes popped wide open. What he inhaled was snuff—pulverized tobacco packed with nicotine. Ever since that day, a pouch of snuff and a large red handkerchief into which he loudly blew his nose became part and parcel of Óli's persona.

Being the skipper's son earned him no privileges. On the contrary, a father's discipline was harsher than a skipper's, as this incident proved: "Once, Papa called me to him," Óli says. "But I was so busy catching fish, I didn't go to him immediately. He grabbed a fish and whacked me on the cheek with it."

On the topic of personal hygiene, the interviewer suggests that perhaps he used a frayed bit of rope to clean himself. Óli's chuckling reply is, "Oh no. As long as you have a left hand and there's plenty of seawater around, you didn't need anything else." He also talks about lice infestation, a collective problem, for if one man had it, everyone on board would be scratching too. The interviewer discreetly avoids asking for the itchy details.

Once the ship reached a fishing ground, the workday didn't end with darkness, for the sun barely sets in the summer in this part of the world. The end of the day was whenever you dropped from fatigue. After a few hours of sleep, your work began again. Mealtime was the only break, and it consisted of fish and potatoes, or potatoes and fish. On holidays, such as Easter, the men were treated to lamb.

Fishing was by hook and line, usually with herring as bait. But when the fish was plentiful, all that was needed was a hook to snag the catch. Fishermen with this special talent were in high demand, and they didn't catch just any fish. To be worth their wage, they had to haul in cod, which would be salted and exported as *bacalao*. All other fish was "trashfish" and was eaten aboard by the crew, used as bait, or thrown back into the sea. A fisherman marked each cod he caught by making a distinct cut on one of its fins. At the end of the trip, each person's catch would be added up. The tally would determine the share of the proceeds for each crew member and the ship's owner.

Another trove of information I discovered was a logbook left behind by *Gyða*'s first captain, Veturliði Ólafur Bjarnason. His family had saved it for posterity and made it available online. The log, which records every detail of *Gyða*'s voyages in 1900, ten years before she foundered, gives us a flavor of life on a fishing boat of that era. The moment a boat left harbor, she wouldn't dock again unless somebody was seriously injured, the catch needed to be unloaded, provisions needed to be replenished, or a storm blew it back. Otherwise they would work through the season with hardly any time off. In one log entry, the captain writes, "On April 28, the ship returned to the fjord to replenish her water supply (two barrels). Stormy weather forced the boat to anchor overnight." It was a lucky break for the crew—their first day off since the start of the trip almost three weeks earlier.

The log is typically terse and dry, recording the weather, the catch, and the ship's location, which ranged from Breiðafjörður Bay in the south to the Polar Circle in the north. The entries for one trip, however, were unusually exciting. On May 18, *Gyða* set sail for Látraröst, the treacherous but fish-rich clash of ocean currents off the westernmost tip of Iceland. The crew returned to Bíldudalur on May 31 to unload the fish. A few days later, they left harbor again, but *Gyða* ran aground. The usually clipped log uses a few more words to explain the incident. Referring to himself in third person, the skipper lays the blame on himself: "As the flu was rampant on shore, the skipper stupidly decided to drink strong camphor-laced liquor, rendering him seriously drunk as now is common knowledge."

Since there was nothing to do until the tide rose to lift the stranded boat, most of the crew went home on a dinghy. The skipper and a couple of others remained on board, and according to the log, "nothing further, good or bad, happened this day." The next day, June 3, was Whitsunday, so the crew took a day off. On June 4, the weather was too still for sailing, but a departing steamship hauled *Gyða* out into the fjord. By her departure, three men had come down with the flu, and a fourth would join them by the time they reached the fishing grounds. Despite good weather and an abundance of fish, the lines were idle because all but the skipper and one crew member were in bed, delirious with fever. When the skipper finally succumbed to the flu, some of the other patients had recovered sufficiently to execute the sailing chores. On June 10, the crew was still weak but well enough to resume fishing. However, the bait, herring, had gone bad because the ice had melted while they were ill. *Gyða* returned to Bíldudalur on June 15 to replenish the herring. She made four more trips that season, returning to Bíldudalur in September to enjoy a well-earned winter vacation.

Understandably, Icelanders have a healthy respect for the sea. We fear its dangers, but we also know it can be a powerful ally. The sea is the highway that can lead us to treasures beyond our imagination, as our ancestors have shown. We have a word for stupid, *heimskur*, which literally means "homebody." Anyone who stays home is dumb. Only by traveling far and wide can one gain fame and fortune and make something of oneself.

The first settlers came to Iceland some 1,100 years ago from Norway, where people lived in villages along the many fjords. A fjord is a deep, long valley of water carved by a glacier millions of years ago. During medieval times, the best way for these villagers to travel was by sea. Necessity compelled them to build better boats and hone their seafaring skills to an unsurpassed level. In the eighth century, these Norse sailors ventured on their brave new ships to what is now called the British Isles. From that point, there was no stopping them. They plowed on in their ships and riverboats to Russia, the Middle East, Central Asia, and North Africa. Some sailed west and landed in North America. The first white child in America was born of Icelandic parents in what is now Newfoundland, shortly after the year 1000 AD.

This Nordic expansion was the beginning of the Viking era. How that name came about is up for debate. Some say it is derived from the word *vík*, which means creek or small inlet, while others say it refers to a long sea journey. These Vikings came from what is now known as Norway, Sweden, Denmark, and Iceland.

The reputation of the Viking varies, depending on whose side you're on. When my son Steinn was nine years old and attending a British-run school in Africa, he came home rather distraught one day. "Dad," he said. "The Vikings I'm learning about in school are horrible guys. But the Vikings I learned about in Iceland are good guys." I had to explain to him the role of perspective in historical interpretations.

To the people of Scotland and Ireland, the Vikings were villains who raped and pillaged up and down the coast. In Iceland, however, children are taught that Vikings were heroes who sailed to distant lands in search of adventure and trade. The truth probably lies somewhere in between. No question about it: the Vikings plundered, raped and abducted women from the British Isles. My family tree includes an Irish princess named

Melkorka, daughter of King Mýrkjartan. Around a thousand years ago, my forefathers kidnapped her and brought her to Iceland, where she spent the rest of her life, never to see her homeland again. Yes, the Vikings were brutes, but they also contributed to the development of commerce, transport, and cultural exchanges throughout Europe and beyond. They established trading posts, which later became vibrant cities, such as Dublin in Ireland and York in England.

I feel that my youth in Iceland was really a preparation for my own voyage. I left home at nineteen to pursue a plan that had all the elements of a Viking exploit: going overseas to improve my fortune (without the pillaging and raping) and returning home after accomplishing my goals. However, the winds refused to cooperate and kept blowing me offshore. The pull of my roots is strong, though—no matter how long I live abroad. My cosmopolitan lifestyle in the U.S., which I thoroughly enjoy, has the ironic effect of bringing me back to my origins. Perhaps it is because as a nation of 350,000, at last count, Icelanders must either cling to their heritage or cease to exist. I visit Iceland every other year. During these trips, I sometimes go to my parents' hometowns to pay my respects. Unlike their childhood when the sea was virtually the only connector between communities, a ring road now encircles the country. My parents began their lives on opposite ends of the island and under very different circumstances, which I believe explains why their outlooks were poles apart. But their difference didn't prevent them from sharing the same dream. Through hard work and the courage to seize the day, they contributed to the Icelandic Miracle and paved the way for my journey.

CHAPTER 2

BÍLDUDALUR: MY MOTHER'S HOME

Bíldudalur sits on the narrow shores of an ocean cove carved by ancient glaciers. Towering over the settlement is a sheer-faced plateau created millions of years ago by volcanoes. Sheltered by a mountain called Bíldudalsfjall, the deep-water cove provides a natural harbor, the reason for the town's existence. It is no more than a sprinkle of quaint houses around a center called Crossroads, where the two main streets meet. Until the 1950s, connection with the surrounding settlements was exclusively by sea or foot. To walk from one town to the next, one had to climb up the highland, hike across it, and scramble down another escarpment. A one-way trip took days. The surrounding mountains also cast a permanent shadow over the town for some ten weeks in winter, meaning the sun is never visible during this period. Sometime in late January, the sun's brows peek above the mountains, and the village breaks into joyous celebration. Young and old congregate for the *sólarkaffi*, which started out as a sedate afternoon of coffee and cake but gradually evolved into a jubilant evening of music, dancing, and carousing.

Bíldudalur in the foreground with Arnarfjörður (Eagle Fjord) on the right.
Courtesy of Mats Wibe Lund.

When I was a child living in Reykjavík, certain behaviors of my mother's always alerted me to the advent of *sólarkaffi*. Although the sun in Reykjavík never completely disappears for weeks, as in Bíldudalur, this minor detail didn't affect my mother's attitude. And she wasn't the only one. An association of the Bíldudalur diaspora in Reykjavík rented a hall every January for their *sólarkaffi*. The week before the event, my mother would go to the hair salon, iron her special red dress, and call up her friends to see who was going. Dad would dutifully escort her to the event, and she would return beaming as though the sun shone out of her. This was the highlight of her year, more than Christmas, New Year or any birthday. Although she had left her hometown at eighteen and lived sixty-some years in Reykjavík until her death, her heart never left Bíldudalur. To my mother, Bíldudalur was heaven on earth. Colored by her rosy reminiscences, and reinforced by my own delightful childhood visits to the town, I have always shared her bias. But it wasn't until researching my roots that I realized the full extent of the greatness of this little town.

When my grandparents moved there in the early 1890s, Bíldudalur was already a boom town. This may sound like an odd description of a fishing community of two hundred seventy souls in the northwest corner of Iceland. But the term "boom town" is entirely appropriate if you compare it with a decade earlier, when the total population of the place was twenty-eight, and their only source of living was a desolate farmstead that ran a sometimes-active trading post.

For several hundred years, Iceland's trade had been strictly controlled by Denmark, its colonial master. The island came under foreign control in 1262, when the population of about 50,000 was caught in a spate of bloody clan wars. In desperation, the chieftains turned to their former homeland, Norway, for help. They agreed to pay taxes to the King of Norway in return for a guarantee of peace and order. In other words, Iceland gave up its sovereignty to become a vassal state of Norway. About a hundred years later, when Norway and Denmark entered a union, Iceland changed hands and eventually became a Danish territory.

Since the early 1600s, Iceland had been a province within the Kingdom of Denmark. Its capital was Copenhagen, not Reykjavík. The Danish government appointed a Danish company to monopolize Iceland's exports and imports. This meant that Icelanders couldn't trade with anyone else in the world. This Danish company sent agents, usually Danes, to oversee the licensed trading posts in Iceland. Bíldudalur was one of them.

Trade with Denmark was in the form of barter. For example, one cow was worth two hundred forty fish. The Danish company dictated the terms of trade, and it was, of course, in its interest to mark down the value of Icelandic imports and send low quality goods to Iceland. This grossly unfair exchange was simple highway robbery, and it was inflicted on a people who were already living hand-to-mouth.

Terrible weather and deadly epidemics, such as smallpox, exacerbated the nation's wretchedness. Then in 1783, Iceland experienced a calamitous volcanic eruption that caused one of the largest lava flows in human history. The poisonous gases and ashes killed most of the livestock in the country, resulting in widespread famine. Some Danes proposed sending food to Iceland; others even suggested resettling the entire Icelandic population of 80,000 in Denmark. In the end, however, the words didn't translate into deed. The Danish government stood by while its Icelandic subjects starved to death. An estimated quarter of the population perished.

When life became unbearable, Icelanders took matters into their own hands. Smuggling became rampant. In a country with so much access to the sea, Danish authorities were hard-pressed to stop these illegal activities. From ships that plied their wares along the coast, English and French merchants conducted trade with their local accomplices.

One smuggling magnate was Ólafur Thorlacius, an Icelander with a Latinized last name, a then fashionable practice for the elite. He bought the trading post in Bíldudalur—no more than a dilapidated shed on a farm—and revitalized it. He violated his trading authority by exporting cod directly to Spain, using his ship *Bildahl*. Because of the enormous Spanish appetite for salted cod or *bacalao*, he became one of the richest men in Iceland. But, in 1815, he accidentally stepped in front of a carriage in Copenhagen and was killed. After his death, Bíldudalur's fortunes declined, until the 1890s when a man with a vision brought the defunct trading post back to life and built it into a town. His name was Pétur Thorsteinsson, founder of the town of Bíldudalur and one of the trailblazers of modern fishing in Iceland. Without him, my family's fortunes and those of many others would have been very different.

Whenever my mother got together with her hometown friends, the name Pétur Thorsteinsson would be invoked so many times that one would think he was their patron saint. As a child, I thought he was part of the family because of the intimate way my mother talked about him. She gave me the impression that she had dined regularly with Thorsteinsson and listened to his plans for improving the lot of his fellow townsmen. But I now realize

this couldn't have happened; she was only a baby when he left Bíldudalur to divert his energies to a new business venture in Reykjavík.

Pétur Thorsteinsson's achievements are a rags-to-riches story. He was born in 1854, an out-of-wedlock son of a rich merchant and a maid. To cover up the illicit liaison, his father sent him to a foster home in a distant county when he was three—just old enough to be separated from his mother. At seventeen he started working as a shop assistant at a trading post immediately south of Bíldudalur. At twenty-six, after a decade of learning the ropes of commerce on the job, he was ready to move into the big league: the risky-but-lucrative business of fishing and fish trading. Around that time, he married an Icelandic woman from a wealthy family. Almost certainly with the help of his well-heeled father-in-law, he purchased the trading post at Bíldudalur.

Soon after settling at Bíldudalur, Thorsteinsson began transforming the place into a company town. The beginning was rocky. When he arrived, commerce at the place had virtually ceased. To further aggravate matters, the winter of 1880–1881 was an unrivaled monster that locked Iceland in the grip of sea ice that was solid all the way to the North Pole. Polar bears traipsed across the frozen highway for an Icelandic tour. Some also ferried over on the abundant ice floes. There were sixty-three sightings of polar bears that year, instead of the normal one or none. The hungry visitors devoured livestock and terrorized humans. The ice kept its grip until June. When the thaw finally came, it was too late for the thousands of livestock that had died of starvation. That year, many Icelanders gave up their struggle against nature and moved to North America.

Commerce froze too, and Thorsteinson's business teetered on bankruptcy. He loaded all his fish on his only vessel, the twenty-four-ton sailing cutter, *Pilot*. Braving the icebergs, he set sail for an extended voyage of six weeks to Copenhagen with his wife and pretty much everything he owned. During that winter in Copenhagen, he sold his cargo and used the profits to purchase a consignment of goods to take back to Bíldudalur. Most importantly, he entered into partnership with two Danish merchants, thus infusing his enterprise with much-needed capital. He certainly didn't dawdle away his time in Denmark.

Thorsteinsson returned to Bíldudalur pumped up with money and energy. For the next two decades, he whipped up a frenzy of investment activities. By the turn of the century, Thorsteinsson's enterprise owned ten fishing and cargo vessels; *Gyða* was one of them. The company built a quay with equipment to load and unload oceangoing vessels—the first in Iceland. To put this achievement into context, Reykavík didn't have the facilities to service oceangoing vessels until 1915. Thorsteinsson was at least ten years ahead of the rest of the country. His company also installed a railway link to the fish-processing plants; constructed numerous residential and commercial buildings, all served by a piped-water system; and built roads to connect the town with the surrounding areas. Thorsteinsson, who is sometimes hailed as the "King of Bíldudalur," even established a currency, or scrip, usable only in his stores.

Through an odd twist of fate, I came into contact with members of Pétur Thorsteinsson's family almost a century later. In the mid-1990s, I had occasion to entertain at my home a senior official of the Icelandic embassy in the U.S. His wife and three young children were there, too. He was a tall, handsome young man whose name happened to be Pétur Thorsteinsson. I didn't think anything of it since both names, especially the first, were common. He noticed an old pendulum clock hanging on my living room wall and asked me about it. I told him my aunt had bought it at the bankruptcy proceedings of a company in Bíldudalur. The discussion went on, and I mentioned that my grandfather had been the skipper on a ship called *Gyða*. At that point he said, "My great-grandfather built *Gyða*." It was then that I made the connection.

My grandfather, Afi

My grandparents moved to Bíldudalur during its heyday. My grandfather (*Afi* in Icelandic) lost his father at the age of eight and his mother at thirteen. The family farm, which was a fairly substantial one based on fishing, changed hands. Afi stayed on as an orphaned farmhand. When he was sixteen, census data shows him as a resident at the farm and also in Bíldudalur. He probably spent time in both places, depending on the seasonal workload.

My grandmother, or *Amma*, was named Ingibjörg Siguðardóttir. She was the daughter of a sheep farmer. In those days, a sheep farmer in Iceland was a poor man. He and his family subsisted on whatever he could wring out of the harsh environment. The growing season was only three months, and the land was often scraggy mountainsides or water-logged bogs. He would count himself lucky if he could grow enough grass to keep his livestock alive through win-

My grandmother, Amma

ter. Sheep farmers and their families were always one storm away from starvation.

When my grandparents got married, they became hired hands at a farm close to Bíldudalur. But they weren't willing to accept their lot. The burgeoning town beckoned. They packed up their belongings, probably a few clothes and their individual *askur*—a wooden bowl, often intricately carved, which a farmhand took to the farmer's wife at mealtimes to receive his portion of food. He then retreated to his built-in bed to eat. Afterwards, he cleaned the bowl by letting the dogs lick it. Life on the farm was a study in minimalism. My grandparents had nothing to lose, for they had already lost what they cherished most—their firstborn, Jón, who died in infancy. They probably didn't look back as they walked away from the farm and headed for the big town.

Afi seized with both hands every opportunity to advance himself. He apprenticed with a nearby jewelry master and graduated in March of 1891 as a certified goldsmith. In those days, every respectable Icelandic woman wore a national dress to church or to festive occasions that featured elaborate silver and gold filigree, called *víravirki*, stitched into the bodice of the dress. The picture shows my grandmother's national costume with ornamentation made by my grandfather.

Amma's bodice

Afi also sought gold in another form—cod. He worked as a seaman from April to September. And of course, he wasn't contented to stay at the bottom of the ladder. According to Uncle Óli, my grandfather apprenticed with a local skipper to learn the use of navigation tools, such as a compass and octant, to triangulate a ship's position. In addition, Afi took a maritime course in Ísafjörður, the largest town in the region, and passed a junior seafaring examination. All these endeavors got him to where he wanted to be—a skipper controlling an oceangoing sailing vessel.

Afi held a third job repairing ships in the winter. As a farmhand, he had acquired carpentry skills by making and mending farm implements. In Bíldudalur, he applied these skills to ship repairs.

The tide of my grandparents' fortunes turned quickly. A few years after they arrived in Bíldudalur, they could afford to build a modest house, which they named *Jaðar,* meaning "edge," because it was located on the edge of town. The babies tumbled out in two batches. Magnús, Halla, and Óli were born within five years (1891–1896), and after a decade's gap, Erlingur and my mother, Hallfríður, came along. Aside from their firstborn, another infant died shortly after birth. The others survived infancy and grew to be strong and healthy.

While Afi was at sea, sometimes for weeks in a row, Amma was a homemaker. She made sure her children went through primary school and were proficient in reading and writing by the time they graduated. Literacy was compulsory in Icelandic society, as every child had to go through catechism studies in preparation for confirmation. Although Icelanders weren't particularly devout churchgoers, confirmation was a rite of passage for every fourteen-year-old. Because of this, the literacy rate in Iceland has always been high. Amma also worked in fish processing during the fishing season, as did the other womenfolk in the town.

Thus after twenty years of steadfast labor, my grandparents had achieved everything they could hope for. But in one day, the sea swallowed it all, together with *Gyða*.

After the tragedy, life became harsh for Amma. To add insult to injury, she was subjected to an inquiry by the local judge. He conducted an evaluation of Amma's ability to fend for herself and her family after her husband's death. I don't know what the process involved and what its intention was. Thankfully, the judge concluded that Amma was a sensible, capable woman and issued her a "license letter" permitting her to handle her own affairs. She and her younger sister, Bjarnfríður, who was thirty at the time, became the breadwinners and guardians of the four surviving children. Bjarnfríður stayed with the family for several years until she married Jón Jónsson Maron, a businessman in Bíldudalur.

The women's income from fish processing, and the boys' from fishing (although Erlingur had to wait until his tenth birthday), kept the family afloat. In addition, Amma and her sister augmented their income by mending and washing clothes, helped by the teenaged Halla, who was an excellent seamstress. My mother, the baby in the family, often bemoaned the stink of the laundry sent to their home. The worst were the pants that the patrons wanted pressed only, not washed. She said the steam wafting out of the trousers reeked of urine.

Life was tough, although from my mother's descriptions, her hometown sounded like paradise. She described a place where grownups were kind, and children under ten met and played all day. In the winter, they skated on the pond. They also skied downhill on barrel staves tied to their shoes. In summer, life revolved around the delights of the seashore—fishing, collecting shells, boating, stone-skipping, or just watching the crabs and other sea creatures scrabbling on the beach.

For as long as childhood lasted, the children of Bíldudalur, poor or rich, had a great time. However, childhood in those parts lasted only ten years; after that, a child became part of the workforce. The girls, aside from looking after their younger siblings, processed fish while the boys went to sea.

Amma struggled for a number of years. Even as her children were growing up and contributing to the family income, her life didn't get any easier. Bíldudalur was on the decline, and by 1914, the parent company of the town's fishing fleet, of which Thorsteinsson was part owner, had gone bankrupt. He had moved to Copenhagen, probably for his children's education, and his partners' stewardship was no match to his. Then in 1916, after the First World War broke out, Iceland became isolated from the rest of the world and suffered a significant drop in its living standards. The country's treasury became highly indebted and food was scarce. Bíldudalur wallowed in a deep recession during this period.

Prospects of a better livelihood for Amma were bleak. Óli left Bíldudalur in 1916 at age twenty-one to study seafaring in Reykjavík. On graduation from the Seafaring Institute of Iceland, he obtained the title of "helmsman." After that, he went to sea but never rose above the level of deckhand on oceangoing trawlers. He eventually left the sea and became the owner-operator of a truck. By the mid-1920s, my grandmother was facing a momentous decision. Her two youngest children—my mother and Erlingur—were at the point of make or break. One was in her late teens and the other his early twenties, and both were bright and ambitious. If they didn't leave then, their future would be limited to the stagnant waters of Bíldudalur. At her children's prodding, Amma sold *Jaðar* and moved her family to Reykjavík in 1927.

CHAPTER 3

BÖÐVARSDALUR: MY FATHER'S HOME

My first and only trip to Böðvarsdalur, the farm where my father was born, was in the summer of 2000, at the ripe age of sixty-one. I thought it was about time I paid my respects to this branch of the family, although I didn't expect to meet anyone at the abandoned farm. Since Dad's parents died before my birth, I didn't have the close ties with this side of the family that I did with my mother's. I set off from Reykjavík in a rental sedan and drove on the ring highway to the northeast end of the island. My father's spirit must have smiled on me, for the weather was unusually nice, which made the three-day drive very pleasant. From the highway, I veered off along a smaller road to the town of Vopnafjörður. After that, the tires of my car crackled on a narrow gravel road alongside the fjord. As my father had described, Böðvarsdalur appeared shortly after a wide turn toward a mountain pass called Hellisheiði. I eased down the access track, careful not to damage the rental car. But a huge gash on the rugged dirt path blocked my way. Nothing less than a tractor could get across. I got out and walked the rest of the way, about a kilometer.

Böðvarsdalur is an ancient farm on the remotest corner of Iceland. Located on a fjord called Vopnafjörður in the northeast, it was mentioned in the Icelandic Sagas as the venue of a battle fought around 1000 AD. This means the farm has existed for at least a thousand years and was, at one point, among the most substantive in the area. Aside from the land, it also bordered the bountiful sea. My family acquired it in 1751. From time to time, more than one family would share the farm. Although Böðvarsdalur was considered prosperous, this prosperity was tenuous and easily disrupted by the whims of Mother Nature. An 1886 feature article in the Canadian newspaper *Lögberg-Heimskringla*, which serves the Icelandic diaspora in Canada, told this heroic tale of devastation and salvation.

During the exceptionally difficult winter of 1880-1881, which featured heavy snows and an iceberg-filled fjord, the livestock at Böðvarsdalur had to be fed exclusively on hay, rather than a mixture of grazing and hay as was customary during most winters. Late in the winter of 1881, Runólfur, who was then an old man in poor health, foresaw a shortage of hay later in the spring and asked for assistance from farmers in the Jökulsárdalur valley on the south-east side of the mountain above the farm. Through the vagaries of the weather, the farmers in Jökulsárdalur had experienced a relatively mild winter, with the result that they had hay to spare. They responded well to Runólfur's request, and sheltered, fed and grazed his sheep at their farms. Assuming that the cold weather was over, they sent the sheep back in early May of 1881. But shortly thereafter the weather in Böðvarsdalur again took a turn for the worse. Local snowstorms covered the farm in four feet of wet snow, which then froze into a solid sheet of ice that lasted well into June. Grazing the livestock was out of the question, and even travelling on foot or skis on this sheet of ice was well-nigh impossible. By the time the neighbouring farmers discovered the plight of the Böðvarsdalur farm, its people and animals were half-starved to death. A concerted rescue action by the neighbours in Jökulsárdalur involved crossing the snow and ice-covered Hellisheiði mountain pass on foot and skis, breaking the ice cover, tamping down the snow, and then herding the starving sheep back across the pass. To keep the weak sheep moving, the rescuers fed them hay from sacks that they carried on their backs. During the crossing they emptied the sacks at short intervals to entice the sheep to keep moving. Unable to cope with all the livestock in one trip, the rescuers then backtracked and repeated this trek across the mountain pass to rescue the remaining cattle, horses and sheep. At the end of the bleak-looking adventure, the neighbours managed to save both the people and the livestock on their twin three-day treks across the mountains.

My grandfather, Runólfur Hannesson, born in Böðvarsdalur in 1867, was the nephew of his namesake in the above story.

My grandfather, Runólfur (left), my father (center), and Uncle Hannes (right) at Böðvarsdalur around 1930.

As I approached the farm, a painting sprang to life: the old farmhouse was the same as the one in the oil painting in my parents' living room, an image I had looked at every day for the first nineteen years of my life. The house was a wooden two-story building, clad in corrugated iron, which was the standard weatherproofing material in Iceland in the early twentieth century. When Dad was growing up, the livestock lived on the ground level. Their body heat (and odor) rose up to warm the upper floor, the abode of the family. The rest of the lot was a patch of earth where only grass grew, and children—plenty of children.

My grandfather married Kristbjörg Pétursdóttir, my grandmother, and they were blessed with nine children. Dad, named Sigurður, was the eighth, the oldest being a girl named Lára, followed by eight brothers. They were the envy of the neighbors, for males could do heavy work. The sixth boy was given to a childless couple on the next farm. He was named Sveinn after his foster father and knew no parents other than his adoptive parents. Such adoptions were a common practice in Iceland through the ages. Farmers took in other people's children either out of their own desire for descendants or charity to destitute families.

A large family also meant many mouths to feed. Most of the farm's operations were for subsistence. According to Dad, the family raised a couple of hundred sheep for meat and wool. When a lamb was slaughtered, nothing was wasted—the head, stomach, intestines, kidneys, and liver all made for good eating. One traditional delicacy was black pudding—blood and barley wrapped in cow's stomach and pickled in whey, the sour, watery byproduct of cheese production. They also kept a cow or two for milk, butter, and cheese. The rest of the farm's resources depended on nature's gifts: fish, eider eggs, seagulls and other wild birds, and the occasional beached whale. Food preservation was by smoking, salting, drying, or pickling in whey.

The farm made some cash income from eiderdown and wool. Both were lightweight and could be easily transported for sale in the nearby town, Vopnafjörður. There were no roads, so horses and rowboats were the only means of transportation.

Dad and his brothers sometimes went fishing on a rowboat. The family consumed whatever they caught, even sharks, always with hook and line. Nowadays, shark meat has become a famous—or notorious—national delicacy that is all the rage among tourists. You either love it or hate it, but the only way to find out is to try it. This gourmet food is called *hákarl,* Icelandic for shark. The preparation requires a year-long process to get rid of the poison in the Greenland shark, the prevalent species in these waters. Its meat is loaded with urea and a chemical called trimethylamine oxide, which acts like anti-freeze. The first people to nosh on a Greenland shark must have had quite a surprise. They probably stumbled around wondering why they felt as if they had guzzled a bottle of aquavit. Extreme drunkenness is the effect of this poison, and death when ingested in larger quantities. But where there's a will, there's a way. Somebody, or more like a number of bodies, through trial and error and a lot of persistence, concocted an elaborate treatment to get rid of the toxins. After catching the shark, you cut it up and bury the chunks in soil for several months. You then hang the meat to dry for another several months. The result is a soft, fermented whitish meat. When people ask me what *hákarl* tastes like, I say, "Imagine blue cheese marinated in ammonia." Which is why it is served cut into tiny cubes. You eat it with a toothpick and wash it down with a shot of *brennivín* ("burned wine").

To get to the site of the fishing activities, I scrambled down the bank to a narrow black beach covered with basalt pebbles. I stood facing the gently rolling sea, listening to its heavy sighs. The pebbles under my feet clicked like castanets as the waves lapped them. The fresh briny air, as sharp as only the Icelandic brand could be, awakened some dormant brain cells in me, and I could hear my father's voice murmuring in my ear. He was reminding me of his encounter with not just one but two sea monsters. He usually spoke in a calm and measured manner, but recounting this incident always brought out a panicked tone.

One day when he was around ten, he and his father rowed out to inspect the shark fishing gear they had anchored near the farm. The contraption was a baited hook and line attached to a wooden beam, which was then fastened to a buoy. The lines were iron chains, and the hooks were crowbar size. When the two of them arrived at the buoy, the sea was blood-red and boiling with violent activity. As they carefully hauled up the gear, they found that three sharks had taken the bait on adjacent hooks, and that the two larger sharks had eaten much of the third. These Greenland sharks were every bit as fierce and enormous as great whites. There they were, thrashing in primeval fury around a flimsy rowboat carrying a scrawny boy and his father. Dad said he had never been so scared in his life. Rowing with all their might, they managed to tow the frenzied beasts to shore. When they gutted the sharks, they found perfectly edible remains of the third shark inside the other two.

Eider harvesting was a much safer occupation, but even so, my family was acutely aware that the sea has the power to give or take. My uncle Sveinn disappeared when he was in his early teens. The theory was that a rogue wave pulled him out to sea when he was collecting eider eggs on a rocky reef.

The eider ducks live in colonies along the shore. The males sport a splashy black-and-white coat, while females are more sensible, wearing a dull, striped brown jacket that doesn't attract predators' attention. According to my dad, the eider were as tame as pets. He could lift an eider off her nest, gather the eggs and down, and place her back on the nest. She wouldn't put up the least resistance. In the process, the eider would also generously donate untold numbers of lice, which meant that the collectors had to be deloused before entering the home.

Hunting was another source of food. The guns were primitive, so accidents happened. Once, when my uncle Halldór was hunting, the breach mechanism of his gun malfunctioned and crushed his eyeball. He managed to crawl back to the homestead and spent weeks recovering. Since then, he always wore a black patch over one eye. His piratical look fascinated me when I was a child.

My dad told this story of a plentiful, serendipitous hunt. A large piece of driftwood had landed on the farm's shores. The residents were ecstatic at such a find. When the Vikings first arrived in Iceland, they reported the existence of flourishing forests, but they cut the trees to make charcoal, a necessary component for forging iron. They also brought sheep to the island, and over the years, the animals chewed up every sapling. For centuries, the principal source of timber in Iceland was driftwood brought by ocean currents from Northern Scandinavia and Siberia.

The tree trunk that floated to my father's farm, however, was unusable. Thousands of sea worms had burrowed into it, and hundreds of seagulls were feasting on the crawly creatures. One of my uncles took out his shotgun and, aiming along the trunk, felled the gulls, dozens at a time. Cleaning them was a lot of work for little meat, but Dad said with the right recipe, gull breast could taste all right, rather like a gamy version of chicken.

When the children came of age, education was compulsory by law. According to the 1907 legislation on education in Iceland, home schooling was permitted for children aged seven to nine, while enrollment in a proper school was required for those aged ten to fourteen. The nearest primary school to Böðvarsdalur, however, was in the town of Vopnafjörður, several hours walking distance across a moor. It was impossible for even the older children to make this trek every day. So, instead of them going to school, the school came to them. A teacher (always male) traveled to the farm and spent a couple of days there. He would examine the progress of each child, assign homework for the next two months, and then continue to the next farm. I am sure the principal teacher was really my grandmother. After all, a literate mother usually raises a literate child. At the end of this homeschooling process, Dad went to the town of Vopnafjörður to sit for government administered tests. He passed with flying colors and received his primary school leaving certificate. In 1927, age nineteen, Dad left Böðvarsdalur to board a coastal steamer with a one-way ticket to Reykjavík. The country's only teacher training institution had accepted him. Three years later, he would graduate at the top of the class, proving there are different ways of acquiring a solid education.

As far as I know, Dad returned to the farm only once after that, sometime in the early 1930s, when he introduced his bride to his family. I don't know any details of this visit, but judging from the fact that the two of them never returned, I can only guess that the get-together wasn't much of a success.

The exodus from the farm happened gradually. In the years after Dad's departure, some of his siblings stayed on, but soon more and more of them decided agriculture wasn't a viable enterprise in this harsh environment. They settled in different towns and found jobs in the school system, postal service, and construction. His one sister married into another farm. The only sibling to remain at Böðvarsdalur was his eldest brother, Hannes. After my grandfather's death in 1936, Hannes took over the farm, which was shared with two other families. By the 1970s, his son Héðinn Hannesson was the sole remaining person at Böðvarsdalur. He built a new house but lived without electricity, telephone or other modern conveniences. His only company was a couple of hundred sheep. In December 1997, a kerosene lamp exploded in his hands, burning down the house. Héðinn managed to escape with relatively minor injuries and returned to the farm a few days later. He used the same fuel canister to fill a second lamp, which also exploded, this time with fatal consequences. An official inquiry established that the store-bought kerosene had accidentally been laced with gasoline.

Wandering around the farm, I looked for signs of the cottage that Héðinn had built, but all I found were the fire-scarred remnants of a concrete slab that once had supported a house. As far as I could see, the vicinity was eerily empty. I shouted to whoever spirit was hanging around and imagined myself standing here in medieval times. The place would have looked the same. Humans had tried to scrape something out of this land for a thousand years and finally gave up.

CHAPTER 4

SETTLING IN REYKJAVÍK

No two people could be less alike than my parents. My mother was a big-town girl. Having grown up under the entrepreneurial sway of Pétur Thorsteinsson, she was a dyed-in-the-wool capitalist. My father, on the other hand, was an unabashed socialist. While studying at the Teacher Training Institute, he adopted the causes of leftwing intellectuals. He later became a board member of the teachers' union. At home, the socialist and the freewheeling capitalist subscribed to their respective left- and right-wing papers. They voted their separate ways, but as far as I know, their disagreement didn't seem to bother them. I never saw them quarrel over politics, or anything else for that matter. I believe the reason was that neither of them was an ideologue. As much as my mother believed in self-reliance, she wouldn't deny help to those who had fallen on hard times, and my father, as much as he was for spreading the wealth, wouldn't want undeserving people to live on handouts.

The only time I detected any tension between my parents was during a discussion I had with my sister, Gústa. To earn pocket money, I delivered Dad's paper, the communist *Will of the Nation*, and she delivered Mom's conservative *Morning Paper*. Gústa lamented that the bundle she lugged around was much heavier than mine. I explained to her, "That's because my paper is a lightweight." (It had no ads except for those promoting cultural relations between Iceland and the Soviet Union). Mom cackled and repeated my statement with glee, but Dad kept his mouth tightly shut.

My parents, who came from opposite ends of the country, met at the Teacher Training Institute in Reykjavík. They started courting while studying in the same class. Mom was an upbeat, extrovert, and strong-willed young woman. Dad was more introverted, studious and athletic. He was always one of the highest ranking in the class. Midway through the program, he was offered a scholarship to study in Denmark, but he turned it down to stay close to his girlfriend. After graduation, Mom and Dad worked as teachers in the same primary school and married in 1933.

My mother and her family had moved to Reykjavík six years earlier. Using the proceeds from the sale of Jaðar, my grandmother bought a cottage on Hverfisgata in a working-class part of town. A new world of opportunities opened up, and the person who exulted in them most was Erlingur. I remember my uncle Erlingur as an expansive man in both physique and personality. He was generous, jolly, and intensely driven. If somebody were to tell him the sky was the limit, he would reach up and shove it with both hands to see if he could raise it. Once in Reykjavík, he wasted no time in improving himself. First, he enrolled in the Industrial Training Institute, a general three-year vocational school. He then went on to the Machinist Training Institute, Iceland's premier engineering school at the time. After graduation, he started out as a machinist on an oceangoing vessel and was at sea for long periods. In 1934 he joined a firm specializing in the safety of marine engines and vessels. He stood out wherever he went.

For his sisters, however, the options were far fewer. Halla, who was in her thirties when she arrived in Reykjavík, had already missed the boat. She remained an unmarried seamstress until 1930, when she died at thirty-six of an acute intestinal illness. My mother went to work at a fish-processing plant, but after a couple of years of washing and salting fish, she decided there were better things to do in life. Only two professions were available to women at the time, nursing and teaching, and she went for the latter. Her six-year primary education in Bíldudalur made her eligible for enrollment at the Teacher Training Institute. It is worth noting how tiny the entire teaching establishment in Iceland was then. Reykjavík had only one trained mathematician, who rotated between my mother's Teacher Training Institute, Erlingur's Machinist Training Institute, and the city's only senior high school, which I would attend years later (but with a different math teacher).

When my parents got married, they settled in my grandmother's tiny house, where Erlingur also lived. Though the quarters were cramped, the four made do. The following year, a fifth tenant moved in—my sister Gústa was born. Around that time, Erlingur also invited a penniless and homeless classmate, Oddur Oddson, to share his room. Finally, in 1936, the proverbial straw broke the camel's back when Erlingur married Kristín Kristvarðsdóttir, a student at the Women's College in Reykjavík.

The two young couples decided to explore larger joint accommodation. The housing market in Reykjavík was extremely tight. The urbanization movement, which had been happening slowly, was now in full swing. The industrial revolution arrived late in Iceland, but when it did, in the early twentieth century, it transformed the fishing industry. Sailing vessels like *Gyða* were replaced by steam trawlers, most of which were docked near Reykjavík. Liberated from the Danish monopoly on trade by then, Icelanders were free to export their products to more lucrative markets. As commerce expanded, so did banking and other occupations in the city.

Many in the country's population, which finally breached the 100,000 mark in 1926, migrated to Reykjavík to seek a better life than farming. However, the supply of new homes lagged: a chronic migraine for many young couples. I can imagine my family's elation when they discovered a building that fit their needs and more. It was located near Tjörnin, the large pond that forms the heart of the city. The street, named Tjarnargata (Pond Street), was one of the poshest in Reykjavík. At the grandest part of the street stood the Minister's Residence, a three-gabled chateau inhabited by successive ministers and prime ministers of Iceland. Nowadays, this mansion is used as an official meeting place and reception hall for foreign dignitaries. The blocks flanking Tjarnargata were also home to financial moguls and industrial barons, as well as the bishop of Iceland. However, only the swanky part of the street was paved with asphalt. The building my family was interested in was on the gravel side, which might explain why two middle class families could dream of living there. The difference in social strata didn't matter; in our tiny nation, everybody was somebody. The prime minister living diagonally across the street from my home was just a neighbor like any other (and his son was known on the block as Dennis the Menace).

Access to credit was the next hurdle—another demand-supply problem. Other graduates of the training institutions, as well as arrivals from the countryside, were trying to establish homes too, and all needed credit. I have no doubt that Erlingur was the driving force behind the financial finagling. He had been working for a few years by then and most certainly built a network of business contacts. According to my cousin Þorkell, his father might have gained access to credit via his employer, Gísli Jónsson, a fellow townsman from Bíldudalur. Gísli was a successful businessman and a rising political star who later became a member of parliament and speaker of the upper house.

Tjarnargata 43. Courtesy of Þorkell Erlingsson

That same year, the two couples and my grandmother moved into Tjarnargata 43. It was a three-story building, each floor a small self-contained apartment. A dark, unheated attic provided storage for all the units and space for the mangle, a machine to torture bedsheets by flattening them between wooden rollers. The basement housed a laundry area and, most importantly, a small wood and metal workshop. This tiny room—jampacked with an assortment of both hand and power tools—would shape my destiny. It was there I discovered my interest in all things related to woodwork and construction. It was there that the seeds of my future career in architecture were sown.

This property was an exceptionally lucky strike for the two families. In the beginning, they crammed into one unit so that the other two could be rented out, thus offsetting the mortgage payment. Every penny counted, for the Great Depression had spread from the United States to the rest of the world and nipped Iceland's economic growth in the bud. A decade later, however, the onset of the Second World War would transform the country in ways that no one could have imagined. Overnight, Iceland turned from a backwater to a front of resistance against Hitler's mammoth war machinery. The job market became overheated, inflation shot up, and rentals and property prices skyrocketed. My family's investment in real estate before the world turned topsy-turvy was, indeed, timely.

Tjarnargata 43 was where I spent the first nineteen years of my life. Every time I visit Reykjavík nowadays, I make a point of strolling on Tjarnargata, now completely paved, and reliving my fondest childhood memories. On the outside, the building looks remarkably unchanged, the same homely concrete box topped with a pitched roof. On one recent visit, somebody told me the third floor unit of Tjarnargata 43 was for sale. I checked it out online and found that the asking price was half a million U.S. dollars! The visuals showed a modern luxury apartment featuring an expansive living room (where two rooms used to be) and a soaring cathedral ceiling (where half the attic used to be). The other half of the attic had been remodeled into a bedroom with a sumptuously staged queen bed basking between a pair of skylight windows. I couldn't believe this was the apartment that my family and my uncle's family had sardined into. In those days, so much space for one to two residents would have been unthinkable.

The boys of Tjarnargata 43. Left to right: Kristinn, Kristján, Ólafur, Þorkell, me, and Agnar.

My extended family eventually occupied all three units. As the two couples continued to multiply, they needed the additional space. By the mid-1940s there were seven children between them. In addition to Gústa and me, there were my brother Kristján and my four cousins, all boys: Agnar, Þorkell, Ólafur, and Kristinn. Poor Gústa, the oldest and only girl, had to put up with six rascals.

The two families were like one. My father and Uncle Erlingur got along famously in spite of their stark differences. Dad's roots were rural. He was of wiry build, active in gymnastics and cross-country running, loved nature, excelled at woodwork, and

My father
in the 1930s

was acutely concerned about social justice. Erlingur's roots were more urban, having grown up in Bíldudalur. He was heavyset and sedentary in nature, his sport being driving around the countryside and photographing with one of his many cameras. He excelled at working on metals and machinery and was powered by an all-consuming desire to succeed. The two men's friendship was based on mutual respect for each other's abilities and accomplishments. Both were highly regarded by their peers in their respective occupations. Both had graduated top of the class at their respective training institutions. They spent many hours together in the basement workshop and the garage, each creating with his own preferred medium.

My mother, around 1930

The only conflict in the extended household was between my mother and Aunt Kristín, Erlingur's wife. I remember my aunt as a shy, reserved person. She was originally from a farm, and although she had gone to a women's "college" (the equivalence of middle school then), she must have felt overshadowed by the siblings from the "big town." It didn't help that my mother was on the domineering side, which, combined with her adoration of her older brother, must have chafed on the younger Kristín. The two women put up a friendly front, though. They maintained the shared building facilities flawlessly. The two families celebrated Christmas and New Year together in accordance with well-choreographed rituals, and the children ran in and out of the two apartments at will. I was oblivious to the existence of any tension. It was only as a grownup that I learned from my cousins that my mother had often driven Kristín to tears.

To the staid elderly and affluent residents that occupied much of the neighborhood, the influx of six unruly boys must have been a rude shock. As if we weren't raucous enough, we also attracted children from the vicinity, turning the unpaved street into a noisy softball field, and quiet backyards into a hide-and-seek playground. When I was around ten, I was loafing around with a group of boys at a new-home construction site. A pile of gravel inspired a rock-throwing contest. I picked a stone that felt just right in my hand, wound my arm back and flung it with abandon. The stone traveled a beautiful arc through the air, farther than anyone else's—I was sure I was going to win—and smashed into a bedroom window. Dad was furious. He had to apologize to the neighbors on my behalf and replace the windowpane.

My childhood was happy and "normal," which meant I was adequately loved, clothed, and fed, as every child should be. Looking back, though, I realize my early years were anything but normal. In fact, my life revolved around scenes of war: foreign soldiers patrolling the streets, air-raid sirens, war planes crashing into the neighborhood, submarines sinking our ships, and so on. At the time I thought such carnage was normal, because it was all I knew.

CHAPTER 5

THE WAR YEARS

Friday, May 10, 1940 was a momentous day in the world's history. Nazi Germany unleashed blitzkrieg attacks against Western Europe. Columns of Panzer tanks aided by dive-bombers raced through the Netherlands and Belgium to point their spearhead at the vulnerable border of Northern France. That same day, Prime Minister Neville Chamberlain of Great Britain resigned and Winston Churchill, then the First Lord of the Admiralty, took his place as both Prime Minister and Minister of War. Chamberlain's dovish tactics were obviously not working. The British had come to realize that Hitler wasn't content with gobbling up neighboring countries with German-speaking populations: his ravenous appetite was driving him to go after the whole of Europe and perhaps the world.

May 10, 1940 also marked a turning point in Iceland's history. In the wee hours of that day, an officer at the meteorological station in east Reykjavík spotted a flotilla in the distance. Visibility from the hilltop was poor, but the silhouettes showed three large warships and several smaller ones. He couldn't see what flag they were flying but probably guessed they were German. A month earlier, Germany had invaded Denmark and Norway. And now could her warships be surging straight for Reykjavík harbor?

The ships turned out to be British. Around 4 am, some seven hundred British marines poured out of a destroyer, bayonets mounted to fend off resistance. But what defense could Iceland put up against warriors of the mighty British Empire? The island was just a jumble of rocks that wasn't even an independent country and didn't have an army. The few people who had gathered at the harbor could only watch helplessly as the marines filed down the gangplanks. According to a contemporaneous account of the British occupation, one angry bystander grabbed the rifle of a disembarking soldier, stuffed a lit cigarette into its muzzle and threw the gun back, shouting, "Remove it before you shoot."

Once ashore, the marines marched off in groups to their assigned destinations. Following crude maps, they fanned out all over Reykjavík. Twenty-five armed soldiers made a beeline for the German envoy's home. They broke down his door and barged in. Forewarned by his secret transmitter, he had started burning documents in a bathtub. The British arrested him. In the course of the day, British troops rounded up other Germans as well as Icelanders with any German association.

The invaders seized the radio station, post office, telephone central and telegraph exchange, rendering the island incommunicado. Even domestic calls were cut off. At the telegraph station, a marine started to hack down the sturdy oak door with an axe. A bystander intervened, saying, "Wouldn't it be simpler to use the door handle to open the door?" The soldier tried it, and the door opened.

British soldiers took over schools and lodging establishments for their temporary housing and turned the half-completed National Theater into a storage for military matériel. They commandeered private cars, trucks, and trawlers to transport their equipment. The locals were skeptical about the invaders' promise of compensation and were pleasantly surprised that the British kept their word a while later.

Until then, Iceland had tried to stay out of the wars in Europe. Neutrality had served the island well during the First World War. It had avoided destruction and bloodshed, suffering only economic damage from the recession. At the start of the Second World War, Iceland was hoping history would repeat itself. Even when Germany invaded Denmark and Norway, bringing the war to its doorstep, Iceland hung on to its neutrality. It rebuffed the British government's invitation to join the United Kingdom as a "belligerent ally."

Map of Northern Europe, dated 1938. By mid-1940, Germany controlled the western seaboard from France to Norway.

As the military situation in Norway deteriorated, the British admiralty concluded that the U.K. had to force itself on Iceland, otherwise the entire North Atlantic would be open to German domination. Winston Churchill presented the case to the War Cabinet on May 6, maintaining that if further negotiations with the Icelandic government were attempted, the Germans might learn of them and act first. A surer and more effective solution was to land troops unannounced and present the Icelandic government with a fait accompli. The British War Cabinet approved the plan and a similar plan for the Faroe Islands, another Danish territory. This decision turned out to be provident, for six weeks after the British occupied these islands, France fell to Germany, making Britain and the two Viking outposts the Allies' last stand on the Western Front.

When my family woke up that morning, word of the occupation had whirled through the city. I was only fifteen months old, and Gústa was six and had started school. It was clear she wasn't going to school that day. My parents turned on the radio and got only static. The station had been shut down.

According to my aunt Kristín, whom her son Agnar interviewed in 2017, shortly before her hundred and third birthday, Icelandic authorities had been expecting aerial attacks from the Germans since their invasion of Denmark and Norway. To prepare the population, the Icelandic government had established "home defence brigades" on every block. Uncle Erlingur, a member of our block brigade, was equipped with a helmet and gas mask. A room in our basement had been converted into an air-raid shelter with sandbagged windows, and a siren installed next door. Early in the morning of May 10, Erlingur received a phone call informing him that an invasion was underway. Kristín recalled that it soon became clear the invaders were British, not German. Unable to contain himself, Erlingur ventured out to see what was going on. He brought back a leaflet that had been dropped by a British plane. In terribly mangled Icelandic, it read:

„*Tilkynning.*
Brezkur herliðsafli er kominn snemma í dag á herskipum og er nuna í borginni. Pessar ráðstafanir hafa verið gerðar bara til þess að taka sem fyrst nokkrar stöður og að verða á undan Pjóðverjum. Við Englendingar ætlum að gera ekkert á móti íslenzku landsstjórninni og íslenzka fólkinu, en við viljum verja Íslandi örlög, sem Danmörk og Norvegur urðu fyrir. Pess vegna biðjum við ykkur að fá okkur vinsamlegar viðtökur og að hjálpa okkur. A meðan við erum að fást við Pjóðverja, sem eru í Reykjavík eða annarsstaðar á Islandi, verður um stundarsakir bannað.
(1) að útvarpa, eða senda símskeyti, að fá símtöl.
(2) að koma inn í borgina eða fara út úr henni fyrir nokkra klukkantíma.
Okkur þykir leiðinlegt að gera þetta ónaeði; við biðjum afsökunar á því og vonum að það endist sem fyrst.
R. G. *Sturges, yfirforingi.*"

The invasion leaflet

"A British war contingent is arrived today in warships and now in town. These arrangements have been made in order to take as early as possible a few places and be before Germans. We English men are not going to do anything against the Icelandic government and Icelandic folk, but we want to guard Iceland against the destiny that Denmark and Norway suffered. Because of that we ask you to give us friendly reception and help us. While we are dealing with Germans in Reykjavík or elsewhere in Iceland, there will be temporary ban on 1) radio transmissions, telegraph transmissions or receive telephone calls. 2) to enter the town or leave town for a few hours. We are sorry to make this inconvenience and we apologize for this and hope it ends as soon as possible." It was signed by Major R.G. Sturges.

Kristín said she didn't feel assured at all, quaking every time a squad of leather boots stomped past. Troops marching past our home soon became a common sight. The British commandeered the University of Iceland buildings a couple of blocks away and set up an army camp on the university grounds. Sometimes, drunken soldiers found their way into our building and banged on doors "demanding company," as Kristín put it. The women cowered, knowing what kind of company the soldiers wanted. The men braced for a fight, but fortunately the drunks never went beyond being a nuisance.

Kristín told of one harrowing incident involving a tenant in our building whose husband had taken ill and was hospitalized. When visiting him, the woman would take a shortcut on foot through the park. For some reason, the army had declared the park off limits at night, but she cut through the park anyway, as it was the shortest way home. One night, she saw a group of soldiers marching toward her. Terrified, she threw herself into a ditch and stayed there until the danger had passed. Crying, shivering, and soaked in mud, she ran home, where Kristín and my mother attended to her, calming and cleaning their distraught neighbor.

Physical assaults by British soldiers were extremely rare, but the emotional assault on the nation's psyche was damaging. Icelanders felt unsafe, defiled. It was true, however, that the economy picked up. Unemployment plummeted from double digits to zero, with all hands on deck to construct airfields, roads, and buildings for the military. Fish prices soared, and Icelanders loaded their catch on ships bound for food-strapped Britain. But no money could make up for the loss of dignity. The people of Iceland had lost control of their lives, the freedom to move around, act as they pleased, and speak as they pleased. Although the British occupiers had promised to stay out of the internal affairs of the country, their actions proved otherwise. They threw people into jail without due process, for reasons such as being married to a German, having German friends, or even just talking to a German. The British detained the crew of an Icelandic cargo ship returning from neutral Spain, all because they had talked to some German seafarers. The worst incidents involved the persecution of the Icelandic political left for daring to speak out against the occupiers. The British closed the newspaper that was the mouthpiece of the Socialist Party and arrested its journalists. They also took into custody a prominent socialist member of parliament. The detainees were sent to prison in the U.K., where they were incarcerated for months.

Although relations with the British improved over time, wariness of the occupiers never went away. My mother became very upset with me when she discovered my prank of rapidly switching on and off the lights in our bedroom. Our bedroom window was clearly visible from the army camp, and she feared that the camp authorities might interpret my antics as spy signaling. She was afraid that soldiers would burst into the apartment and arrest us. Sometimes I also overheard my mother and Aunt Kristín talk in hushed tones about a topic obviously not meant for my ears. They were gossiping about the young woman next door, who was running around with British soldiers and had been disowned by her parents. I had no idea back then why people shook their heads at what they called "The Situation." But now I do. The sudden influx of thousands of young men could only lead to the inevitable. Sexual liaisons, including prostitution, became a national scandal, especially when married women were enticed into the glamor of cavorting with members of a powerful foreign nation.

Nonetheless, as much as Icelanders resented the occupation, they much preferred the British to the Germans. Having lost its neutral status, the Icelandic government feared a backlash from Germany. This fear was far from baseless. Research after the war indicates that Germany had plans to invade Iceland in 1940 and later in 1942, dubbed Operation Ikarus. However, the German High Command found neither plan feasible because of British naval strength in the North Atlantic. As a precautionary measure, the Icelandic government evacuated two thousand children to the countryside. Gústa and I spent the summer of 1940 at Staðarfell in Western Iceland, returning to Reykjavík in the fall when the panic had subsided. All this action was lost on me, as I was too young to remember anything.

My memory began to form impressions when my mother started to allow me to explore the world outside. For an Icelandic child, that age was three. Even during wartime, Iceland was a safe country. Of course, I didn't go out alone. My cousin Agnar, a whole year older, always accompanied me. On our way to our favorite playground, we had to walk through the British army camp a block from our home. This was one of hundreds of barracks that the British army had plunked down all over Iceland. The standard structure of these camps was the ugly semi-cylindrical Nissen hut. Although the occupants tried their best to beautify their surroundings with decorations, such as picket fences and empty bombshells or torpedo casings near the entrances of their dwellings, the result was dismal. The huts looked like a row of knocked-over trash cans. Ever since that time, Icelanders have harbored a deep dislike for structures with curved roofs.

Nissen huts in Reykjavík. In Icelandic, they were called *braggar*. Courtesy of Páll Sigurðsson.

Agnar and I rarely passed these huts without bouquets of buttercups and dandelions in our hands. We presented them to the soldiers, uttering the only English word we knew at the time: CHOCOLATE. When our mothers discovered this chicanery, they sternly forbade us to beg. After that we only handed the flowers to the soldiers without uttering a word. The result was the same, of course, but now we could report to our mothers with a straight face that we didn't beg.

Our playground was a horseshoe-shaped area of about four acres. It belonged to the university and was sandwiched between the army camp and the airfield. This wasteland of mud, rocks, gravel, and puddles was our paradise. Here we built roads for our toy trucks, which my father had made from scrap wood. Toys were in limited supply, so one can imagine our excitement when we uncovered our first ammunition casing. It was a metal cylinder about the size of a small wine bottle and probably originated from an anti-aircraft battery. We knew immediately what it was. Other children had found them and carried them around to show them off—the bigger the better. We brought it home and proudly presented the trophy to our mothers. They were horrified, citing reports of children getting maimed or killed by unexploded ammunition. To our chagrin, they confiscated it. We later found more of these "treasures," but we no longer advertised our find. We kept them, altogether maybe half a dozen, in a secret cache in the backyard.

Another entertainment at our playground was watching planes take off and land at the airfield nearby. The only airstrip that existed in Reykjavík before the war was the grass-surfaced runway in the Vatnsmýri bog, suitable only for light planes. One of the first tasks of the British was to upgrade it and turn it into an all-weather, concrete-surfaced airfield fit for any aircraft. (This airfield is now the core of today's domestic airport of Reykjavík). Every time a plane took off or landed, Agnar and I would look up, watch it for a while, and return to our playing. Little did we know these were bombers shuttling back and forth on lethal missions. Their job was to hunt down German U-boats and destroy them before they destroyed Icelandic and Allied ships.

A particular catastrophic event is forever seared into my memory. One day in April 1944, I arrived at the university playground to find an airplane engulfed in flames at the far end of the field. Fire shot into the air about twice as high as the three-story dormitory close by. The entire sky was black with smoke. From the steps at the university entrance, I watched the crackling inferno, feeling the heat on my face and the sting of acrid smoke in my eyes. Shivering with horrified fascination, it occurred to me there were people trapped inside. I was on my own, having lost Agnar to kindergarten, a misfortune that had caused me no small amount of grief. Facing the conflagration alone was too much for my five-year-old soul to bear; I would wake up with nightmares for months after.

Gústa was similarly spooked when she was on her way to school on a dark winter morning. Her trek to school took her across the causeway that bisects Tjörnin. This little lake in central Reykjavík was on one of the flight paths to the airfield. On that occasion, an airplane with all four engines ablaze flew low over her head as it approached the nearby runway. Years later she told me the hair-singeing incident had given her nightmares too.

Reykjavík was never bombed or strafed, unlike Icelandic towns further east that were within striking distance of German bombers taking off from Norway. Only reconnaissance planes overflew Reykjavík, and they posed no bodily threat. However, some of the spent anti-aircraft shells used by the British could do damage. During air raids, anti-aircraft debris rained over the town. After one such raid, my cousins and I found a shell fragment in our backyard that weighed about one pound. Our parents had always said we had hard heads, but our skulls would have been no match for these metal chunks.

I remember only one time when we used the air-raid shelter in our basement. It was on my fifth birthday, and my mother had invited friends to our home to celebrate. One of the guests was Helga, who was nine and Gústa's best friend. She was very sweet to be willing to associate with a snot-nosed boy like me. When the siren interrupted our festivity, she cried out with indignation, "This is Sverrir's birthday. How rude of the Germans to ruin his party!"

I was scared out of my wits by the scream of the siren, which was just next door. Long after the war ended, the emergency vehicles in Reykjavík changed their sirens from a two-tone BAA-BOO to an undulating screeching wail, similar to that of the air-raid siren. This bloodcurdling yowl always made my arms break out in goose bumps.

The real danger to Icelanders during the war lurked in the sea. Icelandic ships were bombed, strafed, and torpedoed, their crew and passengers maimed or killed. For an island nation that depended on the sea for everything from transport to livelihood, the threat was a chokehold on our lifeline. No casualty befell my family directly, but one incident brought the tragedy of war close to home. In February 1945, the Icelandic freighter *MS Dettifoss* either hit a mine or was torpedoed shortly after leaving Britain. A nearby British warship rescued thirty survivors, but fifteen perished. Before the war, Erlingur had served on *MS Dettifoss* as an engineer. Several of those who perished had been his colleagues.

Ordinary Icelanders did what they could to coexist with the invaders. Many worked in war-related occupations. During summer vacations, my father toiled in the local shipyard in Reykjavík. He crawled into the still hot boilers of transiting steam ships to chisel away the accumulated mineral deposits. Most of these were merchant ships that had come from America and were carrying war matériel to the Soviet Army on the Eastern Front. They had crossed the Atlantic in convoys under the protection of American warships. After the stopover in Reykjavík, British warships would carry on the relay and escort the merchant vessels to Murmansk in northern Russia. If not sunk by German forces, the ships would deliver to the Russians crucial munitions and supplies for their fight against Hitler.

Other convoys assembled in Hvalfjörður (Whale Fjord), the beautiful, deep, mountain-ringed fjord half an hour's drive north of Reykjavík. During the occupation, Hvalfjörður sheltered hundreds of Allied warships and was, at times, the home port of *HMS Hood*, the world's largest-ever battle cruiser. She left port in May 1941 on her fateful mission to engage her German counterpart, *Bismarck*, west of Iceland. At the end of this fiery engagement, the two leviathans were destroyed, and most of their combined crews of over three thousand killed.

The British army was the first foreign military to arrive in Iceland, but other forces soon joined them. When Western Europe collapsed, the U.S. and Canadian governments began worrying about a German invasion into North America via Iceland and Greenland. In early July 1941, the U.S. and Canada sent troops to reinforce the British military presence in Iceland, this time with the consent of the Icelandic government. At its peak, foreign soldiers based in Iceland numbered about 50,000, more than the total number of able-bodied Icelandic men. But while the male population doubled, the number of women remained the same. The social disruption caused by this gender imbalance was enormous. One can imagine the stiff competition Icelandic men faced. While the British were generally regarded as stingy, the Canadians and Americans sent the women over the moon with their gifts of nylon stockings and other acts of generosity.

When the U.S. Navy started escorting shipping convoys across the North Atlantic in the summer of 1941, Germany attacked them with U-boats, triggering U.S. counterattacks. By the fall of 1941, the U.S. Navy had engaged in several battles against German U-boats not far from Iceland. The U.S. was thus technically at war with Germany well before any formal declaration. That came several months later. On December 11, 1941, three days after the U.S. had declared war on Japan for its attack on Pearl Harbor, Germany declared war on the U.S. The U.S. returned tit for tat the same day. One of its first moves in Iceland was to build a naval air base to protect the North Atlantic air and sea routes.

The newcomers from Canada and the U.S. settled into camps further away from my home, so my contact with them was limited. I only noticed the Canadians during the winter months when I skated on the frozen Tjörnin. There they played ice hockey, which I found fascinating. They also played curling, a game of slinging heavy stones along the ice and furiously sweeping their paths with brooms to make the stones slide further. I found this sport peculiar and not very appealing.

My cousins and I made up our own games, and they were often war inspired, which should come as no surprise. I remember playing radio with my cousins. The older boys, i.e., Agnar and I, were the radio announcers, disembodied voices coming out from under a cloth-covered table. Since the invaders lifted the communications ban, families often huddled in front of a radio, straining to catch news of the battlefronts. Our game was a copycat of such adult behavior. Our announcement would go something like this: "In Blueland (a make-believe country), 200,000 soldiers were killed." The greater the casualties the better the news. Upon overhearing us, Aunt Kristín chided, "Can't you invent some more cheerful news?" I was totally baffled. What other news could there be?

As it turned out, there was actually other news. Good news, too. Toward the end of the deadliest war in human history, the Republic of Iceland was born, following almost seven hundred years of foreign domination. An important step in the independence struggle took place at the end of the First World War in 1918, when Iceland and Denmark signed a treaty stipulating that an independence referendum would be held after twenty-five years, which was 1943. But when 1943 came, Denmark was occupied by Nazi Germany, so the Icelandic government decided to postpone the referendum by one year. One year later, Denmark was still occupied, but political pressures in Iceland demanded that the referendum be held anyway. An overwhelming majority of Icelanders voted for independence.

The inaugural activities took place on June 17, 1944, at Þingvellir, the site of Iceland's first parliament and an hour's drive from Reykjavík. It is also one of the geological marvels of the world, where the North American tectonic plate meets the Eurasian plate. Huge cracks traverse the earth, the largest as wide as a one-lane road and tramped on by millions of tourists today. My family traveled to the site the day before the celebration, and we erected our tent with thousands of others. My memory contains a few "snapshots" of the event. One of them was waking up to a loud patter on our tent the next morning. I opened the flap and saw rain pouring in sheets, and the nearby Öxará waterfall tumbling in a ferocious brown torrent. I also saw tents floating on little ponds here and there and bedraggled people trying to rescue their soaked belongings. Fortunately, our tent was on higher ground. My fondest images of that occasion are of Dad performing synchronized floor gymnastics with his teammates. They moved like one body, tumbling, twisting, and twirling in unison. The crowd went wild with applause, and my little heart swelled with pride.

The other piece of good news was delivered to me on May 9, 1945. When I woke up that morning, my mother told me, "There were fireworks last night to celebrate the end of the war." The news about the war flew over my head. All I heard was that I had missed the fireworks. "Maybe there will be more fireworks tonight?" I said hopefully. Not wanting to get my hopes up, Mom said, "I don't think so." But that night, I stayed up. My reward arrived with a boom! I ran to the window of our third-floor apartment and saw a flower of light bloom in the sky, then another and another. Watching the rockets shoot off from the airfield, I silently thanked my British pals for putting on the spectacle for me.

The effects of the war on Iceland continued for a long time afterwards. The camp between my home and the university was torn down, but many other camps, with their ugly Nissen huts, remained for decades as emergency housing in the fast-growing capital. Another remnant of the Second World War was the drifting mines that continued to sink ships and kill seafarers around Iceland. My first full sentence in the English language was a routine radio broadcast to seafarers: "A floating mine was seen today at—" followed by the latitude and longitude. Less visible effects also remain. Shellfish from the idyllic Hvalfjörður still contains excessive lead and mercury dumped by Allied warships.

Most of all, the war ushered in a new era for Iceland. That era started with the landing of British soldiers in 1940, followed by the establishment of a U.S. naval air base. During this period, the country was transformed from an obscure island dangling like a rag just off the polar circle to a strategic hub at the center of superpower attention. To counter the Soviet Union in the ensuing Cold War, the U.S. continued to develop their air station at Keflavík, expanding it into an important base for NATO. This newfound geopolitical status brought Iceland plenty of economic windfalls, without which it wouldn't be the prosperous nation it is today.

For me personally, peacetime spelled the end of an exciting period in my life. In the fall of 1945, I joined the ranks of the masses, trudging to school every day, doing homework and growing up. My parents enrolled me in first grade in the primary school where my father taught.

CHAPTER 6
EAST TOWN SCHOOL

I remember vividly my first day in primary school, Austurbæjarskólinn (the East Town School). I was six years old, one year younger than other first graders. That was because my schoolteacher parents, who had been practicing their craft on me, thought I could skip kindergarten and leapfrog to the next stage.

On the first day of school, all the first graders assembled in the asphalt schoolyard. It was a gray autumn day, as usual. The head teacher stood at the top of the stairs, read the names of the newcomers, and assigned each one to a first-grade class. There were eight in all, labeled alphabetically from A to H. This process reminds me of Icelandic sheep roundups. After the sheep have been gathered from the mountains in the fall, they are herded into a common pen. Each farmer sorts through the animals and drags those bearing the earmark of his farm into a small, farm-specific corral. In our school's replica of such fall roundups, the number of children in the common pen gradually diminished until only a handful remained, most with lumps in their throats or openly wailing. Does the school not accept us? Does this mean there's no room for us in the school? What will happen to us now? After a short while, teachers came out to the playground and hauled most of the remaining sheep into their classes. These were the inattentive ones who hadn't heard their names read.

But no teacher came out to collect me. I stood there with one or two other weeping rejects. The reason was, I later learned, that we were from outside the school district. My address placed me in the downtown school district, but my father had obtained special permission to enroll me in the school he taught in. I was in pretty bad shape when Dad finally came out to the schoolyard, took me by the hand and brought me to his colleague, and said: "Jón, I'm sure you're going to take good care of my boy!" And thus I was enrolled in Jón Þórðarson's G class.

The first graders were placed in the various classes according to scholastic aptitude. G and H were the high performing classes. Nine years later, it was no coincidence that they were the only students to gain admission to senior secondary school, while those from A to F either quit school to start working or went into the vocational stream. I don't think that students in the lower achievement classes were shortchanged. In fact, some of the best teachers taught these classes. Dad, for instance, who had graduated first in class from the Teacher Training Institute and had a sterling reputation as an educator, was a teacher for the "A" and "B" classes throughout his forty-five-year tenure at the school. His students simply lacked the head start some others had and weren't able to catch up.

Austurbæjarskólinn was a very special education project. Established in the fall of 1930, it was an avant-garde school for piloting new pedagogics. My parents, who had graduated from teacher training in the spring of that year, were some of its first recruits. My father must have liked it there, since he stayed until his retirement in 1976. At one point, he even gave up the opportunity to become headmaster in another school in order to continue teaching at Austurbæjarskólinn. My mother suspended her career in 1933 to take care of her children. She resumed teaching at the school in 1961 and remained there until her retirement in 1978.

Austurbæjarskólinn was innovative in every way, starting with the building. Designed and built between 1925 and 1929, under the guiding hand of the renowned architect Sigurður Guðmundsson, the school was the first building in Reykjavík to be heated by geothermal energy. One of Iceland's best-known artists, Ásmundur Sveinsson, sculpted bas-reliefs over the three entrance doors that depicted children studying at the feet of the goddess of learning. The school had thirty general purpose class-rooms and many specialty rooms: an arts room, home economics rooms, a wood workshop, music room, gym, movie theater, and even an indoor swimming pool. It also had well-equipped laboratories for natural science and geography. Unfortunately, the labs and specialty rooms soon became nothing more than general purpose classrooms because the school was grossly overcrowded after the war. During my time there, the enrollment swelled to 1,800—roughly twice the capacity it was originally designed for.

I remember the health clinic well. Students had regular checkups, and if the nurse thought one looked too pale, she sent him to the tanning room. I spent some time lying naked in the room, soaking up the warm rays of the tanning lamp. Sun deprivation in the winter could cause depression and vitamin D deficiency. For the latter, the remedy was a product in abundance in Iceland—cod liver oil. Therefore, every single day during class, a nurse went down the rows, pinched each student by the nose, tilted his head back, and poured the fishy oil from a beaker into the gaping mouth. The health clinic also had a dental chair. A dentist visited from time to time to perform checkups on the students.

Commensurate with the excellent building facilities, the first principal of the school, Sigurður Thorlacius, was an enthusiastic pioneer in new approaches to education. He had studied child psychology and pedagogy in France and Switzerland before his appointment. True to the mission of the school, he encouraged unorthodox teaching methods and developed a progressive culture. He hired highly qualified teachers, many of whom had published well-regarded educational material. He introduced a liberal environment based on mutual respect between teachers and students. For example, in those days, it was common practice for Icelanders to use the respectful plural form to address elders, similar to the French *vous*. In the beginning, I had a hard time addressing my teacher in the familiar *þú*, rather than the reverent *þér*. But this was the new rule in our school and, by and by, saying it to my congenial teacher, Jón, felt natural.

Jón took good care of me, as my father had said he would, and my thirty-plus classmates. He was my homeroom teacher for the next six years, which meant I had the same teacher, sat in the same classroom, and shared the same desk with the same boy, Atli, all that time. Jón taught all subjects except gymnastics and arts and crafts. His teaching methods were remarkably advanced. They were creative and entertaining, getting results without us noticing that we weren't only having fun but also learning in the process. We all loved him. Decades later, after Jón passed away in 1992 at age ninety, four of my fellow students, now respected members of the community, wrote obituaries to reminisce about the marvelous time they had in his G class.

One of the class activities was collective poetry writing. A student would compose the first line of a stanza. Jón would write it down on the blackboard; another would suggest a follow-up and so on until a four-line stanza was complete. All stanzas had to comport with the rigorous conventions of formal Icelandic poetry. On other occasions, Jón would split the class into groups to compete on a variety of subjects, such as the names of the many tributaries of the Danube. The winner was the group that shouted out the most right answers. Sometimes the grouping was by seating and other times by gender; in the latter case, the girls always won.

Jón was always coming up with new teaching methods. Once, in fourth grade, he gave us a long-term assignment. Instead of a page or two at a time, he assigned us an entire book and a list of two hundred questions to answer. He gave us two months to complete it. Days went by, and suddenly I was looking at a looming deadline. I realized I couldn't put it off any longer. I strapped myself to a chair for three days and finished the assignment ahead of time. The experience taught me the concepts of time management, self-discipline, and responsibility—all keys to success.

Jón also built a little library in our class and encouraged students to donate books from their homes. The collection filled two bookcases, alleviating the shortage of books and other teaching materials that plagued all schools in Iceland those days. When a student felt he already knew the material covered in class, Jón would happily allow him or her to sit at the library corner and read quietly.

Extracurricular activities in Jón's classroom were plentiful. There was the chess club, of which I was elected president. However, it met a premature death because I failed to organize any matches. I had meant to but never got around to it.

In our final school year, 1950-1951, Jón wanted to give the class a memorable sendoff. His plan was to take us on a three-day school trip to Snæfellsnes, the western peninsula and volcano that inspired Jules Verne's novel, *Journey to the Center of the Earth.* He came up with a brilliant idea for raising funds: a money-making publication. Students wrote articles, essays, and poems, which were printed and bound into a booklet. We went around the little shops in the area and solicited payment for advertisements. This was an exciting introduction to the world of business for twelve-year-olds. We then sold copies to a captive clientele of friends and family. Although our revenue fell short of target, our parents chipped in to make up the difference. Thus, on a beautiful day in May, we set out for Snæfellsnes. The weather was unusually good, which allowed us to visit the glacier-covered volcano and a mineral spring with carbonated water bubbling out of the ground. We even went birdwatching in a fishing boat that took us around the nearby islands. It was an experience that would stay with us the rest of our lives.

Jón's teaching style can be summed up in one word: partnership. He didn't impose his will on his students, as many teachers do. He did his part, inspired us to do ours, and together we learned. Jón's teaching methods clearly had long lasting effects on his students. In those days, only a fraction of Icelandic children attended senior secondary school. Getting into the premier senior high school in Iceland, Menntaskólinn í Reykjavík, was like winning the lottery. However, about one half of Jón's graduating class of 1951 were among the hundred students admitted to Menntaskólinn in 1954. Many alumni of that primary school class have stayed in touch. The most recent reunion I attended was in 2012, at a little café in downtown

Reykjavík. Some twenty of us turned up, including Atli, the boy who was my desk-mate for six years. We stared at each other for a while, each wondering who that gray-haired old man was.

In contrast to the fun-filled days at school, these were trying years at home. Dad suffered from kidney stones, and the only remedy then was surgery. Dad was in and out of hospitals and endured several operations on both kidneys. Eventually the left kidney became so diseased that the doctors had to remove it. I vividly remember the frightful scars that circled Dad's waist. It was as though he had been cut in half. As an eight-year-old boy, I was most impressed that my dad could survive such butchering. He was tougher than the toughest Vikings.

Between hospital stays, Dad continued to teach, but on days when his infection recurred, he could only lie in bed, delirious with fever. He became allergic to sulfa drugs, as well as penicillin when it came along. But, miraculously, he could tolerate another drug of the same class, Aureomycin, which also had just come on stream. These medications had to be injected every few hours, and it befell my mother to learn how to sterilize the syringes and administer the injections.

By late 1949, the medical profession in Iceland had conceded defeat. Dad's doctor told us that a hospital in London had developed a technique to flush out the kidneys to prevent the formation of new stones. He thought it would be worth sending Dad to London. Thus one week before Christmas, I said goodbye to my father. Early in the morning, Mom and her brother Óli bundled up the sick man, who was shivering from the bitter cold and a burning temperature, and got him into Óli's delivery truck. The day before, our family doctor's parting words to Mom had been: "You have to be strong now, Hallfríður." In other words, Dad's odds of returning home alive weren't that great.

Óli drove the patient to the nearby airport. After an eight-hour flight on a Second World War bomber converted into a passenger plane, Dad dragged his 105°F body into the London terminal and found his way by bus to a downtown station. A visiting Icelandic doctor met him there and took him by taxi to the hospital. A couple of days later, he underwent surgery to remove the stones in his remaining kidney. He survived the operation and began receiving the leading-edge treatment that he had traveled to London for. Doctors inserted a tube into his kidney and flushed it periodically.

During his recuperation, Dad kept a diary, which was spiced with his typical acerbic wit. London was still recovering from the devastations of the Second World War. His diary contained some snide remarks about the hygiene in the hospital. For instance, the windows were caked with a layer of soot so thick that only a faint glimmer of light could penetrate. Being an avid bird-watcher, he cleaned a small part of one windowpane to get a better view. Afterwards he felt ashamed that he had ruined the evenness of the dirty windows. Of the attendant doctors and nurses, he noted that they all smoked like chimneys. By the end of his stay, he wrote in his diary, "My body smelled like a smoked leg of Icelandic lamb." But he was deeply impressed with the chief surgeon's cutting skills. On Christmas Day, the patients in the ward gathered to watch him use a scalpel to slice the turkey on a gurney into precisely equal portions. Dad took time to admire his helping before demolishing it.

That Christmas was a dreary affair for the rest of the family. The weather was no worse than usual, but Dad was absent. My misery was best represented by the sorry state of our Christmas tree. Saving pennies wherever they could, my parents had stuffed last year's tree into the attic. When Mom took it out, it was like a mangy animal, its needles brown and half gone. But this was no time to spend money on frivolities. We put decorations on the raggedy branches and observed the occasion as best we could.

The family's finances were also in tatters because of Dad's long absences from work. I found myself an unwitting courier, carrying envelopes from a well-off family friend to my mother. How much money was involved, I'll never know. What is for sure, though, is that my family owed much to the generous socialized medicine in Iceland. Without it, Dad's miraculous cure in London would never have been possible. The flushing procedure worked because he never had a kidney stone again.

After two months in London, Dad was ready to come home. However, a strike at the Icelandic airline had suspended international flights. This was when Uncle Erlingur came to the rescue. Shortly after the war, his firm had landed a plum government contract to oversee the reconstruction of Iceland's fishing fleet. He became the supervisor in charge, a job that took him on extended travels to countries where the ships were built. At the time of Dad's stay in England, Erlingur was working on a project in Scotland. He took a train to London and brought Dad to his quarters in Aberdeen. A contact in Erlingur's network told him that an Icelandic trawler had just sold its catch in Aberdeen and was about to return home. He spoke to the captain and negotiated a free berth for Dad. According to Dad, the voyage home was a three-day drinking party, as was customary after a whopping payday.

My mother stoically endured this somber period of her life. In 1948 she wasn't only dealing with her husband's illness but also her mother's death. My amma, who lived with us, had been a most helpful, loving and beloved member of the family. One day Mom told me to go into Amma's room to say goodbye. I did as told, not realizing the gravity of the moment. She passed away at home a few days later. These events took a heavy toll on Mom, both physically and emotionally. It had, therefore, left her susceptible to the next disaster that struck us: she contracted polio during the spring of 1951.

I was devastated. My mother—my strong, take-charge mother—became helpless as a baby. Her leg muscles were paralyzed. The doctor visited regularly, but there was no cure for polio; the only treatments were time, hope, and love. Everyone in the family pitched in. Since I attended school in the afternoon, my last year in primary, I was Mom's nurse in the morning. I did the daily grocery shopping, lugging home a pail of milk in one hand and, in the other, a whole fish strung on a wire threaded through the eyes. I cleaned and gutted the fish, cut it into steaks, and boiled them together with potatoes. Before I left for school, I shared with Mom the lunch I had cooked—she ate in bed while I sat in a chair munching glumly by her side. Mom often apologized for being a bother to us. Other than that, she said little, her lips clamped tight and thin. Dad and Gústa took over when they came home in the afternoon. Kristján, then five, was left to his own devices much of the day.

If Aunt Kristín had been around, she would certainly have lent a hand or two. But about a year previously, she had taken the boys to join her husband in Aberdeen. Tjarnargata 43 had been depressingly quiet since my cousins left.

My mother was nothing if not determined. Gradually she got out of bed and took one baby step after another, hanging on to furniture and walls. We were all rooting for her in our hearts. Our stoic culture frowns on any outpouring of emotions, but I'm sure our silent cheering didn't go unnoticed. Mom pushed ahead. After about six months, she could walk again. Our mother was back, cooking, cleaning, taking care of everyone as before. Except we knew she would never be the same. She tired easily and could no longer go hiking with us.

The dark period of my family was over. We could glimpse light again at the end of a long, gloomy winter. But the sun couldn't have shone brighter than when the news of my cousins' return reached us. Uncle Erlingur had finished his job in Aberdeen and was coming home with his wife and four boys, the boisterous cousins I had missed so much. This was just in time for Agnar and me to enter junior secondary school together.

CHAPTER 7
GAGGÓ VEST

T he name of my lower secondary school is a mouthful: Gag-nfræðaskóli Vesturbæjar (Lower Secondary School of the Western District). Which was why it got the nickname Gaggó Vest. Gaggó doesn't mean anything, but it is short and has a ring to it.

Gaggó Vest.
Courtesy of Minjastofnun Íslands (Cultural Heritage Institution of Iceland).

It was originally the only middle school in Reykjavík, but during my time, others had cropped up, so Gaggó Vest served only the westernmost part of town. The three-year institution had a reputation for the quality of its student body—or lack thereof. Behavior and scholastic aptitude scraped the bottom, and I was shocked at how rowdy many of my classmates were. They were disruptive inside classes and fought each other outside during breaks. Even teachers dared not intervene, as some of them were as large as grown men. These ruffians had no intention of going on to senior high and were only biding their time because the first two years of middle school were compulsory.

The picture shows how tiny my school was. It had a total of five class-rooms for 150 students. There were two parallel classes in each of the two lower grades and one in the third grade. The building, dating from the turn of the twentieth century, originally housed the Seafarers' Institute, where aspiring captains and mates learned navigation and other facets of seamanship. Uncle Óli graduated from that highly respectable institution in 1918. The balcony at the top is a remnant of its seafaring days. This was where students learned to use sextants and octants to measure the position of heavenly bodies, such as the sun and polar star.

Gaggó Vest introduced me to teachers who were renowned authorities in their fields. Contrary to the common belief that bad students are products of bad teachers, the school was actually endowed with excellent teaching staff whose qualifications were wasted on the unruly student body. Among them were nationally acclaimed historians—Guðni Jónsson, Óskar Mag-nússon, Björn Þorsteinsson, and Sverrir Kristjánsson. They taught us, or rather, tried to teach us, not only history but also natural science, Icelandic and Danish. Our headmaster, Guðni, later became the editor-in-chief of the forty-two volumes of the Icelandic sagas, the pride and joy of many an Icelandic home, including mine in the U.S.

I was particularly fond of the woodwork and metal craft classes. As tiny Gaggó Vest lacked the space, these classes were taught in two nearby schools. I had learned much of these trades from my dad and Erlingur in our basement workshop, and now the school added to my skill set. I also became fascinated with physics. The school had no laboratories, but I loved to experiment on my own, mainly to validate information in textbooks. For example, according to my physics primer, when you send an electrical current through two carbon electrodes and pull them slightly apart a second later, the current will continue to flow through the gap, creating an intense white light. This is called a carbon arc lamp. To test this concept, I constructed such a lamp by using the carbon cores of two D batteries and the heating element of a space heater, and then plugged the contraption into a 220-volt outlet. The heat of the light was so intense that I could melt pebbles in it. Dad was so impressed that he invited several colleagues to view it.

It was a miracle that I didn't fry or blind myself during my experiments. The arc lamp project treated me to more electric jolts than I care to remember. But the worst accident happened in a chemistry experiment, when a flash and bang singed my hair and erased my eyebrows. Fortunately, Dad wasn't around to witness the explosion, I didn't set the workshop on fire, and my eyebrows grew back.

The headmaster summoned me into his office on the first day of my second year. Anxiously expecting a berating for some infraction, I was surprised by his question: "Do you have a watch?" I proudly displayed my bright new watch. "Great," he said. "From now on you are the *Inspector Platearum*." This was my introduction to the Latin title, Inspector of the Bell, whose job was to ring a large copper bell at the beginning and end of each class period. This title was usually bestowed on a respected member of the school. Granted, I was at the head of the class, but without my watch I wouldn't have qualified. It was a present from my parents for my confirmation earlier that year. I had resented the weeks of catechism, but I could now see the benefits.

The weightiness of the responsibility wasn't lost on me. The operation of the school lay squarely on my shoulders. There would be total breakdown if teachers and students had no idea when classes began or ended. I took my job with utter seriousness. While trying to pay attention to the teacher, I kept an eye on my watch. One minute before the end of class, I got up quietly and headed for the bell in the school lobby. After ringing the bell, I had to make sure to come back to ring it again to signal the end of the break and the beginning of the next class. Of course, I had my lapses, as all humans do. Fortunately, classmates eager for the period to end always nudged me if I didn't get up in time.

To the teaching establishment I was a model student. At graduation, the headmaster presented me with a couple of autographed books, noting that this was reward for good behavior and academic progress during the 1951–1954 school years. If he only knew about some of my physics experiments! After learning about the function of electrical fuses, I was eager to test this knowledge in school. Taking an ordinary electrical plug, I wired the prongs of the plug directly to each other. As my seat in class was close to an electrical outlet, I could push the doctored plug into the socket without anyone noticing. I waited for a moment when the class proceedings were exceptionally boring to conduct my test. I shoved in the plug. A little "pop" sounded, so little that only I could hear it. But nothing else seemed to happen. The lights stayed on. During recess I learned that something had indeed happened—the lights in the class below mine had gone dark. Of course, I had to do my experiment a couple of more times to confirm my findings. The school authorities were hopping mad. They believed a student must have sneaked out of class and replaced the fuse with a blown one, and it went without saying that the culprit must be a member of the disrupted class. The administrators put a padlock on the fuse box. But the fuse continued to burn out from time to time. To this day, the authorities never discovered who the prankster was, since I had the sense to stop before I was caught.

The transition from second to third year was a crossroads for all middle school students. Education was no longer compulsory, and the students could choose between three paths: academic studies, vocational education/ training, or joining the labor market. Although I did very well in academic subjects, I was much more interested in making things, especially out of wood. My childhood dream was to become a woodworker. I was, therefore, seriously considering the vocational stream, particularly carpentry. My parents didn't object, since they had bred in me a respect for manual labor and skills. However, my older sister thought I was aiming way too low. Gústa said, on more than one occasion, "Why don't you give senior high a try? See if you like the idea of learning a trade that's a step beyond carpentry. I'm talking about architecture or engineering." I listened to her arguments, but my pull toward wood was strong.

"Are you interested in building houses or furniture?" my mother asked me. These were the two main branches of woodworking that she was aware of. Neither occupation appealed to me. My interest was more unconventional, such as making wooden toys, sculptures, and on a grander scale, bridges. "I would like to become a bridge builder," I answered my mother. She took it allegorically rather than literally. "Oh, he wants to build bridges between people," she told others.

Actually, my passion was wood sculpting, carving, and turning. I still have the chess set I crafted at age twelve, as well as the lamp and bookshelf made a couple of years later. My hero in those days was Ríkarður Jónsson, one of the premier woodcarvers in the country. His best-known work was Iceland's coat of arms, which won first prize in a national competition in 1918. He also carved the gavel used at the United Nations General Assembly Hall in New York. Unlike other rounded, mallet-like gavels, his was carved in the shape of a Nordic dragon. At a UN Assembly in 1960, Nikita Khrushchev could have banged this gavel to protest another delegate's speech, but he preferred to pound with his shoe.

I once had the chance to visit Ríkarður's workshop. This lucky strike came about while Dad was scouting for pieces of mahogany to build a bench for his foot-pump organ. Somebody told him Ríkarður regularly imported exotic lumber of all shapes and sizes. Dad approached the master sculptor and got an invitation to his workshop. He brought me along for the treat of my young life. As I stepped into the studio, my first impression was: what a mess! Wood chips were scattered all around the floor, and sculptures in various stages of incompletion cluttered the smallish room. My eyes landed on the bust of an old man, and I couldn't tear them away: the bony contours of the face, the rheumy eyes, and wrinkles that looked soft to the touch. The master wasn't just a carver but a magician who could breathe life into wood. I would give anything to be able to carve like that!

Dad found and purchased the pieces he wanted. We engaged in a bit of shoptalk, and I was thrilled to be included in the conversation. Ríkarður gave us tips on the kind of carving tools we might want to get and where to find them. When we shook hands before parting, I noticed how powerful he was. His grip was crushing, and his arms rippled with muscles developed from all that hammering and chiseling.

Meanwhile, Gústa continued to nag me about my future, but she did it in a respectful way that didn't turn me off. At the time, she was in the last year of senior high and ranked number one not only in her class but the entire school. I was in awe of her brilliance. She also admired me for my practical skills, lamenting the "ten thumbs" protruding from her hands, and recognized that my manual dexterity was as valuable as her book smarts. Nonetheless she fiercely advocated that I continue on the academic track for at least another year. She pointed out that if I became a carpenter, I would be building structures designed by others. If, on the other hand, I continued in the academic stream, I would be designing structures for others to build.

I hesitated at first, but the longer I thought about her argument, the more convincing it became. I loved woodwork of all kinds, but I also liked to be in charge of what I was making. To simply copy designs created by others, such as the embroidery that my mother stitched from ready-made patterns, wasn't my thing. After much mulling, I came around to my sister's point of view. I decided architecture was my path, and I am forever thankful to her for that.

A number of my classmates, including the ruffians, dropped out after second year. An influx of students from other schools took their places.

These third-year students were serious about going on to senior high and eventually university, and their behavior showed it.

I discovered I had much more in common with the newcomers. One of them, Björn (Bjössi) Ólafs, became my buddy, a friendship that would last through four years of senior high and beyond. We discussed novels, which we devoured like hot-blooded young men in search of the deeper meaning of life. We went to tear-jerking Italian movies that were all the rage. I also did something that required a lot of mutual trust—teaching him to drive Dad's car. After we had warmed up to each other, I confided in him my dream of being an architect. Bjössi returned the confidence by telling me he too was interested in architecture. He later studied it in France and I in Finland.

Another notable newcomer to Gaggó Vest was Bryndís Schram. She was much admired for her looks and superb dancing skills. A few years later, while still in high school, she entered a beauty pageant and was crowned Miss Iceland. The straitlaced among us, of whom I was one, frowned at the thought of our classmate parading in a swimsuit at the Miss Universe Pageant in California. At the same time, plenty of others harbored secret crushes on her. Decades later, I would reconnect with Bryndís when she came to Washington, D.C. as the wife of the Icelandic ambassador to the U.S.

In 1954, I passed the National Examination Test, the filter for selecting the best performing middle school students for further studies. I was on my way to academia, but in my heart, I would always love to make things with my hands.

CHAPTER 8

MÝRDALUR

During my youth, Icelandic parents often sent their children to work on farms in the summer. The idea was to expose city children to fresh air and life in the country, teach them where our food came from, and cultivate a work ethic. Icelanders had always regarded children as valuable members of the workforce, and in a culture toughened by severe spankings from Mother Nature, the difference between a ten-year-old and a grownup was just size.

After I celebrated my ninth birthday, my parents decided I was old enough to work. That summer, they sent me to Mýrdalur (Bog Valley) in central South Iceland. Their classmate at the Teacher Training Institute, Sigríður Ólafsdóttir, was from Mýrdalur, where her parents owned a farm called Eystri Sólheimar. Sólheimar, a popular name for Icelandic farms, means "sun world," and Eystri, which means "east," distinguishes this Sólheimar from three others in the valley. Given the country's rainy climate and dark winters, the name is more wishful thinking than false advertising.

The glacier Mýrdalsjökull, covering the caldera of Katla. The farm, Eystri Sólheimar, is in the foothills to the left. The sparse, dry grassland in the foreground is a part of the farm holdings. It was scoured clean of all vegetation in the 1918 eruption, when the Klifandi river canyon, seen in the upper right of the photo, belched out an enormous mass of floodwater and icebergs.

My parents started visiting Eystri Sólheimar well before I was born. The first time they made the 180 km trek from Reykjavík was in 1930, shortly after they had graduated. With not a penny to their names, they decided the cheapest means of transportation was their bicycles. The trip lasted two days, with an overnight stay in a hay barn. They didn't say much about their accommodations, but it must have been quite romantic as they were still courting. They traveled on the national highway, which in those days was just a trail. Depending on what the bulldozer had plowed over, some stretches were gravel, others compacted dirt. Toward the end of the trip, imposing glaciers towered over them, those mighty frozen rivers with fat tongues lolling down and carving out the mountainsides. Here in south Iceland, where the annual average precipitation was six feet, the glaciers were well fed, their crowns bulging like paunches of sleeping giants.

This area is one of the foci of activity in the volcanic belt. Once in a while, my parents stopped to identify famous landmarks from the map. One is a volcano named Hekla, which means "cloak," for the cloud covering its top. Internationally, it's known as the Gateway to Hell for its spectacular eruptions. But none loomed as large in my parents' consciousness as Katla (Female Kettle). In this case, molten lava isn't the element people worry about. On top of the kettle sits a glacial lid hundreds of meters thick. When fire meets ice, the explosions belch gargantuan amounts of volcanic ash and gases into the atmosphere and even the stratosphere. The upheaval sends a flood of icebergs, water, and mud into the valleys, wiping out farms and rearranging entire landscapes. As my parents cycled through the scene, they were fully aware of the havoc that Katla had visited on the region a dozen years earlier. Neither of my parents came from the volcanic belt, so they were learning firsthand why Iceland was dubbed "land of ice and fire."

According to my mother, the toughest part of the journey was crossing the glacial rivers. The cyclists waded with their bikes across the smaller rivers, but when they got to the raging Markarfljót (River of the Forest), they knew they needed help. They found a farmer who was willing to ferry them and their bicycles by horse-drawn cart. Like most glacial rivers, it is full of silt and other glacial debris that constantly accumulate on the bottom, causing the river to find a new path rather than flow in an established bed. The river guide, therefore, didn't have a proven ford. Rather, he had to learn to "read the river" every time he crossed. In the middle of the river, the horse stopped suddenly. My parents could see its legs were stuck in the mucky bottom. Meanwhile, the water gushed and swirled around the cart. My mother panicked, while Dad rubbed his hands with excitement. But the farmer and his horse remained calm. They stayed still and waited. Then, the horse extracted its legs one by one from the quicksand before finally moving ahead again. After they were safely across, the farmer explained to his passengers that the horse was trained to bide his time until the liquid sand had solidified. If it had struggled, it would only have sunk deeper.

As my parents crossed the river, they were gazing at a full frontal view of the now-famous Eyjafjallajökull. At the time, this pointy ice-capped mountain was an inconsequential volcano that had sputtered only a few times in the last thousand years. My parents would never have imagined the international ruckus she caused in 2010, when she blew ash columns into the atmosphere and disrupted air traffic in northern Europe for six days. From America, I listened with amusement to newscasters struggling to pronounce Eyjafjallajökull. It is really not so difficult if one realizes the impossibly long string is a compound of three words, eyja-fjalla-jökull, which can be translated as island-mountain-glacier.

Pétursey

When my parents finally arrived at their destination, they spun around to take in the strange and magnificent landscapes enveloping them. In the immediate vicinity, a mountain rests serenely on the glacial rubble plains. This is Pétursey (Peter's Island), which, once upon a time, was a volcano submerged in a glacier or the ocean and thus considered an island. (Who Pétur was is anyone's guess.) At the edge of the ocean a spectacular gateway stands like an entrance to Iceland. Called Dyrhólaey (Door Hill Island), it is a coastal cliff where the sea has eroded a hole large enough for a small plane to fly through. Directly east of it, rock pillars called Reynisdrangar stick out of the ocean like spikes on a dragon's back. What my parents saw was the wild and wonderful creations of violent volcanic activity. The region is full of fissures; like the grate of a barbecue grill, it smokes and sizzles, ever ready to serve up what's cooking. Each of the outcroppings mentioned above once sat on a fissure and was formed when fire met ice or seawater, causing the rapidly cooling lava to turn into a rock formation called "tuff" or palagonite.

Dyrhólaey

Eystri Sólheimar is a sprawling 2,800-hectare estate, 2 km wide and 14 km long, stretching from the shores of the Atlantic Ocean to the edge of the Mýrdalsjökull glacier. The national highway cuts right through it.

My parents found a populous dairy and sheep farm that required intense manual labor. Apart from a small amount of root crops for family use, the only crop produced here was grass for animal feed. Ólafur Helgi Jónsson and his wife, Sigríður, were the farmers. They had only one surviving child, the daughter who was my parent's classmate. She was also named Sigríður, Sigga for short. She was never in want of company, though, for she was raised with four foster siblings—two brothers and two sisters. They were one big loving family that paid no attention to the "foster" label.

Ólafur was a giant in the community, well respected for his farming skills and compassion. For many years, he was the chairman of the district council, a body of elected officials responsible for the community's welfare, particularly the care of the disenfranchised. The farms in the district did what they could to accommodate the displaced, and Ólafur usually ended up taking in the oldest and weakest.

After that first trip, Sólheimar became a regular holiday spot for my parents in the summer. It was a working vacation, for this period was the labor-intensive haymaking season. They brought along their three children, who became good friends with the five born to Sigga and her husband, Þorsteinn. For me, the highlight of those delightful visits was playing with the elderly folks who lived as wards on the farm. I loved hanging out with them in the *baðstofa*, the long communal attic room flanked by a row of built-in beds on each side. *Baðstofa* means "bathing room," since it started out as a sauna brought to Iceland by Norwegian settlers. But as Iceland's forests became denuded and fuel got scarce, it evolved into a general purpose room where people slept, ate, and carried out menial tasks in winter, such as combing wool, spinning and knitting.

I remember at least five ancients, some still able to do light farm work. I became particularly fond of a ninety-year-old woman called Ásta, who had worked most of her adult life as a farmhand at Eystri Sólheimar. She played games with me using leg bones of sheep and seashells. She also gave me treats when Mom wasn't watching. I recently looked her up in a census and found that she was born in 1853!

Not all of the old folks, however, were capable of taking care of themselves. The oldest, Runólfur, became

Me and Sigga, Sigríður's oldest daughter, sitting at the entrance to the front parlor.

a hundred years old during one of my visits. He was blind, and his feet were missing, which I found rather creepy. He sat on his bed all day and stared sightlessly at those around him. The most challenging one was Jón, a deformed, scary-looking old codger who had a habit of defecating in his pants when angry. Every time Gústa had to pass him, she would do so gingerly and muttering, "Jón is a good man."

The farm thus doubled as a nursing home, and also tripled as a school. The schoolhouse, which stood apart from the farm buildings, was a one-room affair with capacity for about a dozen students. This was where we stayed when we visited in the summer, when school was out. Sigga was the only teacher there, as well as principal, nurse, and stable girl. Every morning, children ages seven to thirteen rode their horses from nearby farms, fording rivers and arriving at the school cold and wet. Sigga once told me: "It wasn't enough to teach the children the fundamentals of reading, writing, and arithmetic. It was equally important to ensure that they didn't get sick from sitting chilled and soaking wet in the drafty and poorly heated schoolhouse. And somebody had to attend to their horses." I wouldn't have minded having Sigga as my teacher. She was a slight woman with a big laugh. Whatever life threw at her, good or bad, she would tell a funny story about it and then let out an infectious chuckle.

Up till the age of nine, my trips to Mýrdalur had been all fun and games. The summer after I turned nine, however, my parents left me there for three months while they drove back to Reykjavík. I was to work as an errand boy on a farm a few kilometers east of Sólheimar. The owners were Sólveig Kristjánsdóttir, or Solla as she was commonly known, and her husband, Sæmundur Þorsteinsson. Solla was one of the foster children at Eystri Sólheimar. Her biological mother was an unwed woman at a nearby farm and incapable of raising the child. Solla grew up to be a big-hearted, thickset-but-agile woman who had a special knack for breaking horses, even the nastiest ones that everyone shied away from. And she did it by gentle persuasion, not brute force. Sæmundur, from a neighboring farm, was tall, fit, and movie-star handsome.

Their farm was named Hryggir ("Ridges") for the couple of ridges at the homestead. When I first came to Hryggir, the farmhouse was an ugly gray concrete box with a steep, red-painted corrugated iron roof. Solla, Sæmundur and their toddler slept in the living room, while an elderly couple they had adopted occupied the master bedroom. The old folks were in their mid-eighties and had formerly been farmers in the area. When they were too old to fend for themselves, the young couple at Hryggir volunteered to shelter them.

I had the best room of all, the garret room—and what a view it commanded! On one side, Pétursey and the Mýrdal glacier dominated the landscape, and on the other loomed the postcard-perfect Dyrhólaey. (Nowadays these are some of the sites that attract as many as two million tourists to Iceland a year). I fell in love with Hryggir at once. It was definitely a change in scenery from my city home. It had neither electricity nor telephone, and the only heating was from a coal-fired stove in the kitchen. Drinking water was the collected runoff from the roof, and the bathroom was an outdoor privy. Farm machinery was operated by horses. The farm raised five milking cows, eighty sheep, four horses, a dog, a cat and a gaggle of chickens. For a nine-year-old, this was a fine playground.

In the beginning my duties were light, mostly confined to herding the cows and horses to and from the pastures. But as I returned to the farm summer after summer, each time taller and stronger, I began to actively seek more demanding tasks. While Solla treated me with motherly affection, my relationship to Sæmundur morphed gradually from that of a father figure to a colleague. When Sæmundur discovered that my carpentry skills surpassed his, I became the de facto carpenter on the farm. My most taxing task in that capacity was to mend the wooden boom of the mowing machine, which broke during a terrifying event in the middle of the haymaking season.

The boom is the wooden shaft that connects the two-horse team and the cutting machine. It snapped in two when the newly trained horse, Nasi, got spooked. The crazed Nasi (named for the spot on his nose) dragged his partner and the machine on a wild chase. I watched heart-in-throat as Sæmundur clung to his bucket seat while the scythe-like blade jumped and pitched all over the grassland, emitting an ear-splitting screech that terrorized the horses even more. While hanging on to dear life, Sæmundur struggled to reach the lever to disengage the blades. He finally succeeded. The noise ceased and the horses stopped, trembling and frothing at the mouth. It was a miracle nobody was hurt. However, a broken mowing machine spelled disaster for the haymaking program. I took one look and visualized ways to make the boom whole again. I bravely stepped forward to do the job, and Sæmundur agreed. He had seen my carpentry skills from the playhouse and wooden toys I had made, or perhaps he just wanted to humor me. Using bits of wooden planks and scrap steel lying around the farm, I bolted the two pieces together. My repair held up until the machine was retired many years later.

The success emboldened me. Here I was, a mere twelve-year-old, holding my own among grownups. The next year, I approached Sæmundur with a more ambitious project. I had noticed how time consuming it was to unload hay from the wagon into the shed, one pitchfork at a time. Drawing on the rudiments of physics recently acquired in middle school, I came up with a plan to streamline this process. To my pleasant surprise, Sæmundur gave me free rein.

The hay shed was a gable-roofed concrete building that cut into the side of a ridge. A large door opened at the triangular gable at the hilltop, and hay from the wagons was forked into the barn through this door. The task was relatively easy in the beginning of the season, when the hay dropped to the floor a couple of meters below. It became more exacting when the shed began to fill up and the hay had to be pushed further and further into the barn.

The lessons of middle-school physics were fresh in my mind. I understood how pulleys worked and what leverage was. Instead of forking the hay in manually, I thought of a way to toss the entire wagonload of hay into the barn in one go. I reasoned that, given enough leverage, the two horses could muscle up enough power to do the job. The first step was to lay a sturdy rope sling on the bed of the wagon. The second step was to fashion a block and tackle system that would be firmly anchored to the far gable of the shed. After eyeballing the strength of the structure, I asked Sæmundur to help me reinforce the gable with a wooden beam. The scheme would require a lot of lateral pressure on the building, and the last thing I wanted was a collapsed structure.

When the fully loaded wagon arrived at the upper barn door, we hooked the tackle end of my contraption to the sling. I got the honor of leading the horses that pulled the towrope, while Sæmundur stood by, ready to handle any disaster. As the rope stretched tight and the leverage of the pulleys set in, I was in effect doubling the power of the two horses. The smaller horse, Gráni, was bucking about as he exerted all the power he could muster, while the stronger, Rauður, leaned steadily into the harness. Gradually the load of hay was squeezed into a tight ball, which then made a slow somersault through the opening of the barn, falling to the floor with a resounding whoosh. The system worked! A whole ton of hay had catapulted into the barn! Later in the season, when the barn began to fill, the horses had to drag the hay further into the shed. To make this possible we added wheels to the pulleys. The increased leverage towed the bundle deeper into the shed on top of the earlier pile. The system still worked!

Every summer for six years in a row, I arrived in early June. This was the time when we sheared the sheep, earmarked the lambs, and sent them to fend for themselves in the mountains for the rest of the season. That's why Icelandic lamb meat is prized for their brawny, free-range texture and clean, wholesome taste. This period after the harsh winter was also a time for repairs of leaky roofs, broken down farm equipment, and torn fencing. (I have a four-inch scar on my right calf, a souvenir from fixing a barbed wire fence.) Fertilizing the fields, using both farm animal waste and chemical fertilizers, was another chore that greeted me on arrival. Farm work was unrelenting, and every night I flopped into bed, exhausted.

I participated in all the above activities in addition to my daily chore of helping to milk the cows. The matronly bovines could be tough customers. During the first few days, my amateurish squeezing and pulling irritated them, and they kept trying to slap me with their tails, kick me with their hind legs, and knock over my milk pail. Fortunately, Solla had warned me of their antics and taught me how to avoid mishaps. With practice, my hand developed the right muscles and the right touch, and my clients became much more satisfied.

The haymaking season began in late June. From then until sometime in August, mowing, drying and collecting hay were the primary tasks. This is a life-and-death operation, for if the farm ran out of hay during the long winter, which can last anywhere from four to eight months, the livestock would starve. Most of the cutting was done by the horse-drawn machine that spooked Nasi. On land that was too steep or hillocky for the machine, we resorted to the scythe. Sæmundur had a special scythe made to fit my small size. During wet summers, the process dragged on. The hay would be raked in mounds and topped with jute covers. A myriad of these hayricks would dot the fields until the rains abated, and then the hay would be spread out to dry. A second harvest was cut in August, when the grass was wet and dense and couldn't dry easily. It was ideal, though, for silage, a process of preserving fresh grass in an airtight silo.

Early September was the time for celebration, when the last of the hay had been gathered, the potato fields harvested, and the sheep collected from the hills. Sheep gathering was an exciting communal event. Every able-bodied male climbed high into the foothills of the Mýrdal glacier to look for sheep. But the dogs were the stars. Whenever we spotted a sheep perched on a cliff or ambling across a slope above us, we would whistle to our dog and point to the sheep. The dog would then run up the hill and drive it toward the flock.

Once we had rounded up the sheep, they were driven into a communal pen, from which the farmers claimed their earmarked sheep and drove them back to their farms. Before the party broke up, the men lingered to chitchat and take glugs of *brennivín* from their hip flasks. They went home jolly and well lubricated. Watching them with sober eyes, I shook my head at the grown men horsing around like adolescents.

But the real celebration was a day or two later. The local population assembled in the community hall at Pétursey, dressed in their Sunday best. It was supposed to be an alcohol-free event, but right outside the hall, the participants generously shared the stuff in their hip flasks with all comers. Nobody offered me any, since I was a minor. Besides, I was more interested in the sweets and cookies. There was entertainment too, such as lotteries, dancing to accordion music, and horse races just outside the hall. But my best amusement was watching the goings-on among the young men and women of marriageable age. Sometimes, fistfights broke out among the guys, most likely over who was going out with whom.

The roundup was a joyous time, but one year, an epidemic dampened our spirits. In the early 1950s, Icelandic sheep suffered from an incurable disease, a contagious viral infection of the lungs known locally as *mæðiveiki* (sheep rot). To get rid of the disease, the government carried out a draconian method of slaughtering all sheep in an infected area. A year had to pass before a section could be repopulated with a healthy flock. I was close to tears to see the truck carry my pet sheep, a gift from Sæmundur, to the slaughterhouse.

Sæmundur was a larger-than-life figure to me. He was father, friend, teacher, coworker, and hero. During the sheep epidemic, one sick sheep lost its footing when crossing Hafursá and was carried downriver by the powerful current. I remember watching with dropped jaw as Sæmundur vaulted in and out of the fast-flowing, thigh-deep river, grabbed hold of the horns of the drowning sheep, and hauled it across to the far shore. He reminded me of the Saga heroes performing superhuman feats.

Sæmundur was a genial, outgoing man who wasn't shy about speaking his mind, although he always prefaced his statement with a self-effacing, "I'm just a stupid man." When others mouthed their opinions, he would be all ears, and one could see him weigh every word with care. I'm most grateful for his deep well of patience with my shenanigans. Aside from putting up with my experiments, some of which worked and others didn't, he never had a harsh word for me, even when I deserved it—such as that time I went on a mountain hike with Eyþór, a boy two years older than I from a neighboring farm. As boys will be boys, we wanted to enhance our adventure by cutting across a glacier tongue. To improve our footing on the ragged ice, we tied to our shoes cleats I had made with metal spikes. The cleats functioned poorly, and we kept slipping into the lips of crevasses. In the end we gave up and backtracked our steps. As a result, our hike became much longer than planned, and we were finally slogging through the moonlit night. We hadn't brought any food with us, and I became so shaky from exhaustion that I had to lie down and nap for a while. In the meantime, people back on the two farms were worried. As the late summer day gave way to night, Sæmundur and Eyþór's older brother came searching for us. From a distance, we spotted the lights of their jeep on the gravel track. The vehicle stopped, and in the glow of the full moon, we saw the two men exit the vehicle. We waved and yelled at the top of our lungs, but our rescuers were walking in a direction away from us. They never heard us. We scampered down to the jeep. To let them know we had been there, we opened wide the front doors and tied them together to look like a pair of wings. We picked up our bicycles and cycled home. Passing a stand where large canisters of milk awaited the arrival of the early morning milk truck, Eyþór and I threw morals to the wind. We stole from the next-door farm. Never has milk tasted as good as what I slurped from the large lid of that canister.

I was already asleep when Sæmundur returned. The next morning I told him what had happened. He accepted my explanation graciously, without the least sign of reproach or annoyance.

Eyþór and I had many more escapades, some of which I shudder to think of now. Suffice it to say that we survived. Of our weekend forays into the mountains, my all-time favorite was the river canyons. Sheltered from the blustery weather, they were oases of extraordinary beauty and tranquility. Fulmars and other birds sought shelter there, and the result was a guano-rich soil that allowed a gorgeous subarctic flora to flourish. Blue carpets of the delicate harebell and starbursts of white angelica flowers blanketed the rock shelves, which were inaccessible and thus spared from the destructive appetites of the free-range sheep roaming nearby. It was a magical, enchanting place, and I was always sorry to leave it to continue my trek.

The friendships I made at the farm have lasted a lifetime. Until his death in 2019, I kept in touch with Eyþór and visited him at his nursing home on my trips to Iceland. Hryggir, of course, is also on my itinerary. But the farmhouse I enter these days is a spacious rambler with all the modern conveniences of electricity and Wi-Fi connection. All agricultural activities are mechanized, including the milking system, tractors, and equipment that shrink-wraps hay bales into giant marshmallows. But a shadow hangs over this prosperity. Both Solla and Sæmundur have passed away. Four of their five children have settled in the city. The youngest son, Ásmundur, runs the farm competently and is a well-respected member of the local community. But he is unmarried, a common plight of Icelandic farmers, and close to retirement. Nobody in the next generation is interested in a 24/7 occupation; they prefer a nine-to-five city job with vacation and overtime pay.

Icelandic agriculture faces many challenges. The economics of a global market is one major factor and the other is the flight of the young to the cities. Many dying farms have converted to bed-and-breakfast accommodation to cash in on the tourism boom. Eystri Sólheimar is now a successful B & B run by one of the farmer's daughters, Sigrún. The future of family farms is uncertain. I am most fortunate to have experienced a lifestyle that originated with the first Viking settlers as they battled a hostile environment to coax something out of the land. My summers at Hryggir cultivated in me a love of nature, respect for physical labor, and a farmer's resourcefulness and do-it-yourself independence. These qualities have served me well throughout my life.

CHAPTER 9

MENNTASKÓLINN Í REYKJAVÍK

Menntaskólinn í Reykjavík
(From the cover of *Saga Reykjavíkurskóla*, Volume IV.)

V isitors to downtown Reykjavík will see a barn-like structure set back on one of the main streets. Its plain broad face looks incongruous against the row of fancy shops and restaurants across from it. But in the eyes of Icelanders, this is a revered institution—our very own Harvard. It is called Menntaskólinn í Reykjavík (Reykjavík's School of Learning). Though no more than a senior high school, it is our training ground for presidents and prime ministers. So far, its alumni boast of two prime ministers, four presidents, and two Nobel Prize laureates. Prominent alumni also went into academia, pioneering advances in sciences and engineering and passing their knowledge to future generations. Iceland owes its economic advances and excellent education system to them. I was honored to join the ranks of this illustrious crowd in the fall of 1954. This was then the only senior high school in Reykjavík. Three others served each region in the country.

Menntaskólinn is the country's oldest education institution. By some accounts the school traces its roots to the year 1056, when it was established as a seminary in the southern farm of Skálholt, the seat of the bishop of Iceland. The school was moved to Reykjavík in 1786, then relocated two more times. Finally, in 1846, the government constructed a building for it. At the time, it was the largest edifice in the country.

By the time I enrolled, Menntaskólinn had added three more buildings, but the original construction remained the core of the school. The largest room is the Grand Room. This was where school assemblies were held, as well as special events, such as author readings, music appreciation, and weekend school dances. As a youngster, I never appreciated that I was rock'n'rolling on hallowed ground. My school's assembly hall was a crucible of the island's independence.

It was here that Jón Sigurðsson, the principal leader of the Icelandic independence movement, dared to defy the Danish crown. In August 1851, the Icelandic parliament met in my school's Grand Room because the makeshift parliament didn't have its own quarters. There, the Icelanders rejected a new Danish legislation regarding the status of Iceland. Instead of fulfilling their rubberstamping duty, they had the temerity to present their own bill, demanding complete autonomy in its internal affairs while sharing a common king and foreign affairs with Denmark. Displeased, the king's agent called an abrupt end to the meeting. At this point, Jón Sigurðsson declared, "I protest in the name of the King and the nation, and I proclaim that the congress has the right to complain to the King about the injustice that is being inflicted." Thereupon, the other members of parliament stood up and proclaimed, "*Vér mótmælum allir.*" ("We protest in unison.") Their battle cry marked a milestone in Icelandic history that is learned by all Icelandic school children.

I entered Menntaskólinn in high spirits. I had graduated at the top of my middle school class at Gaggó Vest. What could possibly go wrong? Plenty, as it turned out. Some of the social studies in which I had excelled were no longer a part of the curriculum, whereas topics in which I was weak, math in particular, became more demanding and began to drag down my overall performance. The competition was also much fiercer. Menntaskólinn was the country's premier learning institution, while Gaggó Vest was a holding pen for roughnecks. To top it all, I broke my right wrist within a month of arrival when playing a brutal game of handball during gymnastics class. Being right-handed, this handicap seriously affected my studies. In class, my whole attention was focused on the art of taking notes with my left hand, to the detriment of learning the material. The combination of all of the above resulted in a collapse of my grades at the end of the first semester.

I hung my head in shame at having to show my parents barely passing marks at Christmastime. My mother's chiding was bad enough, but what stung me most was her self-reproach: "I shouldn't have sent you to primary school a year early. You're just too immature. Maybe you should repeat the year." That did it. From then on, I doubled down on my studies. My grades bounced up the next semester and continued to improve the subsequent school years. Overall, my marks became pretty decent. Unfortunately, my mother was used to seeing off-the-charts scores from Gústa. Once in a while, she would remind me that Gústa had graduated at the top of her class *and the entire school* the year before I entered.

My freshman class had one hundred twenty-seven students in six parallel classes. Girls constituted about a third of the cohort. After the first year the cohort split into a language and a math stream. With my sight set on becoming an architect, I chose math. Ironically, the math stream had to deal with more languages than the language stream. Both streams studied Icelandic, Danish, English, German, French, and Latin as compulsory subjects, but a dearth of Icelandic textbooks for many subjects led our teachers to use foreign-language textbooks. Thus, we in the math stream studied calculus and chemistry in Danish, physics in Swedish, and for learning French, we used a Norwegian textbook. Multilingualism is a fact of Icelandic life; for a country as small as ours, learning to communicate with other people in the world is a necessity.

The teaching staff at Menntaskólinn was outstanding. Most were alumni of the school, and several had been at the top of their graduating class. For example, Einar Magnússon, who taught us Danish and history, had ranked first in the class of 1919. Einar often went out of his way to assist students and accompany them on field trips. He was also renowned for his stinging wit. He emphasized in particular the virtue of loud and lucid diction. He once touted as model for clear articulation a student named Ragnar Arnalds, exhorting others to "speak like Ragnar Arnalds, who expresses his non-sense loudly and clearly!" I am not sure how Ragnar took this backhanded compliment. He later became a politician, including a stint as Minister of Education, and no doubt continued to speak loudly and clearly.

Another first-rate teacher was Sigurkarl Stefánsson, who taught us astronomy. He had graduated at the top of the math stream of Menntaskólinn in 1923 and was a pioneer in developing math curriculum and textbooks for the country. The emphasis on math was a fairly new phenomenon in Iceland. Because of its religious roots, Menntaskólinn had traditionally focused on the humanities and languages such as Latin, Hebrew and Ancient Greek. Although there had been earlier attempts to improve math education, they hadn't gained traction. In a country of horse carts, dirt roads, and sailing ships, people didn't see much use for advanced math. At the turn of the twentieth century, however, Icelandic authorities realized they needed math and hard sciences to gain entry to the modern world. In 1904, after the Danish king granted home rule to Iceland, the nation regained its power to run its own affairs. One of the policies the government implemented in earnest was education reform, which called for emphasizing math and the physical sciences over Hebrew and Greek. Fifty years later, the math instruction at Menntaskólinn had become truly superb, maybe too superb for me, for I was constantly struggling to stay afloat. A few years later I began to appreciate its advantage when studying at a foreign university where I didn't speak a word of the language. Math is the same everywhere, and thanks to my teachers, my foundation was as solid as bedrock.

The instructor I was most impressed with was Ólafur Hansson, top graduate of the language stream of Menntaskólinn in 1928. Though a historian by training, he taught us German to fill a vacancy. His claim to fame was his participation in a radio program similar to the U.S. television quiz show *Jeopardy*. Since nobody could defeat him, he was a permanent contestant on the show. Every time I tuned in, my mind would be blown by the vast warehouse of information stored in one man's head. He knew every trivia in the fields of history (his specialty), literature, music, philosophy, science—you name it. He was ordinary-looking, round-faced, round-bodied and most well-rounded in his knowledge. I later discovered the secret to his genius. On a "saga tour" led by him, we struck up a conversation while walking from one farm building to another in an area where the *Nial's Saga* took place. I told him I had been working at a garage in the summer and was fascinated with the transmission of power from the engine to the wheels. Apparently, he didn't know much about the subject. He probed me for information, and I was both delighted and flattered to watch him savor the tidbits I fed him. By the end of our discussion, I had the feeling Ólafur could dismantle and reassemble a differential transmission with his eyes closed. I then understood why I enjoyed his classes so much. His omnivorous curiosity was the spice that livened his lectures and made the most onerous German grammar palatable. Ólafur later became a professor of history at the University of Iceland.

I can go on and on listing the top graduates who returned to teach at their alma mater. These highest performing students were called the Dúx, from the Latin word *ducere*, "to lead." They were Iceland's best and brightest, and many chose to join the faculty at Menntaskólinn. The salary was modest, but the prestige of working at the ancient institution was enormous. The teaching profession in Iceland was generally well respected, but to be an instructor at Menntaskólinn was a sign that one's career had reached a pinnacle.

Around this time, the country was in political turmoil. Through the ages, all that Iceland had ever wanted was to be left alone. Its strategic location in the middle of the North Atlantic, however, made it red meat for predators. Several years after the Allied occupation of Iceland had ended, the U.S. requested to return and build up its military base to thwart the ambitions of the Soviet Union. Certain camps in Iceland wanted the country to remain neutral, while others, fearful of Soviet invasion, looked to the West for protection. Finally, the latter won out and a treaty with the U.S. was signed. Protests ensued. Icelanders were concerned that the American base would make an irresistible bull's eye for the Soviet Union. The thought of nuclear bombers flying overhead could keep anyone up at night.

Every day, newspaper headlines and radio broadcasts assailed the nation with the specter of holocaust. In my mind, the nuclear incineration of Iceland was only a matter of time, like the eruption of Hekla or Katla. As there was nothing I could do about it, I tucked the worry into a mental back pocket. Luckily, my rich social life provided ample distraction. I built stage sets for the school play and helped to maintain Selið, the school's country retreat in Hveragerði, a small town about 35 km from Reykjavík. It was a dilapidated but substantial building with enough floor space for at least a hundred students in sleeping bags. A weekend visit typically included lectures on geology, since the town sat atop a steamy geothermal area. There was also entertainment such as dances and student performances. It was all good, clean fun under the supervision of a teacher. Sometimes, however, what teenagers consider good, clean fun can produce unexpected results. On one trip, the entertainment committee decided to pull a practical joke on their classmates. They asked a renowned radio anchor to record a fake news item: The U.S.S.R and U.S. have started lobbing nuclear warheads at each other. As the sonorous broadcast echoed through the building, pandemonium broke out. This Armageddon scenario had played out many times in our national consciousness—a mushroom cloud billowing over the American base in Keflavík and the entire country going up in flames. The girls started crying, and the boys looked dumbfounded. Faced with the déjà vu, I felt strangely calm. This was when the entertainment committee realized the joke had gone too far. A juvenile voice on the radio piped: "Just kidding!" I will refrain from naming the masterminds of this terrible gag, but they grew up to fill leading political positions.

My last year at Menntaskólinn was a heady time. We were given several weeks off to cram for final exams, both written and oral. For me, the worst ordeal was orals because of the alphabetical order of my first name, Þórólfur. In the Icelandic alphabet the letter Þ comes after Z. Up till then, I had used my middle name, Sverrir, but there were two other Sverrirs in my class, so I reverted to my first name. I remember envying Agnar when he, the first in the alphabet, finished his oral exam in the early morning. I, in contrast, endured an agonizing wait to finish last in the late afternoon.

Serenading our teachers outside their homes was a graduation tradition at Menntaskólinn. The graduates walked in a group from one residence to the next. With the teachers standing in front of their homes, the students sang in Latin, French, and German. However, by the time my class graduated, the logistics of this tradition had become overwhelming. Reykjavík had been expanding rapidly, and some teachers were located in far-flung parts of town.

A convoy of tractor-driven hay wagons filled with graduating students in 1958, with Pétur Stefánsson driving the lead tractor. I was driving the second tractor.
Courtesy of Agnar Erlingsson.

Shortly before graduation, I became part of a committee to solve this problem. We persuaded several farmers on the outskirts of Reykjavík to lend us their tractors and hay wagons to transport the graduates all over the city. In hindsight, I am surprised that any farmer would accept this harebrained idea. On the day of the event, several of us picked up the vehicles from the farms. I carefully parked my tractor and wagon on the gravel shoulder of the national highway, waiting for the rest of the convoy to catch up. Suddenly, the shoulder collapsed, and my tractor started to tip over. Wrestling with the steering wheel, I righted the vehicle by sheer willpower and forced it back onto the road. I hadn't realized the shoulder was waterlogged and couldn't stand the weight of a tractor. This was a terrifying incident. Had the tractor rolled over, I wouldn't have been singing that year, to say the least. But it didn't, and thus this mode of transportation became yet another Menntaskólinn tradition.

Graduating class of 6-X of 1958. I am standing, half hidden, left of center in the picture. Courtesy of Pétur Thomsen.

Graduation was also a time for serious planning. Which university should I apply to? Since the University of Iceland was limited in its offerings, many of us looked abroad. Finland had held a fascination for me since I was a child. It was the land of old castles and modern architecture; the land of poets, writers, and my favorite composer, Jean Sibelius. As a child, I devoured the five volumes of the *Tales of a Barber-Surgeon*, written by a Finnish author in the nineteenth century and translated into Icelandic. They were filled with action and blood and gore—just right for a boy's literary taste. During my summers at Hryggir, I had read each volume dozens of times, for want of choices in the farm library.

In primary school, I had watched educational films that showed Finnish landscapes and historical buildings. I had fantasized about wandering around these granite buildings and marveling at their grandeur. In high school, this childish fascination matured into admiration for the architects of Finland, Elias Saarinen in particular. His son, Eero Saarinen, is better known in the U.S. as the architect of the Dulles Airport terminal in Virginia, an important gateway to the nation's capital. Finland became a mecca to me, and I desperately wanted to study architecture there.

I also wanted to do something unique. No Icelander had ever studied architecture in Finland. Most of our architects had trained in Denmark, Sweden, and Norway, some in Germany and a handful in France. But none of these places, which I considered part of the beaten path, appealed to me.

Right after getting my final grades, I wrote to the Department of Architecture at the Technical University of Helsinki. I stated I wanted to study at their institution and enclosed my transcript. I thought that since my grades were good and Menntaskólinn was the best school in Iceland, any institution anywhere in the world would accept me. Thus, when the university replied to me within a few weeks, I wasn't surprised that I had been admitted. The letter also mentioned that I would be an "audit" student. Neither my parents nor I knew the term, and we chose to ignore it. I would find out what this special status meant when I got there.

As for financing, my parents had made it plain long before that they could only support the overseas studies of one child, and that child was Gústa, who by then had been studying for two years in France. I, therefore, would have to rely on my own resources: student loans, savings from summer jobs, and working while studying in Finland.

While preparing to leave for Finland, I heard about a fellowship that was part of a cultural exchange program between Finland and Iceland. Every year, one Finnish scholar received financial support from the Icelandic government to study in Iceland and, reciprocally, the Finnish state supported an Icelandic scholar in Finland. The announcement emphasized that preference would be given to those pursuing *advanced* studies in cultural subjects of relevance to the two countries. The grant would amount to 300,000 Finnish markka, or about 30 U.S. dollars per month, and for only the first school year. It was a modest sum by any standard, but when the difference it made was between a half-full belly and an empty one, it was huge. I applied but didn't think my chances were high. After all, I was just a high school kid applying for college.

As a final hurrah, I joined my classmate Pétur Stefánsson on his journey home to Egilsstaðir, the largest town in East Iceland. Five of us crammed into his bright-yellow convertible, a beat-up car known for breaking down in the most inconvenient places, such as a restricted area in front of the main police station in Reykjavík. But on this week-long journey, it behaved flawlessly, if I discount the inconvenience of running out of gas a couple of times and the nine occasions we had to patch the blown inner tubes of its threadbare tires. Our hair whipping in the wind when it wasn't raining, we felt invincible.

At one long incline, we got stuck behind a heavily loaded truck. It was crawling up as slowly as a turtle, and to add insult to injury, it was spewing dust into our open-air cabin. We sat choking and fuming, but the narrow gravel road spared no room for overtaking. A bright idea occurred to me. I jumped out of the convertible and sprinted after the truck, like Superman. Huffing and puffing, I caught up with the truck and jumped on the running board. The driver balked at the face that popped up at his window. I asked him to pause on the side of the road to let us pass, which he graciously did.

On reaching Egilsstaðir, I called my parents to let them know we had arrived. As it turned out, they had been frantically trying to figure out how to contact me. The Prime Minister's Office had called to inform them that

I had been recommended to receive the Finnish government scholarship. There was only one snag. I had submitted an unsigned application. While preparing the application on a borrowed typewriter, I had admired the beauty of the font, and it didn't occur to me that I was supposed to sully the form by scribbling my name on the dotted line. With a deadline looming, the Prime Minister's Office needed my signature immediately. I purchased a plane ticket back to Reykjavík. This was the first plane ride of my life.

I have kept in touch with the Menntaskólinn class of 1958, attending the big-number reunions, such as the fortieth and fiftieth. As far as I know, every graduate of my class went on to contribute to society either at home or abroad. Some made names for themselves in the fields of science, engineering, medicine, and the arts. Several became the country's brightest political stars (members of parliament and government ministers), as well as editors-in-chief of the country's largest newspapers. Predictably, the brilliant students went on to brilliant careers, but some of the lackluster ones sparkled too in their respective professions. It goes to show that talent comes in different shapes, and grades aren't everything.

CHAPTER 10

THE BP SUMMERS

My BP, or British Petroleum, summers began in 1954. I was fifteen, and my parents thought I was too old to return to Mýrdalur, since farm work was like summer camp for children. Although I was still nine months short of the legal working age of sixteen, employers weren't picky given the overheated economy. My mother pulled one of her many social strings and landed me a job at a BP gas station. To tell the truth, I resented her meddling because I had planned to look for a job myself, and my occupation was going to be as exciting as Agnar's. One summer, he worked as a crane operator unloading fish from trawlers, and another summer as a construction worker of a power transmission line. I admired the magnificent steel towers that Agnar helped build and wished I could have been a part of that endeavor. Instead, I spent the summer doing mundane chores—pumping gas, changing oil, and washing cars.

The next summer, I returned to BP but wound up with a totally different assignment. A coworker with a bad back asked me to swap places with him. He was a member of a co-op owned by BP workers. The participants were obliged to provide unskilled labor for constructing an apartment building for themselves. The swap with my handicapped friend meant that he took over my shift at the gas station, and I became a construction worker. The arrangement suited both of us well, as I rather enjoyed assisting the carpenters in building wooden forms for the concrete structure, but I doubt it was legal.

In 1956, during my third summer at BP, the company assigned me to its central depot. This was the site of the oil storage tanks, distribution center, and a variety of workshops to service these facilities. There I met a group of hardcore labor unionists who took the meaning of workers' rights to a new level. Union rules were sacred and strictly adhered to. For example, two people must handle the delivery of heating oil to homes: the driver and a second worker to pump the oil into the residential tanks. Under no circumstance could the driver touch the pumping mechanism. One-person deliveries were allowed only on long hauls, since having an extra person along for the ride would be an indefensible waste. These unionists' motto was: Never go to the toilet during official coffee and lunch breaks. If you really need to relieve yourself during a break, do it in your pants and clean them up on company time. The philosophy was, coffee breaks were too precious to squander on such trifles as going to the loo.

This was the heyday of labor unions in Iceland. A widespread six-week strike the year before had crippled industries and contributed to the fall of the center right government. The new leftist government inherited an overheated economy with skyrocketing inflation. The majority of workers, especially the unskilled ones, were struggling to make ends meet.

The Soviet Union seized the chance to woo discontented Icelandic workers. They invited a select group of unionists to Moscow. These Icelanders returned to Reykjavík drunk on a cocktail of milk and honey from the Soviet worker's paradise, no doubt mixed with a generous measure of vodka. During lunch breaks in the BP cafeteria, there were often heated discussions about the pros and cons of communism. The hardliners who had seen the Promised Land with their own eyes told fabulous tales of their visit. According to them, the Soviet government paid their workers so well that everyone could afford to hire a maid or two. The skeptics teasingly questioned whether these maids also had maids.

Once, on hearing again and again about the fantastic riches Soviet workers were drowning in, I couldn't help speaking up, "But where is this wealth coming from? Don't people have to work hard to produce this wealth first?" I believe this was my capitalist mother talking.

A coworker guffawed at my naiveté. "The state can do anything," he replied. "It prints its own money!" Indeed, the Icelandic government had done just that, and in excessive amounts, bringing the country to the brink of bankruptcy. But I was too ignorant at the time to use it as counterargument.

"Sverrir has a point," somebody said. "You can't get something for nothing." We all turned to the speaker. It was Árni Jóhannesson, foreman of the auto mechanics workshop. Everyone shut up. People respected Árni, who was as dedicated a unionist as anyone else. He was just more sensible, and I was lucky to have him as my supervisor.

Shortly after my arrival at the depot, I was assigned to grease the company's fleet of tankers and trucks under the general supervision of Árni. A master mechanic and an affable man in his late fifties, he sensed quickly that I was bored with just doing oil changes and lubrication. He took pity on the eager beaver in me and started teaching me new skills. He also let me assist the four mechanics in the auto repair shop. Occasionally, I worked in the adjoining metal workshop where highly skilled welders and lathe operators constructed and repaired a multitude of machine parts. They were essential to keeping the oil pipeline flowing, pumping stations going, and every aspect of the facility shipshape.

The BP depot was a major import terminal for fuel oil in Iceland. In the absence of a deep-water harbor, oceangoing oil tankers anchored a couple of hundred meters from our workshops. From there, the oil was pumped through a pipeline into the giant tanks of the depot. Making sure this went smoothly was the most important task of the workshop complex. I have a particularly vivid memory of one occasion when everybody in the workshops, myself included, toiled round the clock for a couple of days to repair the broken main pump. This happened at a time when oil supply was at a critical point.

Most of the time, I worked on repairing the company's tankers and trucks. Much of the vehicle fleet was old, dating back to the Second World War. Because of the severe shortage of foreign currency to import goods, a broken-down vehicle was usually repaired rather than replaced. Substitution, modification and cannibalization of parts were par for the course. Knowing which spare part could be used for what model, with or without modifications, was one of Árni's strengths. Once, I was in need of a brake cylinder for an International-make truck. However, these trucks were rare and the depot had no spare parts for them. Árni directed me to the storeroom to get a brake cylinder for a GMC truck. "Drill two new holes in the torque plate," he instructed me. I did as told, and the transplant was a success.

I loved this work, which was dirty and messy but required ingenuity and inventiveness. As the lowest man on the totem pole, my job was typically one of the dirtiest, such as washing engine parts in a metal tub filled with gasoline. I gradually got to do more challenging work, starting with replacing brake linings. I would be standing in a cloud of asbestos dust, grinding and wire brushing the new brake shoes. In those days, asbestos was everywhere in the repair shop, from brake and clutch linings to heat shields for exhaust pipes. Nobody had yet figured out that exposure to asbestos was a health hazard.

Although I never became particularly good at it, welding became my new passion. By imitation and by trial and error, I learned to use an oxy-acetylene torch to fuse thin materials. The errors taught me the key to gas welding was getting the temperature right. Too cool and the material wouldn't fuse; too hot and it would dribble—I learned this lesson painfully when a droplet of liquid steel dripped on my wrist.

The best toy ever was the torch for cutting thick material. Once the steel started melting under the torch, I would push a lever to cut off the acetylene, causing a surge of pure oxygen and a spectacular shower of sparks as the steel burned. Watching the flame slice through steel as effortlessly as a hot knife cutting through butter gave me quite a thrill.

Fusing thick material was just as fascinating. The method called for electric arc welding, which works on the same principles as the carbon arc light I had constructed at home. I was overjoyed when Árni assigned me the task of reconstructing the broken chassis of a tanker truck. Just like my home experiment, the professional contraption produced a light explosion as blinding as the sun. I wore a welding helmet to protect my face, especially the eyes. My supervisor had also taught me to periodically inspect the quality of the weld by chipping away the crust on the red-hot metal. For this task, I had to raise my helmet. At one such moment, a fragment flew into my right eye. The pain was excruciating. My first thought was, *Have I lost an eye for good?* I opened my eye a crack and was relieved to see shadows of shapes and light. The speck had landed on the white of my eye and not the pupil, thank goodness. A colleague got me a roll of bandage from the medicine chest. I patched myself up and carried on. For three days, my right eye was the color and size of an overripe strawberry.

I was in awe of the plethora of creativity and skills in the shop. Once, the carcass of a wrecked truck was hauled into the workshop. The driver had lost control of his tanker truck at a steep hairpin bend, and the truck rolled over several times. The driver survived. The truck would have been declared a total write-off today, but back then, with all the art and craft they could muster, the workshop crew put Humpty Dumpty together again. Straightening the rear beam axle was the biggest challenge. This was important, because otherwise the inside driving axles would wobble and break when spinning.

I still get goose bumps every time I think of the brilliant solution to this problem. Some genius at the shop came up with the idea. He knew that one of the banes of welding is that when melted metal solidifies, it contracts slightly, causing a tiny twist. Usually this is a nuisance, but in this case it became the source of the repair. The workers placed the axle in a large lathe, welded rows on the warped parts, and let them cool and contract. Ever so slowly, the axle began to revert back to its original shape. That truck went on operating without a hitch for years.

The dozen or so men in the workshops were like family to me. They nurtured me, trained me, and forgave me when I made mistakes. My biggest blunder was the time I set fire to the workshop. While I was using gasoline to wash engine parts, a coworker was welding nearby. A spark ignited a bit of fuel that had sloshed onto the floor. Instead of stamping out the flame, which in hindsight would have been the right thing to do, I pulled my tub of gasoline away, causing more fuel to slosh onto the floor. The tub burst into flames. Five fire trucks, the entire fire brigade of Reykjavík, raced to the scene. They quickly put out the fire, saving the workshop from major damage, and most importantly, preventing the fire from spreading to the oil storage tanks. What a disaster that would have been! Thoroughly ashamed, I felt I couldn't show my face at the depot again. I dragged myself to work the next day, bracing myself for reprimand and snide remarks. To my relief, Árni didn't say a word about the incident, and neither did my colleagues.

The managers at the depot looked out for my interests too. They knew I was headed for higher education and went out of their way to help me earn extra cash. During the summer of 1959, after I had spent my first school year in Finland, my managers offered me opportunities for overtime work and its premium pay. Some of these assignments were enjoyable, too, such as the trip I made with Valdi, a BP veteran truck driver. He was a thickset man, loud and garrulous, and full of cheerful stories. In those days, tiny farm-based gas stations sprouted on the Icelandic landscape like mushrooms. That summer, BP had just changed the color of the company logo. Every gas station had to be repainted. Valdi and I trundled by truck from farm to farm all over western Iceland. The farm mistresses welcomed us with open kitchens, stuffing us with coffee, cakes, and mounds of Icelandic crepes filled with whipped cream and rhubarb jam. For our last stop, we crossed a mountain range and arrived at a gas station in pouring rain. Since we couldn't paint in such weather, we asked the farmer if we could sit around and wait for the rain to stop. "You're most welcome to do so," he replied. "However, on this side of the mountain, it hasn't stopped raining for five weeks." I'm sure the rain eventually stopped, but by that time Valdi and I were already back in Reykjavík.

I feel truly privileged to have worked with the men at the depot. The auto-mechanic skills they taught me would be a lifesaver during my future road trips in god-forsaken parts of the world. Other skills, such as the sense for metals, came to good use in my life as an architect. But the most important lesson I took away from my BP summers was this: while skilled manual labor was admirable, its horizon was limited. A few of the top-notch mechanics I had worked with would be promoted to management, but most would remain in the same spot until retirement. Gústa's nagging had nudged me into the academic stream, but until the BP experience, I had harbored lingering doubts about my decision. Now I was certain I had made the right choice.

PART TWO

VIKING ADVENTURES

CHAPTER 11

FINLAND

I left Iceland to pursue university studies in Finland in August 1958. I was a nineteen-year-old embarking on my quest to see the world. In my youth I had deeply admired the adventures of the Vikings. Even after the Viking Age was over, young Icelanders often did a stint in Norway, serving a king or nobleman and performing heroic feats in battle. In the modern era, this tradition takes the form of studying overseas and competing in international business and professional arenas. Like my forefathers, I needed to travel to distant lands to prove myself, and then I would return home and use my skills to help make my country one of the greatest in the world.

I was giddy with optimism in those days. Actually, it wasn't just me. The whole nation was in a state of euphoria. Everything was going right for our newborn republic. With financial aid from the U.S. Marshall Plan, the country reconstructed the ageing fishing fleet that had been decimated by war and neglect. The World Bank, a United Nations affiliate that would employ me many years later, provided loans to Iceland to build the groundwork for an economic boom. Many more bonuses came our way during the Cold War, when the two superpowers contended for our loyalty. Iceland played hard to get, driving the rival suitors to shower her with gifts.

I didn't have far to go to witness this new affluence. Right in front of my home, the National Museum of Iceland, a solemn building with a church-like tower, took the place of the ugly war barracks. The dirt field

I had played in blossomed into a park, and the airstrip for warplanes expanded into a full-fledged international airport. Success was everywhere; the word "failure" wasn't in our vocabulary.

On the day of departure, reality pulled my soaring spirits back to earth. My flight was delayed. When I finally boarded the plane two hours behind schedule, my stomach was churning with worry. Am I going to miss the connection from Copenhagen to Finland? What happens if I do? Would I have to buy another ticket? But I have no money. Does that mean I would be stranded in a strange land where I don't know anyone and no one knows me? These thoughts kept me on edge throughout the flight.

My fear came true. I missed my flight in Copenhagen. I nervously approached an SAS staff. To my relief, she understood my textbook Danish. My best high school scores were in Danish, but I had never used it on a real Dane before. Without ado, the attendant put me and my cardboard suitcase on a plane bound for Stockholm with a connection to Finland. Communicating in Swedish in Stockholm was somewhat more demanding, because I had never taken lessons in the language. I had only picked it up studying physics from a Swedish textbook. But in the end it worked just fine. With a ticket to Helsinki in hand, my spirits were soaring again … until I settled into my seat on the Finnair plane. Suddenly I felt truly alone. Everyone around me was speaking a language that sounded like gibberish to me. I couldn't pick out a word, not even a prefix or suffix that shared a common root with any language I had encountered. Even the dress code of these passengers seemed alien. The women were draped in long colorful skirts, and the men sported flamboyant vests and jackets. I had no idea at the time that they were gypsies.

The picture that met me in Helsinki was bleak. Finland, a small country with only four million people, was poverty-stricken and still reeling from the ravages of a series of wars. Its tragic history, which I would learn more of during my stay there, would fill me with admiration for the indomitable spirit of its people.

The Finns are a Finno-Ugric people who speak a language that shares the same roots as Estonian and Hungarian, which explains my difficulty in understanding them. Finland became an independent country in 1917 after seceding from the Russian Empire, which collapsed during the communist revolution. A civil war broke out in the new republic, with the communist Red Guards fighting the conservative White Guards. During four months of internal fighting, thousands were massacred on both sides. The Whites won, the two sides reconciled uneasily, and the country settled down, though not for long.

In November 1939, the Soviet Union invaded when Finland refused to cede land Moscow wanted for a security zone. The Finns put up a valiant fight that lasted months instead of days as everyone had expected. But they knew this David-and-Goliath battle wasn't going to have a happy ending. A slaughter by the Red Army seemed imminent.

During my first weeks in Helsinki, I met a young woman who had lived through those times. Tuula Solin was a good-looking, cheerful college coed I had developed a platonic friendship with (since she already had a boyfriend). During one of our long walks together, I learned she was one of the 80,000 children evacuated to safety in neighboring Sweden. She was an infant when she was torn from her parents. A Swedish family raised her, and when peace finally settled in Finland five years later, she was again torn from her adoptive parents to return to her biological parents. This double trauma had scarred her for life, leaving her anxious and insecure. She discovered many years later that she wasn't alone when she joined the Finnish/Swedish Society of War Children and became an active member.

The feared massacre didn't happen because Finland sued for peace and surrendered large tracts of territory to appease Moscow, ending what the Finns call the Winter War. This act of Soviet aggression was bullying pure and simple, causing the League of Nations to expel the Soviet Union from its membership.

The world's sympathy for the victim was crystal clear, but when Finland sided with Germany in 1941, the waters became muddied. It is totally understandable why Finland allied itself with Germany to invade the Soviet Union. The Finns call this war the Continuation War, because they see it as a continuation of their battle with the Russians. Subscribing to the motto, "The enemy of my enemy is my friend," the Finns seized the opportunity to get their lands back. However, Finland lost again, had to pursue peace with the Soviet Union, and even help the Soviets drive the German army out of Northern Finland. The final peace settlement included major war reparations to the Soviets, decimating Finland's economy for years to come. It also meant additional loss of vital territory—Karelia in the south and, in the north, Petsamo with its access to the sea.

The wretched misfortunes of this young nation can bring the stoniest heart to tears. But the Finnish character isn't self-pitying. Centuries of conquest, first by the Swedes and then the Russians, had honed their survival skills. Hardships only harden their resolve. The Finns call it *sisu*, which has no equivalence in other languages and is best described as a combination of grit, guts, and resoluteness, all capped with a measure of coolness in the face of insurmountable odds. Thanks to this national trait, Finland bootstrapped itself into a highly successful advanced nation by the turn of the millennium.

When I arrived, however, Finland was the antithesis of prosperity. The country was flooded with refugees from territories ceded to the Soviet Union. Poverty was visible everywhere in Helsinki, from the cramped, jerry-built housing to the Russian-made clunkers on the roads, and the threadbare clothing on the inhabitants' backs.

One of my first tasks after arrival was to find lodging within the tight budget of my scholarship. My fellow students went out of their way to help me. They showed me where to find billboards with room rental ads. They also helped me with the necessary phoning since many of the landlords spoke only Finnish. Within days, I found a tiny sublet on Lauttasaari, a densely populated island suburb of Helsinki. Connected by bridge to the Helsinki peninsula, it was a mere 5 km west of the Technical University, which I was to attend.

Relatively speaking, Lauttasaari was an "upscale" suburb of red and ochre brick apartment blocks built after the war. Though there was nothing luxurious about these homes, they were decent and safe. My classmates had warned me against wandering into certain parts of town, where knife fights were everyday events. I took their advice to heart, for every Scandinavian knew that a Finn didn't fight with his fists but his sharp *puukko*, or knife.

The flat I stayed at was miniscule and had only one bedroom, which was rented out to me. The owner, Erkki, slept on a wooden bench in the kitchen, while his wife, Saara, and their seven-year-old son camped out in the living room. Erkki was almost blind and physically disabled, which made all his movements slow and awkward. He spoke only Finnish, while Saara was fluent in Swedish. They were poor but kind. Noticing my scarecrow looks, Saara occasionally invited me to share a simple meal in the kitchen, typically a fish soup with rice. Since the sublet didn't include cooking privileges, my daily diet consisted of one meal at a cheap café supplemented with snacks of bread and cheese in my room. The painful boils that blistered my legs were probably symptoms of some nutritional deficiency.

The Technical University of Helsinki is the oldest institution in Finland for training engineers and architects. Originally a vocational training poly-technic institute, the nickname of the university was still "Poly." When I first arrived, it occupied a stately Renaissance-style building situated next to the Western Harbor, a few blocks from the center of town. Its ochre-colored facade was deeply scarred from the Winter War. A 1939 Soviet bombing raid aimed at the Western Harbor installations wound up striking the Soviet Embassy located next door to Poly. As a popular Finnish yarn went, none of the Helsinki emergency services were allowed to enter the burning embassy because of its diplomatic status. When the fire chief spotted a civilian with a fire extinguisher furiously pumping at the flames, he yelled, "Hey, nobody is allowed to extinguish these flames!" "I'm not!" the man shouted back. "I filled the fire extinguisher with gasoline!"

On the day of registration, I wandered around the imposing stark corridors of Poly. Totally lost, I approached a slight middle-aged man and asked in Danish for directions to the admissions office. Not knowing a word of Finnish, I hazarded a guess that he might understand Danish. His eyes lit up, and he responded in Swedish, "You must be one of the two Icelandic students joining the Department of Architecture!" He not only escorted me to the admissions office but also helped me complete the entrance formalities. A few weeks later, I met him again in my freehand-drawing class. Gösta Diehl was my teacher and a painter of considerable renown in Finland. In the following months, he would come to my easel and teach me the finer points of angles and proportions. He would tease out of me drawing talents I had never known I possessed.

Two weeks after I settled in, the other Icelander admitted to the Department of Architecture arrived. He was Gunnar Jónasson, my high school classmate. By then, I was an "old hand." I helped him find lodging and spoke up for him whenever my few words of Finnish came in handy. We were really quite pathetic: two lonely souls with nothing to our names aside from our cardboard suitcases. At the time, the entire Icelandic population in Helsinki numbered three, excluding visitors and a handful of transients. The third member was Benedikt Bogason, a Menntaskólinn graduate five years my senior. He had started his engineering studies three years earlier at the Civil Engineering Department of Poly. He was the real old hand and later introduced me to his circle of friends.

When the semester started, I registered for classes in high spirits. While in Iceland, I had begun perusing the book *Teach Yourself Finnish*, with marginal results. I had also carefully studied university brochures and was comforted to learn that the institution was bilingual, catering equally to both Finnish- and Swedish-speaking students. Finland, which has a significant Swedish-speaking population from the days of belonging to the Swedish empire, has two official languages, Swedish and Finnish. While Finnish was as alien to me as Japanese, I was confident my proficiency in Swedish would improve quickly.

What I discovered on the ground was entirely different. The lectures were conducted only in Finnish. The bilingual part was the individual discussions, coaching sessions, and essay writing, but none of these could make up for missing the lectures. I panicked. Learning Finnish became a matter of sink or swim, and I needed to urgently come up with a plan for my studies.

This was what I decided: Firstly, I wouldn't take all the first-year classes at Poly, focusing instead on topics that required minimal language skills, such as mathematics, physics, chemistry, drawing and so on. This meant I would complete the first two years in three. Secondly, I would enroll in language classes at the nearby University of Helsinki.

The first part of the plan worked well. I attended the courses I had selected at Poly, ignored the fact that I had been admitted as an audit student, and took and passed the finals by the end of the first school year. I then applied for admission as a regular student, fully prepared to participate in the competitive entrance examinations taken by all Finnish students. To my surprise and delight, the university admitted me as a regular student without any fuss, and the credits I had earned during the year were recorded as if I had been a regular student from the beginning. While this was a pleasant turn of events, I felt like an interloper for a long time. All I had done to gain admission was write to the University with my grades attached. No essays, tests or other screening. My Finnish classmates, on the other hand, had to go through a double vetting process. First, they had to apply to a "pre-selection" course. Poly accepted annually about a thousand students to this two-month course. At the end of it, only the top fifty were admitted. They were truly the *crème de la crème*. These students, 90 percent male, were then given a year off to complete their compulsory military service. Women were exempt from the military, but the few females accepted into the architecture program had to wait a year for their male counterparts. The system was unabashedly designed to accommodate men.

When the freshman class started at Poly, the males had completed their training as officers of the Finnish armed forces. They were a formidable lot. The uneasy feeling that I was a wimp both in academics and manhood plagued me. It wasn't until a couple of years later that I realized I wasn't so bad after all. In an architectural competition held by the faculty, my anonymous entry would receive honorable mention, an award that was just shy of the three winning entries. Only then did I cease wondering whether I belonged.

The second, or language part of my plan, was a very different story. For my purpose, the language class for foreigners at the University of Helsinki turned out to be quite useless. Most attendees seemed to be professional students from all over the world, who were in Finland simply to add Finnish to their collection of exotic languages. They were there to learn something unusual, so they could go home and impress their friends with the ridiculously complex construct of the Finnish language.

A couple of examples may best explain why the language is so difficult for foreigners. Take the Finnish word *tottele* (to obey). Now add a couple of suffixes, and you wind up with *tottelemattomuus* (disobedience). Add yet another couple of suffixes and you have a still longer word, *tottelemattomuudestansa* (despite his disobedience). Another hair-tearing element is that each noun has fifteen forms, and some of them are very different from the root. Take the word, *yö* (night). In one form, *öisin,* the word bears no resemblance to the root, making it impossible to find in the dictionary.

For me, Finnish wasn't a luxury but a necessity. I soon developed a plan B, which was to continue to plug away at *Teach Yourself Finnish.* I also discovered a do-it-yourself method that worked quite well for me. My guide was *Reader's Digest*, which published both Swedish and Finnish editions of its monthly magazine. I would pick an article of interest to me and study it in the two languages side by side. This allowed me to understand both the text and structure of the Finnish version and accumulate vocabulary at a much faster rate than before.

Plan C presented itself accidentally. When my geometry teacher noticed my language conundrum, he lent me a geometry book in Norwegian, which was close enough to Swedish and Danish. He was a short, stocky, and gruff man, with a caustic tongue that belied the kindness of his heart. Later, when I took one of his written tests, I tried my best at writing the test in Swedish, which I had thought was passable. My teacher's reaction indicated otherwise. "I didn't know it was so easy to understand Icelandic," he said wryly. Noting my discomfort at his sarcasm, he changed his tone: "I lent you that Norwegian textbook, so let's agree that you wrote the test in Norwegian!" As it turned out, he had written a textbook in Finnish on the same subject. I found his treatment surprisingly clear and easy to understand. It dawned on me that technical Finnish is a much lower-hanging fruit than the literary form. From then on, I was no longer afraid to tackle technical articles in Finnish.

This episode, which happened in early 1959, was a turning point in my language battle. Learning Finnish had been as frustrating as walking blindfolded through a labyrinth. My self-teaching methods were boring and often led me head-on into a wall. I naturally gravitated toward a circle of Swedish-speaking friends, but this only took me further from my goal. My success at understanding technical Finnish was hence a much-needed breakthrough.

My freehand ink drawing of a traditional Finnish smokehouse

On the whole, I did fine in architectural and engineering concepts because they were visual, technical, and linguistically simple. I carried out many hands-on projects, usually under the guidance of teaching assistants who were a couple of years my senior. Their Swedish was often as bad as my Finnish, so misunderstandings sometimes occurred. Once, when showing my latest project to a teaching assistant, he took one look at it and said, "Tämä on erittain hieno." My heart sank. I thought he had said, "Tämä on erittain huono." The two utterances sound similar, but the former means, "This is really excellent," while the latter means, "This is trash." Fortunately, I could tell from his body language and tone that he was pleased with my efforts.

For subjects such as geology, law, art history, and architectural history, my language deficiency was more of a challenge. I coped by going to the library and reading up on these subjects in languages I understood. But I am sure I missed a lot of what my fellow students easily absorbed.

Hrafn and I at Finland's Parliament House in 1959.
Courtesy of Gunnar Jónasson.

In my second and third years, two more Icelanders joined the Department of Architecture. They were graduates from my former high school, Hrafn Hallgrímsson and Sigurður Thoroddsen. The Icelandic population in Finland thus swelled from three to five. Hrafn came bearing a piece of curious news. There was actually an Icelandic woman living on a farm somewhere in central Finland. Her name was Ásta Peltola, née Sigurbrandsdóttir. We couldn't believe it. To see with our own eyes that the report was true, we decided to pay her a visit. We boarded a bus headed for the small town of Sysmä. The driver dropped us off at the entrance to the ranch where this mysterious Icelandic woman was supposed to live. There is a slight variation in the way Ásta and I recall this meeting. According to my recollection, the three of us walked up the entrance road to the enormous log building that was the manor house and knocked on the door. The stout, middle-aged woman who greeted us broke into a smile. I started introducing ourselves in my limited Finnish, and her smile broadened as if she were about to burst out laughing. Hrafn shut me off mid-sentence by saying, "Sverrir, stop this nonsense. This woman is obviously an Icelander." Ásta describes this encounter differently. She recalls in her memoir, *The Silent Tears*:

> I had just finished washing the lunch dishes and was humming a ditty when someone knocked on the door. When I opened, I saw three young men smiling from ear to ear. Their eyes shone like stars, and their whole demeanor indicated that they had just achieved a major victory. Their green, lambskin-lined anoraks bore clear witness to their Icelandic origins. It had been ages since I had seen anything as Icelandic, and I immediately addressed them in Icelandic. They were Hrafn Hallgrímsson, Þórólfur Sverrir Sigurðsson and Gunnar Jónasson. The three had heard that an Icelandic woman was living somewhere in the depth of the Finnish forests and they were understandably proud of having found her. They had just finished eating a major meal in the village, because they had expected to travel tens of kilometers through the Finnish wilderness before finding her. They were pleasantly surprised to discover that her homestead stretched down to the bus station in the village that they had just left.

Ásta was originally from Flatey, a tiny island off west Iceland. She was studying to be a nurse in Copenhagen when Germany invaded Denmark. From there on her story is fit for a movie. While working at the hospital, she fell in love with a German medic, a forbidden romance that was scorned by her colleagues and made her a pariah. The lovers met in secret and pined for peace to arrive. But one day, the young man was deployed to the Eastern Front and never heard of again. Ásta finagled her way to Berlin to search for him, contracting TB in the meantime. As Soviet troops advanced into Germany, she joined a caravan of refugees and *walked* all the way back to Copenhagen. She wound up a patient in a TB sanatorium in Copenhagen. There she met and fell in love with a fellow patient, a Finnish freeholder named Arno Routala, who had enlisted in the German Army during the Finnish-German alliance. The two lovers moved to Finland and married, and she became the mistress of a large farm. While Ásta recovered from TB, Arno didn't. Shortly after his return to Finland, his condition deteriorated, and he died in 1947.

Ásta became a thirty-year-old widow, living in a country where she struggled with a language that, according to her, sounded as if the words were "uttered from the bowels." She chose to stay, and during the next few years she learned enough of the language to manage the farm and navigate the unfamiliar environment. She met another farmer, Jussi Peltola, and they married a year later.

Ásta and Jussi.
Courtesy of Ásta's family.

Jussi was a giant of a man and gentle as a lamb. He was soft-spoken and an attentive listener, quietly soaking in what others had to say. I was most flattered that he could be interested in me and even sought my opinion. Once, he took me on an extended trip to inspect a piece of land he was planning to purchase. For several days we drove on dirt roads through a forest of pines and firs. Columns of greenery rolled by endlessly on undulating terrain, interrupted only by a lake here and there in a country known as the land of a thousand lakes. Forests, which cover 70 percent of the country, are the place of worship for the Finnish soul. This is where they hike, cross-country ski, and get lost in the maze (but with the help of a map and a compass to get them out). The forests are also a valuable source of timber and paper, a major industry in Finland. After our trip, Jussi bought the tract of forest we had inspected. It would provide him with a handsome income for many years.

Ásta and Jussi treated us like we were older brothers to their two young sons. Their home was always open to us, and we loved to spend weekends and holidays at their place. This was a godsend to us poor Icelandic orphans, since we had no homes to return to during school breaks. When Jussi asked me to design a little chalet for them, I was more than happy to put my studies to practice. I saw the chalet for the first time fifty some years later when I arrived at the ranch unannounced in 2018. Ásta and Jussi had passed away, and their eldest, Olavi, who was fifteen when I last saw him, embraced me. He took me through the forests to see the fruition of my design. I was happy to see that it was a well-used family retreat, with an extension added to accommodate the growing clan. The log cabin was as I had envisioned—a novice attempt at practicing the textbook principles of Finnish architecture, mainly simplicity and harmony with the environment. The exterior of the cottage, which is made of logs from the surrounding trees, is practically part of the forest. From the interior, a large picture window connects the residents with nature. A brick fireplace, essential for surviving Finnish winters, commands the center of the cabin. From there the structure blows upward to a cathedral ceiling overarching the living room and a cozy sleeping loft. Olavi told me that during construction, the unconventional roof had caused quite a stir in the community. People wondered if Jussi was building a church. But when they saw the finished product, some expressed approval by building their own "churches."

By the spring of 1960, the end of the second school year, I had completed, as planned, the equivalence of one year at Poly. My mastery of Finnish was also steadily improving. I was feeling more in my element, but there was one pressing problem. My scholarship was only for one year, and the savings I was living on were down to the last few meals. I searched the university bulletin board for jobs and found an ad for an architectural assistant. However it also said only third year and above students need apply. I applied anyway and got it.

This was a summer job in a small company town in the southern tip of the country. It is named Parainen and more popularly known as Pargas in Swedish, being a Swedish-speaking enclave. The town is located on an island in the archipelago close to Turku, the second largest city in Finland. The scenery was spectacular. Like strings of pearls, bridges connected island after island stretching far into the Gulf of Finland. The islands were typically solid granite outcrops covered by tall pine trees. The surrounding brackish water teemed with fish as I found out when I went fishing for perch with colleagues.

The town was a blight on an otherwise pristine environment. Parainen was basically a cement factory situated next to an enormous limestone quarry and surrounded by dwellings that had sprung up haphazardly over the years. The coal-fired limestone kilns in the factory belched out carbon dioxide and lime dust day and night, creating a gray shroud over the pine forest. A color photograph of the area would appear black and white. Surprisingly, the inhabitants seemed rather unperturbed by the pollution, pointing to the fact that the trees were still alive, so the problem couldn't be serious. After all, the factory was their source of livelihood. The only ones who complained were the housewives. Their white bed linen and other laundry hanging out to dry had all turned the same color—dull gray.

My main job was to revise the original plans of the factory to reflect all the alterations and additions that had been introduced over the years. I also helped with town planning, which was hitherto nonexistent. A house was plunked here, another there, to accommodate the growing number of workers for the expanding factory. Vehicular access to a house was often impossible. I tried my best to use my nascent architectural skills to address the mess, but my efforts at town planning didn't amount to much. It was a pleasant summer anyway. The downside was that I didn't get to practice my Finnish because the community was exclusively Swedish speaking.

Until then, my fellow Icelanders and I had socialized mostly with members of the Teknologföreningen, the Swedish-speaking students' union of Poly. Because Poly was mostly male, we invited women from nearby colleges to our dances. The half-a-dozen higher education institutions of Finland were all clustered around downtown Helsinki. Some were predominantly male, others female. To ensure that the budding intelligentsia enjoyed a healthy social life, many of the students' unions held inter-collegial dances regularly. The parties were often raucous and involved alcohol, sometimes in copious amounts. Since few could afford to drink regularly, we binge-drank whenever we had the chance. My poor mother, who had banned alcohol from the home because of her brother's drunkenness, would have died if she had seen me cavorting with this crowd.

It was at one such coeducational party that I met a Swedish-speaking Finn named Monika.

CHAPTER 12

MONIKA

I met Monika Maria Hägg during the fall of 1960. She was a twenty-year-old student at the Swedish-speaking College of Commerce in the same neighborhood as Poly. These two institutions had a brother-sister relationship, or more like boyfriend-girlfriend. At a dance sponsored by the College of Commerce, I picked Monika out of a group of young women. She was a petite and attractive brunette with a cute button nose and hazel eyes. After the dance, we stood around and chatted. She was reserved and quiet, and since I was that way, too, we clicked. I asked her out for a date.

Monika was from Kokkola ("Gamlakarleyby" in Swedish), an industrial harbor town on the northwestern coast of Finland. Originally almost exclusively Swedish speaking, it had grown into a bilingual town. Despite her proximity to Finnish speakers, Monika was never at ease speaking Finnish and never made the effort to improve. As far as I know, all her friends in Kokkola and in Helsinki spoke Swedish. It never failed to surprise me how little socializing there was between the two groups. Swedish speakers made up only 8 percent of the population, but since they had been the ruling class for six hundred years, the smell of superiority lingered like smoke in their hair. Not until the new era, after the Second World War, did the Finns begin to come into their own. The country's president during my time there was Urho Kekkonen, a man of Finno-Ugric pedigree.

In Helsinki, Monika rented a room from relatives who lived in Munk-kiniemi, an affluent suburb. Early in our relationship Monika introduced me to Uncle Eddie and Aunt Sylvia, her guardians in Helsinki. Eddie Berglund, a telephone technician, was a chubby, balding, and jolly cousin of her father's. Sylvia, his wife, was a handsome and bilingually garrulous woman of Finnish ancestry, who took great pride in marrying into the Swedish-speaking establishment.

Eddie and Sylvia's son had emigrated to South Africa to seek his fortune. At the time, South Africa was a bastion of apartheid. Uncle Eddie would tell us about his son's letters, including supposed facts about the superiority of the white race, such as, "The black and white races are biologically so different that the two have difficulties in conceiving children together." I ignored this absurd diatribe from a man I otherwise respected, but Monika regarded her uncle as the fountain of wisdom and swallowed everything he said.

Shortly before Christmas 1960, Monika dropped a bombshell on my lap. She announced she was pregnant. My first reaction was panic. We had known each other for only three months. Although I liked her well enough, marriage had never entered my mind. We were both poor students. Feeding ourselves was hard enough. How could we afford to feed another? But what options were there? We discussed them and realized they boiled down to two and quickly to one. Since abortion was illegal in Finland, marriage was the only option. It never occurred to me that I could walk away.

On our way to Iceland to get married, we stopped in Stockholm, where Monika bought a wedding dress. The final leg of that trip, from Copenhagen to Reykjavík, was a nightmare. Departure was delayed by an hour or two at a time until finally, after some twelve hours of accumulated delay, we stepped aboard a passenger plane that had been converted from one of the very last Second World War propeller-driven bombers. The primitive heating system was uneven, with the result being that our faces were covered in perspiration where the vent blew hot air, while our feet felt like blocks of ice. A furious northerly gale raged over the Atlantic, slowing our plane to about the speed of a car. The prolonged flight forced the plane to stop in Scotland for emergency refueling. Altogether we were on the plane for more than twelve hours instead of the scheduled five. Throughout the trip, the old bomber shook and bucked and tossed our stomachs upside down. Monika, who was already suffering from morning sickness, all but threw up the baby. The cabin stank of digestive juices, hers and others'. To top it all, Reykavík welcomed us with a blizzard, a most apt conclusion to the hellish flight.

Monika and me at our wedding in 1961

We got married in early January in a quiet church ceremony. During the subsequent family gathering in my parents' flat, Monika's wedding band fell into the bathroom sink. I opened the water trap to try to retrieve it, but it was gone, forever. Tearful and distressed, Monika blubbered that this was a bad omen.

Shortly after our return to Finland, Monika took me to Kokkola, her hometown. She had earlier vowed she would never introduce me to her family. She claimed her father was a belligerent man who abused his wife and was bound to brawl with me. On arrival at her home, I found a congenial father-in-law, quiet and low-key, who shared my passion for woodwork. Axel was a short, wizened man of about fifty and a carpenter by trade. I never saw any violence from him on that trip or any other, so I have no idea why Monika issued me that warning.

Axel and his wife, Bernice, lived in a cottage in a tumbledown area on the outskirts of town. I was struck by the crude conditions of their tiny shack. It had only one bedroom, which Bernice shared with her ten-year-old son, Jonnie. Axel slept on a couch in the living room. Monika and I slept in the woodshed that Axel had refurbished some years ago into an extra bedroom for his two daughters. Heating was provided by a wood stove, and water came from a well. The bathroom was an outhouse behind the shed, and telephone lines were nonexistent. The winter of my first visit was mild, but on one of my subsequent trips, the temperature plunged to minus forty. Nobody went to the bathroom unless it was absolutely necessary.

What struck me the most was the behavior of Monika's mother. Bernice, a rotund, slack-faced woman, didn't speak a word to me during my first visit. I was puzzled at first but soon noticed that she didn't speak to anybody else either. She moved around like a ghost, prepared the food, washed the dishes, and then disappeared into her bedroom.

Over the years, I would learn more about this family. Axel and Bernice got married shortly before the Winter War broke out. Axel decided to evade the draft by going to Canada, where he worked for a year as a lumberjack, leaving behind Bernice, who was pregnant with Monika. After the war concluded in 1940, Axel returned to his family. When Finland entered the Continuation War in 1941, Axel dodged it again and returned to his previous occupation in Canada. This time he stayed in Canada until the end of the Second World War in 1945 and supported his family through remittances. His second daughter, Anna-Stina, was born in his absence.

During this period, Bernice suffered from mental illness. She sought medical help and received what was considered cutting-edge treatment for conditions such as depression and schizophrenia. Bernice underwent lobotomy around 1950. For several decades in the twentieth century, drilling holes in the skull and taking out chunks of the brain was hailed as a breakthrough for curing mental illness. Today, of course, lobotomy is banned. The surgery has been discredited after cases of horrific damage came to light, one of which I witnessed firsthand in my mother-in-law.

Years after my first visit to Kokkola, Bernice joined me briefly on the porch and started telling her story. I was surprised because she had never talked to me before, and I listened carefully. She explained in a low mournful voice that she had been ill many years ago and gone to the hospital for treatment. When she returned home, her husband and her three children had disappeared. In their stead, she had found total strangers, a man and three children of similar ages to her own. She didn't know who they were and why they were in her house. They claimed to be her family, but they weren't. She hadn't seen her family since she came back from the hospital. Then she stood up and left. She never spoke to me again. Monika had warned me that this might happen, but I still found the encounter eerie. Bernice's amnesia only started after the lobotomy, so there was little doubt what was to blame.

On our return to Helsinki in early 1961, Monika and I found a small studio apartment in Kivihaka, a new suburb at the northern end of Helsinki. Monika worked hard on finishing her two-year diploma in commerce, and I focused on my studies at Poly while working part time as a draftsman. Steinn was born on July 30 that year. He was an adorable child, and lively—perhaps too lively for his own good. Before he had outgrown his crib, he had fallen out of it several times while trying to balance on its edge. He broke his collarbone twice during these maneuvers. Aunt Sylvia, who lived nearby, was a great help during the early months of Steinn's life. Later, my mother came for a month to take care of Steinn. I was twenty-two, Monika twenty-one. We had no idea having a baby meant that life as we knew it was over.

As we settled into domesticity, I noticed new behaviors in Monika. Once in a while, she would enter a grim mood. Her pinched brows, downturned mouth, wound-up body, and the dark cloud that hovered over her signaled a brewing storm. I soon learned to keep out of her way to avoid getting snapped at. Confrontation had been a missing lesson in my upbringing—it was my parents' fault that they never argued in my presence. Also, having visited Monika's family, I sort of understood why she could be that way. I would be mopey too if I had grown up in wartime, my mother had mental illness, and my father was gone during the toughest times. Being the eldest, Monika must have shouldered much of the burden of daily survival. The worst part was that friends and neighbors shunned the family because they viewed Axel as a deserter. After the war, when Axel applied for a permit to build a proper house to replace the shack on his property, the authorities turned him down. The unspoken reason was loud and clear. It was a slap in the traitor's face: Where were you when the country needed you? Axel had to wait two decades before he finally got his permit. I was then in the middle of my studies at Poly. At my father-in-law's request, I designed a simple three-bedroom rambler, which Axel built. He and Bernice lived there until they passed away.

Monika and I had our first serious argument shortly after Steinn's birth, and it was over our pesky eastern neighbors, the Russians. In those days, political tension between Finland and the Soviet Union waxed and waned like the lunar cycle. Tensions usually heightened during election years, when West-leaning political parties seemed likely to gain power. Once the election was over, and Finland had performed some clever footwork to appease the Russians, the pressure would let off. On October 30, 1961, the Soviet Union sent Finland a diplomatic note, triggering what became known as the "Note Crisis." This was at the height of the Cold War, when Berlin was split in two. In the note, the Soviet Union, citing an obscure clause in the postwar peace treaty, asked for military cooperation from Finland to counter a perceived Western threat. Finnish leaders scrambled for a response. Compliance would mean getting pulled into the Soviet orbit, thus undoing a decade of neutrality. Noncompliance could lead to a Soviet invasion.

Monika wanted to pack up immediately and resettle in Sweden. When I refused, she burst into tears. I tried to console her by pointing out that there was no immediate urgency. The Soviets no longer had a military presence in Finland, and there were no tanks amassed on the border. If and when Soviet troops showed signs of movement, there would be plenty of time to evacuate. She seemed convinced for the moment, but the next day and for several days after, she went to pieces again and again. The incontrollable tears, rants about my stupidity, and shouts of "The Russians are coming!" carried on. She had always touted Sweden as utopia, with its low crime rate, thriving economy, and social sophistication that far surpassed Finland's in every way. But even if Sweden was ideal, I couldn't quit my studies and my job at the snap of a finger. She shouldn't either, what with only one more semester to go.

Her hysteria continued, but gradually the screaming bold font in the headlines returned to normal. Kekkonen had met with Khrushchev and worked out a backroom deal. The Note Crisis faded away, and so did my marital crisis, at least that particular one.

Monika and I were just beginning to get acquainted. We had stumbled into a blind marriage. Before the wedding, I had known absolutely nothing about her background—where she came from and who her parents were. Right after our wedding a third person entered our lives, and we became so sleep deprived that we sometimes forgot our own names. One day rolled into the next, but once in a while an interruption brought the treadmill to a standstill, and we could take a good long look at each other.

I discovered a whole new side of Monika when we went on our first major trip together. In the summer of 1964, when Steinn was three, we decided to take an extended road trip. We drove our beat-up old Austin to Lapland in northern Finland and saw the Saami people roaming with their reindeer herds. We crossed into Norway and visited Hammerfest at the northernmost edge of the inhabited world. From there we wove south around the fabulously scenic fjords, visited Tromsø, Trondheim, and finally Stockholm, and took the ferry back to Finland. We covered three thousand miles in three weeks, quite a feat considering the rough condition of the roads. I knew vacations made people happy, but I didn't know they could change personalities. The moment we left Helsinki, Monika flew out of her dark cocoon, became upbeat and daring, and flitted around with frenetic energy. I could barely catch up with her. Once we reached a destination, she would look around, take a photo, and flutter to move on. When we were planning the trip, I had wanted to spend a few leisurely days at each place, but Monika's goal was "to go as far as possible." I had to put my foot down on the definition of "possible," or we would have driven all the way to the North Pole. Our poor old car was worn to the wire by the time we got back to Finland. It refused to disembark from the ferry and had to be pushed off. With the mechanical skills acquired at BP, I cajoled it back to life for one last leg back to Helsinki.

Monika and I would run up a lot of mileage during our marriage, some of which made fond memories, others not. At least we had one thing in common—our love of travel—and it would fuel our marriage for as long as it did.

CHAPTER 13

PUHUN SUOMEA!— I SPEAK FINNISH!

After two years in Finland, I had all but given up hope of mastering Finnish. I had made language studies a priority, taking all the classes available and studying on my own, but as my third year at Poly began, I still couldn't carry on a decent conversation in Finnish unless the topic involved technical lingo. I began resigning myself to permanent inferiority as far as Finnish was concerned. This state of despair would soon change.

I landed a part-time job as a draftsman. The outfit that hired me had the formidable sounding name of Kulutusosuuskuntien Keskusliito (called KK by everyone), which translates into the Central Union of Cooperative Societies. This organization designed and supervised the construction of apartment complexes for consumer cooperatives all over the country. The language used in the office was exclusively Finnish, which was daunting for me. Fortunately, my colleagues were helpful and my job required mostly graphics. It was to develop the details of staircases, kitchens, doors, and windows needed by the construction crews.

Everything was going splendidly until the telephone rang. It rang and rang. Apparently the boss wasn't in his office to pick it up. I looked at my coworkers, but they were going about their business as though they were deaf. My drafting table was right next to the boss's office. What was I supposed to do? I ran in and grabbed the receiver. "*Tervä*," I blurted what I thought was hello in Finnish. (I later found out it actually means, "Pleased to meet you.") A remote voice drifted through the storm of static. I don't remember how I managed to take down the message.

Three days a week, I labored at my drafting table at KK. Sharing the room with me were three other draftsmen. As the four of us worked at our respective tables, conversations ping-ponged back and forth among my colleagues. Unless spoken to, I just listened. I didn't want to torture my coworkers with my stuttering Finnish.

"Did you hear that Pekka has started working for Alvari?" the colleague to my right said. Alvari was the nickname of Alvar Aalto, the father of modern Nordic architecture.

"Yeah, Pekka wants to become a mini Alvari. Poor guy, he's not going to get paid shit," the fellow in front of me replied. Alvari was known to pay his underlings next to nothing for the privilege of serving him.

Moments later, a colleague said to another, "Have you seen the design of this stupid urinal? It looks as if you're peeing into a rubber boot."

Everyone laughed. So did I. I understood what he said, in fact, everything that my colleagues batted at each other, the jokes, the serious discussions about load-bearing walls and window details, and the gossips about bosses, fellow workers, and girlfriends. I understood everything! A month into the total immersion at KK, I could truly say, "*Puhun Suomea!*"—I speak Finnish! Steeped in the all-Finnish environment, my language ability took off at an astounding rate. I could answer the phone in a calm and collected manner, a pencil in hand to jot down the message. I also began to be bolder in expressing my opinion. Nobody laughed at my mistakes. My colleagues embraced me for trying so hard to be one of them and rewarded me with friendship and professional support. If I had questions about anything, they went to great length to either explain to me or point me to the right source. The Finns are a reserved people, not prone to extravagant display of their feelings. In this case, however, they showed no restraint in showering me with goodwill.

I enjoyed immensely my new status as a competent Finnish speaker, an achievement few foreigners could claim. Understanding the lectures at Poly no longer required heroic effort. I could take notes in a mix of Finnish, Swedish and Icelandic. Socially, I no longer felt like a dimwitted child that grownups had to speak to slowly and deliberately. In fact, my Finnish became so good that people sometimes took me for a native. Although they could tell I had an accent, they mistook my accent for that of a Swedish-speaking Finn. The bilingual ones would switch to Swedish to accommodate me. And then they would realize I spoke Swedish with an accent too. Only then would they realize I was a "bloody foreigner."

A few months after starting my part-time job at KK, a personnel change would have far-reaching impact on my career. KK's chief architect, Esko Korhonen, left the organization to start his own architectural firm. Six months later, in June 1962, he asked me to join him as the sole employee in his new venture. Esko was a well-known architect famous for his apartment blocks, which were honeycombed with compact units designed for low-income families. These were rising up fast to meet the growing demand for urban housing. Instead of decimating forests to make space for humans, Esko's designs embraced the concept of consonance with natural surroundings. He paid great respect to existing structures, trees, hills, and granite outcrops. His buildings were positioned to look as if they had always been a part of the scenery. The interior was the epitome of efficiency, with each nook and cranny tweaked to provide maximum utility. During my apprenticeship, he drilled into me the aesthetics of using the right materials and colors, and the importance of paying close attention to the light and shadows cast during different seasons and time of day.

Esko was forty, compact and muscular, and warm but reticent. The times he opened up were when he told war stories. He had been a first lieutenant on the front lines during the Finno-Russian wars. This was the existential fight that thousands of Finns had died for. Obviously, the life and death aspects of the ordeal were too painful for him to reminisce about. All his anecdotes were humorous, though with a dark tinge. Describing life at the front, he said, "We slept in a circle inside the tent, our feet close to the stove in the center and our bodies radiating out like spokes of a wheel. When we woke up in the morning, our feet were scalding from the stove, and our hair was frozen to the ground. The temperature easily went down to minus forty."

His office was one of the three bedrooms at his home at Lauttasaari. Working conditions in his small house were cramped and became even more so a few months later when his wife presented him with a son. As a result, Esko moved the office to a nearby basement facility. My tasks were more challenging than those at KK, now that I was the sole apprentice to a well-respected Finnish architect. The bulk of my work still consisted of fleshing out construction details of large apartment blocks, but in between these mundane activities, Esko took on some exciting assignments. Foremost among these was a competition for designing a church in Helsinki. While hashing out ideas, I suggested making a miniature model of the interior of the church auditorium, a skill I had acquired from my school projects. Next, I would use my camera to manipulate the image to give the illusion that the model was actually a life-size church, something I had never tried before. I had a state-of-the-art Exakta camera that could take extreme close-ups and create a kind of virtual reality of the auditorium. With Esko's blessing, I exploited the fancy features of the Exakta, the world's first mirror-reflex camera. I also resorted to other photography tricks. To overcome the fuzziness of items outside the focal area, I applied a tiny lens aperture to give a sharp in-depth look to the pews. I also used a fine-grained film and a very long exposure time, both of which had to be supported by a rock-steady camera resting on a stack of hardbound books. The result was something I was justly proud of. In the end, we didn't win the competition, but the process invigorated my creative juices.

My dabbling in serious photography was smashed to smithereens a few months later. That was when my two-year-old got a hold of the fascinating toy his dad had been playing with. Screaming with delight, Steinn ran across the living room with the camera held high over his head and lobbed it against the wall. He turned to me for approval, grinning from ear to ear. I had to wrap my arms around myself to keep from wringing his neck. My precious Exakta was irreplaceable, since I had already broken the bank buying it. We could only afford a cheap replacement, which worked fine for ordinary snapshots, but I could no longer engage in advanced photography and soon lost interest in the hobby.

By the fall of 1963, my fourth year in Finland, I thought I had it all. Monika had graduated and was working full time at an insurance company, and I had an apprenticeship with a renowned architect. Our combined income allowed us to upgrade from our tiny studio apartment to a one-bedroom. The extra space was a lifesaver, as I could use a bookcase to partition the living room and create a study. This was where I would put my nose to the grindstone, so I would one day finish my degree, get a full-time job and live in a proper apartment. The current one had paper-thin walls and was poorly maintained; the cracked and leaking toilet bowl remained cracked and leaking for a long time.

Another advantage of the new apartment was that it was in Lauttasaari, a short walking distance from Esko's office. This saved me a long commute, which was at least an hour each way by bus from my previous home. When the bus drivers went on strike, which could last weeks, service would come to a standstill. On one such occasion, I resorted to an unconventional means of transport—cross-country skis. The winter had been unusually cold that year, and the inland sea surrounding the Helsinki peninsula was frozen solid. Instead of traveling the dogleg of the bus route, I discovered a more direct way by cutting through the islands and gliding across the channels and Helsinki Bay. The 10 km trek took me well over an hour at the beginning of the strike, but after several weeks of the vigorous exercise, I was down to forty-five minutes. Conveniently, Esko's basement office had shower facilities where I could freshen up. The ski commute was actually quite enjoyable, but I couldn't count on Helsinki Bay to be frozen whenever there was a bus strike. A short brisk walk to the office was a much safer bet.

Working for Esko was a privilege, but there was a problem. He had only a couple of clients. The workload in his private practice was erratic and became a trickle shortly after I moved to Lauttasaari. Esko was also becoming increasingly involved with Helsinki's town planning office, where he would become the chief planner a few years later. As a result, he had little time to spare for his private practice. After more than a year of working together, we agreed it was time for me to find another employer. This wasn't difficult because Finland was going through a construction boom. Several architectural firms were looking for senior-year students. One of them was the office of Matti Hakuri.

Matti was almost fifty, craggy-featured, good-natured, and a generous boss who believed that keeping his employees happy would produce the best results. His firm employed six to eight people, whom he managed with minimal supervision. He also made sure they understood that they bore maximum responsibility for the outcomes of their work. He encouraged his employees to give it their all and provided them with the necessary resources to do so. His method of calculating salaries was most irregular. Staff members named their hourly wages based on their own assessment of their value to the company. Every two weeks, each employee would submit a salary request that consisted of the number of hours worked and a self-determined hourly rate. On one occasion, Matti confronted me about my salary request slip. "Your hourly wage is too low," he said and gave me a raise on the spot.

Matti's office, also located in Lauttasaari, was in a separate wing of his home. The facility was a joy to work in. It was one large room explicitly planned and built as an architectural design studio. After working solo at Esko's shop, I had almost forgotten how heartening the camaraderie of fellow draftsmen could be. The place was alive with light banter and serious advice and critique of each other's work (all in Finnish, of course, which I now spoke fluently). We thrived in the atmosphere of solidarity and pride in our creations.

As time passed, Matti assigned me to increasingly complex projects. They included a neighborhood school, control towers at several rural airports, and auxiliary facilities at Helsinki's International Airport. Most of these assignments consisted of fleshing out details of the buildings, often in painfully meticulous fashion. When I hear people say, "The devil is in the details," I always counter with the quote attributed to the famous German American architect, Mies van der Rohe: "God is in the details." I had learned from carpentry that the difference between a humdrum and an outstanding product is the attention to particulars.

In this regard, Matti was an artist without peer. I was speechless with admiration when he showed me the design of his weekend cottage. Every conceivable corner of the cottage was developed down to the finest minutiae. In my entire career as an architect, I would never again see such diligence. Perhaps this was why Matti valued me. He must have noticed that I shared his obsession. Toward the end of my employment, he even let me handle the entire design of a school for agricultural technicians. As a rule, the design concept was reserved for "principals," not "associates" like me.

The combination of practical work and theoretical studies was standard architectural training in Finland. I am sure we became better professionals because of it, but the cost, both emotionally and financially, could be high. Student architects were prone to make mistakes, and in this field, a tiny error can carry an enormous price tag. One such error I made nearly cost Matti a fortune. This was a piece of expensive glass for an airport control tower. I measured its dimension incorrectly, and the contractor ordered it without checking. The case went to arbitration, and in the meantime, I spent sleepless nights beating myself up for the mistake. Weeks later, the judge concluded that the building contractor was liable because it was his responsibility to check the architect's work and catch any error. I can't say who was more relieved, my boss or me! This was a memorable experience, and although it had a happy ending, I didn't appreciate the ulcerous stress. My fellow apprentices encountered similar incidents, which caused nervous breakdowns once in a while.

Another downside to the work-study combination was that graduation was protracted. The program was officially four and a half years, but most students took seven to eight years to complete it, and some never did. Sometime during my work with Matti, I came close to giving up my studies. I had attended all the compulsory courses at Poly, but there was a significant backlog of exams and projects I must finish before receiving my degree. It felt like a millstone around my neck, and I dreaded having to tackle it. "I'm already doing the work of an architect," I rationalized to myself. "So why torture myself by working through assignments and projects that are of little value? I've done them all in real life under the guiding hands of masters." But deep down I knew I was cheating myself. I had to get that diploma, because it is much more than a piece of paper. It is like a pilot's license, without which one cannot fly.

So, I grudgingly carried on at Poly and completed one or two compulsory assignments each semester. At times I made an effort to get a decent or even excellent grade. Other times, in a subject where I knew my talent was meager, such as water coloring, I simply attacked a bunch of canvasses strewn across the living room floor with brushes dipped in various colors, just to produce the required number of paintings. The result was a barely passing grade in that course.

One day in early 1966, I was chatting with Sigurður Thoroddsen, a compatriot who had studied engineering in Iceland for two years before switching to architecture in Finland. We compared notes on our "diploma project," a piece of architectural design equivalent to "thesis" in other fields. It suddenly occurred to me he was close to the finishing line. He had arrived two years after me, and now he was threatening to become the first Icelander to get an architecture degree in Finland! That privilege rightfully belonged to me! Suddenly, I was inspired to get cracking on my thesis.

In May 1966, just short of eight years after I set foot on Finnish soil, I became the first Icelandic architecture student to graduate there, beating Sigurður by a few months. (Since then, many Icelanders have obtained architecture degrees from Poly and other Finnish universities.) My graduation was an anticlimax. It consisted of going to the office of the Department of Architecture, finding the right clerk to talk to, and getting a certificate that listed all the courses and assignments I had completed. It took a while for reality to sink in. I was now a bona fide certified architect, and I never ever had to take an exam again. For many years, decades in fact, my sub-consciousness refused to accept it. I would wake up in a sweat, having dreamt that there was one more course I had to pass.

The next question was what would I do with my life from now on? Staying in Finland was tempting, but I was inclined to think of Iceland as my end goal. After all, I had left Iceland full of idealism and desire to contribute to my country's renaissance. At the same time, I felt I was too green to make much of a difference. Like the Vikings of yore, I must prove myself in battle before returning home. Vastly complicating my planning was Monika. Her end goal was Sweden, the land of her dreams. No matter how many times we thrashed it out, we couldn't arrive at the same destination. Finally, we found common ground in our shared taste for traveling. We agreed it would be a great idea to find jobs in exotic places, thus gaining work experience and seeing the world at the same time. A three-year plan gradually took shape in my mind: one year in another Scandinavian country, one year in a developing nation, and one year in the U.S.A. After this globetrotting adventure, I would be ready to settle in an as-yet undefined home country.

Monika approved, and we scouted around in earnest for openings outside Finland. Then fate stepped in and gave us an unexpected nudge in the direction of our plan.

CHAPTER 14

LIMBO

I like to joke that Destiny came knocking on my bathroom door. I was sitting on the toilet, reading an old newspaper article about a local architect named Jan Thurfjäll. He had just landed a large contract in a far-off land called Kuwait, and the project was the construction of Bedouin settlements in the desert outside of Kuwait City. I must also add the toilet I was using belonged to Monika's Aunt Irene and Uncle Sigurd, who lived in Luleå, a town in northern Sweden. We were visiting them on a trip to celebrate my graduation.

I showed Monika the article. Not quite sure where Kuwait was, we borrowed an atlas from Uncle Sigurd. Kuwait showed up as a tiny raisin at the tip of the Persian Gulf, next to an expansive yellow patch that denoted the desert of Saudi Arabia. We looked at each other, guardedly hopeful. For months we had been scanning trade journals that advertised international postings, but none of our enquiries had panned out. With a shrug, we agreed there was no harm in trying. I found the address of Thurfjäll's firm and paid him a cold call.

This cold call warmed up very quickly. Jan Thurfjäll was a short, rotund man and as jolly as his cheeks were ruddy. He treated me like a long-lost nephew, plying me with questions about my studies in Finland and waxing poetic over the elegance of Finnish architecture. I was flattered by his enthusiasm and would have been more so had I known that this new uncle of mine was a bit of a tycoon in those parts. He had architectural offices all over northern Sweden, plus a prefab housing company, a real estate agency, and even a bed sheet factory.

As our "interview" wound down, I was addressing him as Janne, as he liked to be called. Janne said, "I've always had great admiration for Finnish architecture. I think you'll be a good addition to the team. I'd like to hire you to work on our Kuwait project."

I floated out of his office, hardly believing my ears. Kuwait was Janne's first international contract, and he was willing to stake his success on a newly minted architect from Iceland. He knew nothing about me except what I had told him. Any other employer would have expressed interest pending receipt of credentials, references and so on, but not Janne. He trusted his heart. When not in the office, he was a passionate musician who played piano with a band, and he followed his music wherever it led him. Ten years after my visit, he would give up all his businesses, purchase a former royal yacht from England, convert it into a floating restaurant and nightclub, and operate it in the waters near his hometown until he passed away in 2000. I am sure he died a happy man.

Monika and I returned to Helsinki walking on air. Our dream of working overseas was about to come true. I informed Matti about my impending departure, which he found regrettable but accepted as a natural progression of my career. At home, Monika and I began making preparations for the next chapter in our lives. We then settled down to wait for a formal job offer.

After what seemed like an eternity but was in reality only a couple of months, I got a letter from Janne's organization. The writer was Hans Gauert, the managing director of the company's international operations. He offered me a position at his headquarters in the town of Sundsvall in Sweden. The letter also informed me that the international affiliate had recently changed its name from Thurfjäll International AB to the snappier sounding T-Consult. Monika and I read the letter over and over but found no reference to any overseas posting. We were disappointed, and yet I still had faith in my gentleman's agreement with Janne. Besides, status quo wasn't an option for me. My colleagues had congratulated me about my exciting new job, some of them with outright envy. To backtrack would be an insufferable loss of face. Monika and I thus decided to accept the offer and treat Sundsvall as a waystation. I would find bachelor quarters in the Swedish town, while she and Steinn would remain in Finland until my Kuwait posting came through.

I started working in Sundsvall in early November 1966. This office comprised two branches: one for jobs in the Sundsvall area, and the other for operations overseas. But I soon found out that the international branch was merely a paper creation. Until the opening of its Kuwait office, which was planned for early 1967, it was just Hans Gauert trying to drum up overseas business. Once in a while he would ask me to prepare some material for promoting the T-Consult brand. Most of my work, however, was for the local office, designing and implementing a variety of jobs in the area.

I pored over the newspapers every day for happenings in the Middle East. Arab-Israeli conflicts had been escalating. Palestinian guerrillas based in Syria, Lebanon, and Jordan conducted attacks against Israel, leading to devastating Israeli reprisals. During my first week in Sundsvall, an Israeli strike on the village of al-Sam`u in the Jordanian West Bank left scores dead and wounded.

It became increasingly clear that T-Consult wasn't going to establish an office in Kuwait any time soon. My correspondence with Monika was filled with anxieties. Our lives were in limbo, and there was no telling how long this state of affairs would last. We decided the least we could do was endure limbo together. Just before Christmas, after almost two months of separation, Monika and Steinn reunited with me in Sundsvall. We found a suitable apartment in the suburbs and daycare for Steinn. Monika tried to find a job, though half-heartedly, since we weren't planning to stay long. Sundsvall was a boring medium-sized harbor town in northern Sweden. It was as wooden as the paper and pulp industry that sustained its economy.

As we settled in, news from the Middle East became increasingly ominous. In April 1967, the Israeli Air Force shot down six Syrian MiG fighter jets. In May, Soviet intelligence reports indicated that Israel was planning a campaign against Syria. Although later found inaccurate, the information further heightened tensions between Israel and its Arab neighbors. The saber-rattling grew louder, but most political observers regarded the noise as nothing more than that. They believed the region would calm down after a while and an actual war was far-fetched.

The senior managers of my company must have taken these pundit opinions to heart. Or perhaps they were worried that a competitor might beat them to the Middle East market. One day Hans Gauert called me to his office and told me T-Consult was opening its office in Kuwait that month, April 1967. My heart lifted. Finally my penance in limbo was over. But what Hans said next condemned me to a place worse than hell. The company was sending Clas Göran Blom to open the Kuwait office, he said. My ears rang with disbelief. I knew Clas Göran, who also worked out of the Sundsvall office. He was a young, aggressive Swede who had no more than a two-year engineering degree. How could they pick him over me? Besides, the company and I had an understanding that my assignment was in Kuwait and that Sundsvall was just a temporary post. I had given up job opportunities and a comfortable lifestyle in Finland based on that understanding. And now they were reneging on it.

I protested. Hans' reply was that Clas Göran had been with the company longer and was thus more familiar with its operations. After he had established the office, Hans assured me, I would be on my way to Kuwait. By then, I no longer believed anything Hans told me. He had disliked me from day one. He was German and naturally more formal than the Swedes, but with me, his behavior was stiff to the point of hostile. His body language was bluntly clear: he would never forgive me for going over his head to get the job. Janne, the head honcho of the company, had handpicked me without consulting him.

Monika blew up when she heard the news. "How can they do this to us! They promised you the job!" I couldn't agree more with her, but when she went on ranting against the company, I found myself in the awkward position of defending it. Monika's anger knew no bounds. Once she started, she would rage on like a burst dam, swamping everything in sight, which inevitably included me. It was all my fault: I was too passive, I had misread the situation, perhaps even misunderstood the job offer from Janne. I had got it all wrong. So, now the battle at work had spread to the home front. Squeezed on both sides, I felt like a watermelon caught in a vise, about to explode any time.

Meanwhile, war cries in the Middle East heightened. Egyptian president Nasser, goaded by criticism from the Arab League for failing to aid Syria and Jordan against Israel, now jumped into the fray. On May 14, 1967, Nasser mobilized Egyptian forces in the Sinai; and on May 22 he closed the Gulf of Aqaba to Israeli shipping, thus blockading the Israeli port city of Eilat. On May 30, King Hussein of Jordan arrived in Cairo to sign a mutual defense pact that placed Jordanian forces under Egyptian command. Shortly thereafter, Iraq joined the alliance.

My ears were stuck to the radio. My heart went out to Israel, the underdog, as did most of Sundsvall. Here was a newborn nation, its people still recovering from a brutal genocide, and now all its neighbors were ganging up to destroy it. On June 5, 1967, I woke up to stunning news. Israeli planes had taken off while the region was still asleep. They flew over Egypt and Syria and bombarded the sitting ducks on the tarmacs. This preemptive assault destroyed most of the air force of these two countries, leaving their ground forces without air cover. The Israeli army swept in to finish the job. Within three days the Israelis had achieved an overwhelming victory, capturing the Gaza Strip and all of the Sinai Peninsula up to the east bank of the Suez Canal.

Israel warned King Hussein of Jordan against interfering. Instead of complying, he ordered the shelling of West Jerusalem. An Israeli counterattack drove Jordanian forces out of East Jerusalem and most of the West Bank. Israel also launched an assault on the Golan Heights, capturing it from Syrian forces after a day of heavy fighting. The U.N. called for a ceasefire, and one by one, Israel's vanquished neighbors agreed to lay down their arms. On the sixth day, June 10, 1967, Syria became the last of the hostile Arab states to sign the ceasefire, marking the conclusion of the Six-Day War.

In Sundsvall, the astonishing turn of events left us dumbfounded. We had thought Israel's days were numbered, but it emerged the victor and stronger than ever. The ceasefire was good news for my company. Hans asked me to fly to Kuwait as soon as possible. Monika, who had by now cultivated a deep mistrust of the company, insisted on traveling with me. "Either we travel as a family, or none of us travels," she declared. However, that would mean delaying my trip, as she and Steinn didn't have visas to Kuwait yet. In the end, Hans and I reached a compromise. The three of us would travel from Sundsvall to Rome, where Monika and Steinn would stay on the company's dime. I would continue the journey alone to Kuwait and arrange for the necessary permits for my family to join me.

CHAPTER 15
FINALLY, KUWAIT

I boarded the first commercial flight to the Middle East since the start of the Six-Day War. When my Lufthansa plane stopped over in Cairo, I saw grim-faced, gun-toting soldiers everywhere and carcasses of bombed-out planes littering the airfield. From Cairo on, instead of flying the normal route across the Sinai Peninsula, the pilot made an enormous detour, adding hours to the flight. Israel had seized the entire Peninsula from Egypt. The area was now militarily unsettled, and Lufthansa wasn't taking any chances flying over it.

My plane landed late at night in Kuwait City, the capital of Kuwait. As I exited the aircraft and started descending the steps to the tarmac, a gust of searing air almost knocked me over. I thought it must be the blast of the plane's engine before it occurred to me that it was the hot night wind of the desert.

Climate shock, culture shock, everything about Kuwait slammed me like a sledgehammer. I couldn't have picked a place more different than what I was accustomed to. While Scandinavia was cold, wet, and orderly, Kuwait was suffocatingly hot, bone-dry, and a huge sandy mess. The daytime temperature was 48°C (118°F) and would remain thereabouts for the next few months. The country consisted of the capital city, an oil export terminal, derricks sticking out here and there, and a highway leading north to Iraq and south to Saudi Arabia. The rest was desert—lots and lots of desert. Sand invaded the streets, gardens, and I would soon discover, even kitchen cabinets and my bed. Sandstorms pierced the cracks around windows and doors, depositing layers of fine dust inside the house. There was no getting away from it. The color of the city was a uniform dirty yellow.

I had expected a city worthy of an oil-rich nation, a thriving port on the Persian Gulf, but what I found was a medieval fiefdom surrounded by a desert camp. Although Kuwait struck oil in the 1930s, it would take many decades to develop into the ultra-modern glitzy metropolis of today. Back in the 1960s, the city of about half a million was a sprawl of crude, low-slung buildings. The exceptions were the massive palace compound of the Emir and the villas of the oil rich. Garbage was everywhere, since trash collection was nonexistent. Residents threw their garbage into the street for rats, feral donkeys, and other critters to feast on. The heavier trash piled up to form hillocks of rotting waste, while the lighter refuse, such as paper, was blown around during the frequent sandstorms.

I reported to work at the T-Consult "office" established by Clas Göran a few months before. I use the quotation marks because a tiny ramshackle room crammed with a few desks and chairs could hardly be called an office. It was housed in a corner of a business owned by our sponsor, Ali. In Kuwait, no foreign business could obtain the necessary work permits and licenses without the mediation of a sponsor. The requirement was simply a rip-off to enable Kuwaitis to dip into the revenues of foreign firms. I never figured out what exactly Ali's business was. All he did was sit in his room in his immaculate white robe called the *dishdasha*, smoking cigarettes, sipping sugary tea, chatting with his buddies, and watching a miniature TV.

Hans Gauert gave me my first briefing. The news wasn't good. Our Bedouin settlement project was on hold because of the repercussions of the Six-Day War. For a while, the authorities in much of the Middle East, including Kuwait, touted the war as a slam-dunk victory for Arab states. People cheered and celebrated in the streets, but as economic contractions spread and swarms of refugees fanned across the region, no amount of propaganda could mask the truth. Kuwait saw an influx of Palestinian and Egyptian refugees from the territories lost to Israel. The governing family of Kuwait was getting nervous. To remain in power, the House of Al Sabah had to tamp down discontent among their citizens. People were upset about the defeat, the government's lies about it, and the threat of refugees taking away their jobs. The government had to invest in social programs to appease the populace and also settle the newcomers. Providing permanent homes for Bedouin nomads was the lowest of their priorities.

Only a small part of our contract could be salvaged. It was a study that compared the merits of two different building materials: the traditional sand-cement blocks and the newer sand-lime ones. The subject was as dry as a mouthful of sand, but at least it gave us a toe in the door. The first draft was written by a colleague in Sundsvall, but the company that commissioned the study had rejected it as inadequate. Rewriting this report thus became my first assignment.

As the project was behind schedule, I was given a tight deadline to complete it. Most nerve-wracking of all was that I had to write it in English, my worst language in school. I had always viewed English as a scrappy, undisciplined language that jumbled bits and pieces from the Romance and Germanic schools, with neither the ardor of one nor the structure of the other. I didn't take English seriously until my last years in Finland, when I realized English was the lingua franca of the twentieth century. To prepare for my travels around the world, I gave myself a crash course by consuming every Agatha Christie mystery. And now the time had come to put Agatha to the test. I wrestled with every sentence at first, but the more I kept at it, the easier the prose flowed. The exercise also forced me to pick up the necessary technical jargon, so that my report read like a professional paper and not a murder mystery. Little did I know that the English proficiency I developed during this period would be my passport to many parts of the world.

With the Bedouin project dead in the water, we were left to scramble for pickings in the local market. In spite of my dislike of Hans, I have to admit he was talented and resourceful in this area. He won a contract to design and supervise the construction of luxurious camps for wealthy Kuwaitis traveling on *Hajj*, a pilgrimage to the holy cities of Mecca and Medina in Saudi Arabia. We hired Farouk, a competent structural engineer of Lebanese origin and a Muslim. The last qualification was essential because only a person of the Muslim faith was allowed to set foot on the sacred grounds. His job was to do site inspections in Mecca and Medina and to produce structural calculations. Using his reports, I fleshed out Hans's designs and helped a quantity surveyor prepare the bidding documents. This man, named Cruikshank, was a South African based in Kuwait. He took me under his wing and taught me his trade. This crash course in estimating construction costs and writing contracts, the basics of quantity surveying, would fundamentally change the path of my career.

With business looking up, our office moved to a better space in a brand-new building. We erected partition walls in our corner of the otherwise empty floor. The extra elbow room felt good, but the drawback was that we no longer had access to Ali's phone. Telephone lines were at a premium, with long waiting times for newcomers. And a telephone was, of course, the lifeline of any business. With luck and ingenuity, Clas Göran solved our communication problem. In another corner of our floor, he found an insulated wire that disappeared out a window and entered another window in the building across the street. Noting that the current of the wire wasn't enough to power a light bulb, he went down to the market, bought a telephone handset and connected it. Lo and behold, it worked! We had an operating telephone. There was a snag though—we didn't know our phone number. We eventually got our own line.

I worked long hours to finish the study. For me, a typical workday meant getting up in the early morning, driving to the office in downtown Kuwait, driving back at midday for lunch, trying to sleep in the sweltering heat until four o'clock, then returning to sweat at my desk until late at night. My workweek was seven days. For months, I only knew the route from home to work. The traffic was generally light but ruthlessly fast. There were no speed limits, and drivers behaved like Bedouins on camels. Lanes and directions meant nothing to them. The city had no traffic lights, only roundabouts that invited me to screech and careen through like a racecar driver. With windows rolled down, the wind slapping my face felt good, for the company car I drove was a souped-up Volkswagen Beetle with no air-conditioning.

My home life was equally wretched. After I had secured the necessary visas and permits, Monika and Steinn arrived from their exile in Rome about two weeks after me. Monika tried hard to find a job, but the shrinking postwar economy offered few openings. She was bored into nagging, and there were plenty of peeves to gripe about: Do you have to work late every night? Why do we have to live in this crummy so-called villa while Clas Göran and his wife live in a luxury apartment? We hardly have any furniture and look at the sand everywhere! What stung me most was that she was right. I was the qualified architect slaving to deliver for the company, but Clas Göran was my overseer and got all the perks. To have my wife remind me every day of this injustice was like rubbing salt into my wound. At the same time, T-Consult paid for all our living expenses in addition to a generous salary. It had us trapped in a golden cage. Even though the door was wide open, we hesitated to fly away. And thus I plodded on, while Monika found some relief by hanging out with other disgruntled expat wives. Her friends were mostly Scandinavians. They spent time at the club and beaches, passing empty days devoid of intellectual stimulation. I fully understood her frustration.

Steinn was the only one to adjust well. He was enrolled in a good school, the American-run International School of Kuwait. He was six years old, and an extrovert who believed everyone was a playmate regardless of culture or language. He thrived in school and soon picked up a new language, American English, which he mixed into the Swedish he spoke with his parents. He also learned Arabic from the neighborhood children. Watching him chatter with his friends, we were immensely proud of his linguistic talent. One day when Farouk came to dinner, he overheard Steinn yelling to his playmates in Arabic. He turned to us and gravely advised, "Make sure he never uses this language in grown-up company." We had no idea

Steinn was mouthing the foulest swear words in the Arabic language, of which there are many.

On rare weekends off, I would do my best to entertain the family. I even took them to the cinema several times. But anti-West sentiment in the wake of the war meant that the cinemas showed mostly third-rate Indian films. The audience also had to endure propaganda films showing President Nasser of Egypt barking slogans about wiping Israel off the map. The cinemas were filthy, with countless cockroaches swarming inside the showcases featuring coming attractions. Inside the theater, we had to wade through ankle-deep piles of pistachio shells to get to our seats. Sometimes a rat hunting for uneaten nuts would brush against our legs. Going to the cinema wasn't very pleasant, but it was one of the few diversions in town.

By far our favorite pastime was driving into the desert at night. Following established car tracks, we would drive tens of kilometers until we could no longer see the city lights. These forays sometimes took us far across the unmarked border into Saudi Arabia. Sprawled on a sand dune, drinking in the cool night air, the three of us would gaze at the Milky Way splashed across the black velvet sky; our troubles faded to nothingness in the vastness of the universe. Recalling what I had learned in high school astronomy, I pointed out to Steinn the Big and Little Dipper, North Star, Venus, and so on. It is no small wonder that ancient Arabs were masters of astronomy. This was the sky that Arabs gazed upon for thousands of years. Both sublime and practical, stars were an elemental part of their lives, inspiring their poetry and guiding them at night. Their scenery was unmarred by light pollution, which unfortunately couldn't be said of mine. Although we were far from the city, we still had light pollution from giant gas flames flaring here and there. In those days, when oil was pumped out and harvested, the gas byproduct was simply burned off.

I could take a break at last when the company invited bids for the Pilgrimage Camp project. Monika was desperate to skip town, and so was I. We decided on a four-day vacation to Baghdad. Our map showed that a circular route would be possible. We could travel north along the Euphrates River and return along the Tigris.

I was quite surprised to learn that my car, a Peugeot 404, needed a passport too. It was called a *triptique*, a guarantee that the car would return with us. Otherwise we would have to pay a fine valued at approximately three times the purchase price of the car. The document prevented car owners from selling their cars on the black market in countries with exorbitant duties and taxes, such as those in many countries in the Middle East and South Asia. In this case the *triptique* was issued by the Kuwaiti Automobile Association and guaranteed by the Icelandic Automobile Association. My father signed off as the ultimate payer should I illegally dispose of the vehicle. The risk of losing my vehicle due to theft or accident hung over my head throughout my travels. If anything happened to it, Dad would be liable for a huge sum of guarantee money. As a result, I was very protective of the vehicle wherever I went.

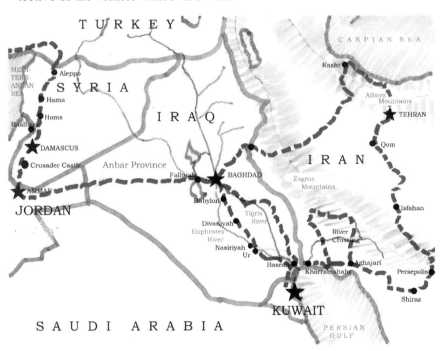

Map of the Middle East. My travels are shown in broken lines.

Our first destination was the ancient city of Ur, the birthplace of Abraham. Just before Basra, we found the exit for Ur. The asphalt strip deteriorated quickly and turned into a maze of dirt tracks. A military vehicle approached and signaled me to stop. I got out of the car to face the four Iraqi soldiers. They told us to return to the main road. Their arguments were: there was no real road for the next hundred or so kilometers, we would get lost among the crisscrossing tracks, and the military would wind up having to search for us if we didn't show up at the next military patrol station.

"I understand your concern," I said, chummily. "But I've always been interested in the history of your country. We're in this area for a short time. This is our only chance to see the cultural heritage sites we've heard so much about. It would be a great honor for us to visit Ur. And this is the fastest way to get there."

My words must have stirred up a swell of national pride. The commander declared, "We will go with you."

The patrol did a U-turn and escorted us for much of the trip to Ur. When the soldiers left us, some 40 km short of our target, their parting advice was to always select the track that veered to the right and to stop if we were caught in a sandstorm. We did select the right tracks, there was no sandstorm, and we arrived safely in the ruins of Ur. I notice from today's maps that this desert track is now a four-lane highway.

As we approached the city, an earth-brown stump jutted out of the bare skyline, its size growing more and more spectacular the closer we got. According to the map, this was the Ziggurat. A *ziggurat* is a massive terrace structure built in ancient Mesopotamia. It was built with sunbaked bricks piled on top of each other in successively receding levels, like a pyramid. The one at Ur, which is about four thousand years old, rests on an enormous base measuring two thirds of an acre and is one of the best preserved in the world. Three theories are commonly put forward about the purpose of the Ziggurat. One, it was a dwelling of the gods and a place of offerings to them. Two, it was a reconstruction of the cosmic mountain from the creation myths. And three, it was a bridge between heaven and earth.

We parked close to the Ziggurat. The area seemed totally devoid of human life. I stepped out of the car and was surprised to see pottery shards strewn all around. These fragments must be thousands of years old, but in this glut of ancient artifacts, they were discarded like debris. Not knowing what the rules were, I resisted the temptation to pick up a piece or two as souvenirs. We wandered around all by ourselves, overwhelmed by the sensation of treading on the same ground as Abraham, founder of the Jewish nation and Judeo-Christian civilization.

A man wearing a *dishdasha* and checkered *keffiyeh* on his head appeared and introduced himself as the guardian of the ruins. A friendly, engaging man, he spouted story after story of the Ziggurat and the village that existed nearby. Wagging his chin like a village gossip, he chattered about the characters as if they were his neighbors. Then he did something that made me question the authenticity of his tales. He pointed at the rubble of a wall and proclaimed, "Right here is the home of Abraham and Sarah." Although the Bible does mention Ur as the hometown of Abraham, how anyone can make such a declaration of a pile of bricks stretches the imagination.

At the end of the tour, I found myself in a quandary. I had changed money at the border, but none of the bills was of small denomination for gratuity. When I handed the curator the equivalence of a US$50 note, he sprang to attention, told us to wait, and hurried away. He returned with two clay fragments, each smaller than my palm and etched with an ancient script. He told us the inscription was cuneiform. We were stunned. Cuneiform is like hieroglyphics, one of the earliest forms of written expression. Still not quite believing our eyes, we dithered over which one to accept. Our guide made up our minds for us. "Keep both," he said. Clearly this was an illegal transaction, but I could hear the ancients whispering in my ear: "It is your destiny to safeguard these relics." I'm also glad he offered us two tablets. When Monika and I divorced, we didn't have to fight over them. Mine now decorates the wall unit in my living room and is quite a conversation piece.

After Ur, we continued north on the desert track. We spent the night next to the track somewhere between Ur and the city of Diwanyia. We slept in the car, since there were no hotels around. It was also a way to guard our vehicle through the night. The seats of the Peugeot 404 were ingeniously designed for camping. By pulling the front seats forward and reclining them all the way, the front and rear seats connected to form a lumpy queen-size bed that easily accommodated two adults and a child. We would spend many nights on this makeshift camper during our travels.

The next morning we continued to our next destination, the ancient city of Babylon. Ishtar Gate, one of the entrances, was a dazzling blue facade made of lapis lazuli. From the gate stretched the resplendent Processional Way, which was lined by walls frescoed with more than a hundred lions. The next stop, however, was a colossal disappointment. It was a place that some archeologists believe was the site of the legendary Tower of Babel. A local guide told me that shortly before the First World War, a group of archeologists excavated a *ziggurat* now known as the Tower of Babel. When they returned to their dig after the war, they found that locals had discovered the excellent quality of the excavated bricks and sold them as building materials. All that was left was the huge hole in the ground for tourists to goggle at.

Shortly north of Babylon, we encountered the sandstorm the soldiers had warned us about. The wind whipped up and turned the desert into a ballroom of waltzing dust devils. I killed the engine, and we watched in dread as the gusts churned sky and earth into a huge pot of pea soup. Visibility went from poor to nil, and the car shook as if it was still running. Even without the soldiers' advice, I knew better than to go on. Driving in such conditions is equivalent to subjecting the vehicle to a sandblaster. It can strip the paint off the body, roughen the windshield until it is opaque, and wreak havoc on the engine.

The wind finally abated, and brown slurry fell from the sky. I soon realized this was the "mud rain" I had read about. I had often wondered about it, and now that my curiosity had been satisfied, I wished never to experience this phenomenon again.

When the rain stopped, I got out to inspect the car. What greeted me was a clay sculpture of my brand-new, once-golden Peugeot. Every square inch was covered in thick glutinous mud. It took us a long time to scrape the dirt off the windshield and windows so that we could see our way to Baghdad. The entire storm lasted about an hour.

Baghdad looked like a chocolate pudding, with everything covered in slimy, slippery goo. I remember in particular the filigreed facades of the old houses. They would have been exquisite, especially the details of the intricate balconies, if only they weren't caked in mud. We returned to Kuwait the next day along the banks of the Tigris River. The trip was a thankfully uneventful drive on a four-lane highway. At the end of it, we were exhausted yet invigorated, our spirit of adventure renewed and ready to conquer new territory in this marvelous, timeless land. All the hardships we had endured had been worthwhile.

The lull at the office continued as the company waited for the returns of the Pilgrimage Camp bid. Other projects remained dormant, and T-Consult's finances were in tatters. As a token of consideration on our part, Monika and I moved into cheaper quarters, a two-story row house closer to town. The place had been occupied by a Dutch acquaintance who was leaving the country. Conveying with the house was a five-gallon glass container and associated winemaking paraphernalia, including a recipe for Indonesian rice wine. This was a godsend. Kuwait was a dry country in more ways than one. Alcohol was banned, and the supply on the black market was of dubious quality and expensive. The ingredients for winemaking, however, were plentiful in the local market. The moment we moved into our new quarters, we set out to brew our first batch of rice wine. Many more would follow, and our popularity among friends soared.

The weather had cooled noticeably by October. One morning I stepped out of the house and felt goose bumps on my skin. I went back in to put on a sweater. The thermometer outside the house read 90°F (33°C). No wonder I felt chilled! After four months of relentless 120°F weather, my body was reacting to the "cold front."

The break in heat also brought the odd shower. At the first drop of rain, people rushed out to the streets, raised their arms to Heaven, and cried with joy. A few weeks later, Heaven sent its blessings again, but this time it went overboard. Swords of light slashed the sky and released a deluge of biblical proportions, though thankfully it poured for only one day rather than forty as in Noah's time. But Kuwait was pancake-flat, and there were no storm drains. As quickly as the flip of a coin, one torrent turned drought into flood. The entire city was inundated. Emergency workers thundered around on rubber boats driven by powerful outboard engines. We were stuck at home for a few days.

Our house had a flat roof, which was delightful to sleep on during cool dry nights but a nightmare after a heavy shower. The parapets held in the water and turned the roof into one big muddy pool. On the day of the rainstorm, I went to check on the roof. I opened the door and was almost bowled over. Water cascaded around me and tumbled down two flights of steps into the living room. I clambered down and opened the front entrance to let out our uninvited guest. And then we started mopping up the mess.

Monika was eager to get away as much as possible. Knowing the trips were her only outlet, I tried to oblige whenever work permitted. At home, Monika's nerves bristled like a frayed power cord. Traveling was like wrapping electrical tape round her ragged wire. It was an easy, though temporary, fix.

Ancient Persia, now part of Iran, was the target of our second trip. This time, we planned a one-week itinerary, throwing in as many sites as logistically possible. As I mentioned before, Monika preferred breadth to depth in her travels. The more area she covered, the higher her spirits. We asked friends and coworkers about what to expect in Iran, but nobody seemed to know anything beyond the Kuwait, Basra, Baghdad axis. No one we knew had traveled that far by road.

We crossed the border from Iraq to Iran at the east bank of the Shatt-el-Arab River. This river is the confluence of the Euphrates and Tigris before emptying into the Persian Gulf. As we walked over to the customs desk on the Iranian side, we had to squeeze by the front entrance of the local jail. Hands clawed between the bars at us, accompanied by high-pitched wails. I peeked in and saw the prisoners crammed together, reaching out and jostling for air. The scene reminded me of the paintings of hell by the Dutch artist Hieronymus Bosch.

After crossing the border, the landscape became marshy, but gradually changed back to the all too familiar desert. The majestic Zagros Mountains towered like a giant fortress in the backdrop. The craggy massifs were the largest in the region and comparable to the European Alps and North American Rockies.

At this point, I must say something about Steinn. He was the best traveler I have ever met. Anyone of any age would gripe about the long rides in a car without air-conditioning, the extreme heat, the lack of space, creature comforts, and so on. But not Steinn. I often forgot I had a six-year-old sitting quietly in the backseat, doing whatever he did to entertain himself. The only time he fussed was during the leg through the marshland. A large beetle got into the car and landed with an audible thud in his eye. He cried out in pain. I stopped the car to check on him. I had never seen him so frantic before. But once it became obvious there was no injury to his eye, he quickly calmed down and became his normal contented self again.

We passed through the town of Khorramshar and continued east toward our destination—the cultural heritage sites of ancient Persia. I stopped at a roundabout to decipher the road signs, which were in Farsi, a language unknown to me. The only human being in sight was a nicely dressed man in Western-style trousers and shirt, and holding a goldfish bowl with a goldfish in it.

I addressed him slowly in English. To my pleasant surprise, he replied in fluent English. He told us which road to take and said he was waiting for a bus headed in the same direction. We offered him and his goldfish a ride. During the drive, he explained he was the pharmacist in Aghajari, a small town at the foot of the mountains. It was his daughter's birthday, and he had been to Khorramshar to buy her a present, the goldfish. When we arrived at his home after about an hour, the birthday girl squealed with delight at the sight of her present. Our hosts smothered us with hospitality. The food and cold drinks were most welcome, but the shower was the best of all. Since we were camping, we could only clean ourselves from a water can. They also offered us a room for the night. But it was only 5 pm, the sun was still shining, and we had an ambitious itinerary to stick to. We declined the gracious invitation and went on our way. This was our first taste of the generosity of the Iranian people.

We traveled deep into the mountains that night. The rock formations were astounding. In some places the tortuous layers looked like stacks of wet newspapers folded and squeezed together with gigantic clamps. What great forces must have been at work to accomplish this! I also saw oil or bituminous substances oozing out of rocks and streaking down cliffs. At nightfall, the brownish mountains became bathed in an orange glow from the gigantic gas flares shooting out of oil wells. The pulsating flames lent a surreal drama to the barren mountains.

When it became too dark to drive on the winding dirt roads, we found an open spot to camp for the night. We put down the car seats as usual. I had stretched out on our "bed" when Monika pointed to something outside. I sat up and saw a couple of shadows flickering in the eerie gaslights. They were moving closer, and then I realized they were people and not ones I would want to meet in the dead of night. My heart beating furiously, I managed to reposition the driver's seat. By the time I was sitting up at the wheel, the intruders were only a few meters away. I turned on the engine and floored the gas, wheels screeching and gravel flying. The intruders must have jumped out of the way, for I didn't notice hitting anyone.

This incident left us quite shaken. We could have been robbed, our car hijacked (which meant my father would have to pay a huge fine), or worse, murdered. That night, I drove until a village appeared. I coasted into the heart of the village and parked on a street surrounded by houses. This became our method for selecting a campsite. From then on, we parked in well-lit parts of towns, typically near a police station.

We reached Shiraz the next day. Nestled a mile high in the mountains, Shiraz is best known in the West for the wine grapes that carry the town's name. After enduring the heat in the lowlands, the cool mountain air was heavenly. We walked around admiring the elaborate architecture, from the mosques to the ornamentally tiled gas stations. We visited the tomb of a famous poet from Shiraz. It was a most pleasant place to stroll around and breathe in the rose-scented air. In fact, downtown Shiraz was a quilt of rose gardens, a hallmark of Iranian culture.

Our next destination, about an hour's drive away, was Persepolis, the capital of the Persian Achaemenian Empire. The site was a large expanse of ruined buildings, the outcome of wanton destruction by Alexander the Great and his army. A few structures survived, including a series of bas-reliefs of Persian warriors that adorned a low foundation wall. The well-preserved carvings were lifelike and went on for an entire block. Pacing in front of them, I felt like a general inspecting my troops before facing off Alexander's men.

While in junior high, I had spent many hours perusing books on Alexander's exploits. The stories about this man who marched his army from Macedonia through Persia, Afghanistan, Pakistan, and finally to India, fascinated me. Even at that young age, I could tell he was crazy. At the same time, I felt kinship between my Viking spirit and Alexander's lunacy. Vikings, too, had ventured incredible distances. The only difference was my ancestors didn't conquer and subjugate other people. We merely looted and raped and hung around for a while. Most of the time, we returned home, leaving a few traces of ourselves, such as when a blue-eyed blond is born in the unlikeliest parts of the world.

After Persepolis, we continued for another hour toward Pasargadae, our final destination. This city was built by Cyrus II the Great around 550 BC. The literature on ancient architecture hails this city as a great achievement in terms of balance, simplicity and beauty, but all I can remember was the boxy stone sepulcher that housed the remains of Cyrus II. By then, I was suffering from antiquity fatigue. One ruin looked much like another. I began to understand why all the sites we visited were empty of visitors except the Sigurdssons. Locals were too jaded to care, and foreigners couldn't easily get to these out-of-the-way places. The upside was that I didn't have to contend with busloads of tourists and shops peddling cheap trinkets. In any case, after a week of time travel to the distant past, we were more than ready to return to our twentieth-century home.

CHAPTER 16

MY FIRST (AND LAST) HAREM

Life in the office picked up as our job hunt in the region began to bear fruit. One of them sounded exciting—supervising the construction of the palace of the ruler of Abu Dhabi. The Egyptian architect who had designed the palatial residence had absconded, leaving no one to supervise the construction. My job was to fill this void, which meant a six-week stay in Abu Dhabi. The project sounded most intriguing, for the palace included a harem, definitely a first for me. Monika wanted to come along but was told that wasn't possible. My accommodations were to be bachelor's quarters, basically one small bare room in a dormitory. Reluctantly, she stayed back in Kuwait with Steinn.

Abu Dhabi is one of seven Emirates that merged to form today's United Arab Emirates. At the time, the whole town was one giant construction site. The main street was a huge sandbox and a trap for unwitting drivers. Even four-wheel-drive vehicles often got stuck and had to be rescued. Foreign workers swarmed the town. The high-level professionals were mostly British, the skilled workers Indian and Palestinian, and the laborers Iranian. The only available lodgings for expats were barrack-like dormitories with broken plumbing.

Abu Dhabi had sprung out of the middle of nowhere. In the 1950s, the area was only a clutter of mud huts, since the population was largely nomadic. The father of the Emir whose palace I was working on was the first generation to enjoy the incredible oil riches of the region. One story about the father claimed that he stuffed all his oil money in his mattress, not knowing what else to do with it. Indian rupee was then the common currency in these parts, and when he found that rats were feasting on his rupees, he sent the Indian government a letter of complaint about the quality of their currency.

I was actually nervous about the assignment, since harem architecture had been absent from my curriculum. I browsed the library in Kuwait and found a couple of books about the life of women in the Muslim world, but there was little guidance with respect to the requirements of our project. The Prophet, says a man is entitled to have four wives if he can treat them equally. *Who is going to be the arbiter of that?* I wondered. According to my Muslim friends, the Emir and other high-ranking members of society treated the four-wife limitation very liberally, typically by having three, more or less, permanent wives and a fourth temporary one who can be replaced at the whim of the ruler.

The new palace was still a skeleton when I started my assignment. It was actually a compound of four mini palaces that radiated from the main edifice. Each was a multilevel luxury mansion occupied by a wife and her children and servants. Connecting all four in the center was the Emir's reception area, consisting of a cavernous ceremonial hall, administrative offices, and security buildings. The Emir wouldn't have his own sleeping quarters but would have rooms in the residences of his wives.

One of my jobs was to figure out what to do with the esoteric building materials that the Egyptian architect had purchased. Under orders to spare no expense to make the place luxurious, he went on a shopping spree that "extravagant" doesn't even begin to describe. Architects normally chafe under the reins of a budget. The opposite—building without a budget—is actually much more trying. It's like sending a child into a candy store and telling him to eat all he wants. The outcome can't be good. Faced with the piles of candy in our warehouse, the decisions that confronted me were daunting. For example, what should we do with the solid gold faucets? There were about a dozen of them, and they had to shine equally in the quarters of each wife, otherwise someone could feel slighted. Another dilemma was where to install the toilet seats that played stereo music when you raised the lid. We had a number of them, but not enough for every toilet. Which wife would like that sort of thing, and which wouldn't? Then there was the batch of elaborately sculpted ceramic tiles. They could form the backsplash to the Emir's ceremonial throne or his personal throne (the toilet). Decisions, decisions, and thus the list went on.

I was fortunately deemed too junior to participate in site meetings with His Royal Highness. After one such meeting, the Agent-in-Charge, a Brit, was ready to tear out what little remained of his hair. The Emir had decided he wanted a penthouse atop the roof of the already-built ceremonial hall. The roof structure had of course never been engineered for such a load, but the Emir considered himself above such trivia as the rules of engineering or the law of gravity. The chief engineer resorted to a remarkably ingenious solution. To test the roof's ability to carry the extra weight, he ordered the Iranian laborers to load the appropriate spots on the roof structure with cement bags of a weight equivalent to the proposed penthouse. At the same time he set up devices that measured the downward bending of the structure. At the end of the day he determined the roof was strong enough to hold up the Emir's wishes. The penthouse became reality.

On the eve of my departure from Abu Dhabi, my coworkers gave me a farewell party at the club, where the all-male expat workforce socialized. Their main pastime was to ogle the British BOAC air hostesses on layovers and get roaring drunk. The liquor laws of this British-dominated fiefdom were much more liberal than those in Kuwait. During my party, I noticed a man, obviously sloshed, crawling out on all fours under the bar's swinging gates. The scene was right out of an American Wild West movie. "Who's that guy?" I asked my colleagues. Somebody answered, "Oh, he's the captain of the plane that will be taking you to Kuwait tomorrow morning."

I returned to Kuwait in one piece. That weekend, I decided to atone for my harem escapade by treating the family to a tour of a special Iranian city—Isfahan, famous for its grand Persian architecture. Cocky from the success of our previous trips, I chose a shortcut that would traverse the mountains and save us countless miles and hours.

Our shortcut turned out to be a gravel road. On top of that, January was the middle of winter, also the rainy season. Watching the sleet and wet snow pelt my windshield, the first pangs of doubt hit me. But, I was twenty-nine years old. My faith in my invincibility swept aside all qualms, and I forged ahead.

After a while, we descended into a deep valley. A river flowed at the bottom, with no bridge in sight. I sized up the obstacle in my path, comparing it with the rivers I had forded in Iceland. "This is doable," I thought and plunged in. The engine died midway. The most potent Finnish cusswords seethed through my teeth. Monika and Steinn were deadly silent.

A desperate situation calls for a desperate solution. I put the car in first gear, pressed down hard on the ignition key, and forced the starter motor to keep the engine turning and dragging the car to the other side of the river. The starter motor survived the abuse, and we made it across. Once on dry land, I checked under the hood and found that one of the spark plug covers had cracked and was causing the engine to misfire on one cylinder. I dried up the parts and got the other three cylinders running. Since I didn't want to turn back and face the river again, the only option was to push ahead up the narrow mountain gravel road. My poor Peugeot stalled halfway up the slope. I grabbed my toolbox, confident I could wheedle it back to life with the aid of "rubber bands and chewing gum," as the gang at the BP repair shop would put it.

While I was working on the engine, a truck came lumbering up the steep slope while another descended on us from above. Both drivers came out of their cabs, which were colorfully painted with sceneries, a common decor for trucks in these parts. They took one look at me, and determined that this foreigner who had driven up this route in an ordinary car in the middle of the rainy season was obviously nuts. We had no language in common, but their body language was clear. They wanted me to step aside, please, and let the experts take over. The truckers got the engine running marginally better than before. With a grand gesture they indicated the road was all mine. But I couldn't leave without showing my appreciation. Their threadbare jackets and pants indicated they were dirt poor. Trying to help a stranded fellow traveler, they had been traipsing around in sandals in the sleet-covered mud for over an hour. I wanted to give them a parting gift and suspected offering money would be seen as an insult. Being a heavy smoker at that time, I had plenty of cigarettes in the car. I presented two cartons to my rescuers. But no, they adamantly refused even this kind of compensation. The last I saw in my rearview mirror was the pair of them huddling in the sleet, waving at me and beaming with pleasure at getting this imbecile moving again.

Driving on to Isfahan was out of the question. Monika's heart was set on seeing the famed architecture, but mine was set too. There was a line between adventure and adventurism, and even I knew it would be unwise to cross it. I promised her many more trips in the future and coasted down the valley to the main road.

Back in the office, the friction between Hans Gauert and me resumed. This volcano had been rumbling a long time. It was bound to erupt, and it did when I least expected it. I mentioned in passing to Hans a job offer I had recently received. It was from the Saudi Ministry of Public Works in response to a job application I had submitted eons ago. The job was low in rank, and the salary a pittance. I thought it was preposterous, but Hans' eyes lit up. "You should take it," he said in all seriousness. "You can be my eyes and ears in Riyadh. If you hear of any consulting possibilities in Saudi Arabia, you can pass the information to me." I blew up at the idea of becoming an industrial spy. Before I knew it, the words "I quit!" flew out of my mouth.

After our tempers cooled, Hans and I realized it wasn't in the interest of either of us to part ways immediately. I continued to work for the company for a few months. On my last day in the office, Hans and I shook hands stiffly. I wanted nothing to do with this man ever again, but apparently the arc of justice had its own plan. During my employment with the World Bank years later, my boss asked me to interview an architect who had applied for a Bank consultancy in Pakistan. Hans Gauert was his name. At the interview, Hans did a lot of smiling and reminiscing about old times as if we had been bosom buddies. To be fair, I assessed his strengths and weaknesses objectively, and he got the job.

CHAPTER 17

HOMEWARD BOUND

I had carried out the Viking tradition of setting sail and proving myself in battle on the world stage. The most decisive struggle was the one with myself, and I think I had won it. Since leaving Iceland, I had fought with the demons in my head who told me I wasn't good enough and would never make it. But here I was, a decade later, a certified architect with a unique and diverse curriculum vitae. (How many architects can claim experience with harem construction?) My future after T-Consult was a question mark, and yet I didn't lose sleep over my next job. The Middle East had revealed to me my strength. I could collaborate with anyone from any background, as long as the person wasn't a close-minded jackass. Professionals of Lebanese, Palestinian, Indian, British, Swedish, and other nationalities had worked by my side. I thrived in their company, their different perspectives, beliefs, and stories. The rich culture made me bubble happily like the yeast in my homemade wine. I have to thank my parents for this. They had taught me to embrace conflicting viewpoints, to listen to every side, and make up my own mind.

Monika and I reviewed my game plan to see the world. I had fulfilled two of my three objectives: a year in a Scandinavian country other than Finland, and a year in a developing nation. The third, which was a year in the U.S., would have to wait. If the opportunity never arose, I wasn't going to carry my regret to the grave. All things considered, it was time to settle down. I wanted to go home to Iceland, and although this wasn't Monika's first choice, she agreed to give it a try.

Before we left the area, however, we wanted to have our fill of it. Who knew whether we would return? After studying the map for days, we charted a grand six-week tour that would take us east through Iran, Afghanistan, Pakistan and India, and back to Kuwait to wind down our affairs. It took a bit of time to acquire all the necessary visas. Then one day in July 1968, we were all set to go. As we were putting our last items into the car, a visitor with a bleeding foot arrived at our apartment, carrying a telegram that blew apart all our plans.

The messenger was Clas Göran's wife, Sonja, a much more congenial person than her "better" half. She was the general factotum at the office, keeping accounts, filing correspondence, and doing other odd jobs. That day she saw a telegram addressed to me, marked urgent. Knowing we were about to leave, she ran the mile over. While jogging along the littered streets in sandals, a glass shard made a nasty cut in her foot. As Monika cleaned and bandaged the wound, I read the telegram. The sender was UNESCO, and it expressed interest in hiring me for the position of quantity surveyor in Malawi. Could I please present myself as soon as possible for an interview at the nearest regional office: Beirut, Lebanon?

After driving Sonja back to the office, Monika and I sat down to ponder the news. Much as we looked forward to our grand tour to India, the prospect of employment with such a prestigious agency was tantalizing. Just consider the name, United Nations Educational, Scientific and Cultural Organization. Every aspect of civilization fell under its umbrella. We simply couldn't ignore its summons. I had applied for the architect opening for the Malawi project some time ago but hadn't received a reply. And now the prospective offer was for the quantity surveyor position, which I was less sure about. In Kuwait I had dabbled in tasks related to that occupation, but did I really know enough about that trade? It took me a minute to persuade myself that I did.

We unpacked the car and made dramatic changes to our travel plans. Instead of heading east, we would drive west to Beirut, the location of my interview, via Iraq, Jordan, and Syria. Our visa application stalled at the Syrian embassy, however, and so we dropped Syria from our itinerary. We would stop at Amman in Jordan, leave the car there, and fly the last hop over Syria to Beirut.

One memorable incident took place during our drive through Anbar province in Iraq. The place was unheard of when I motored through, but after the U.S. invasion of Iraq in 2003, this Sunni stronghold of Saddam Hussein's became world renowned for insurgency and suicide bombings. Even during my days, traveling in this neighborhood was dicey. While guessing my way through the desert of Al Anbar, we passed a ghastly sight. It was the charred remains of what looked like a small industrial complex. The scene evoked news articles about an Israeli air raid on an Iraqi nuclear research facility. I knew we shouldn't be there, but there was no other way out than to keep driving. Soon after, a military patrol pulled up alongside. I stopped the car, and we all got out to show them exactly who we were, a family of dumb, lost foreigners.

A soldier peered into my car. He started shouting angrily in Arabic, his finger jabbing at the camera on the back seat. They hustled us all back into the Peugeot, I in the driver's seat, Monika next to me, while Steinn shared the back seat with the soldier. I felt something hard poke at my spine. I glanced at the rearview mirror and realized the object was the muzzle of the soldier's machine pistol. The drive lasted an hour at most, but it seemed like eternity. To prevent an accidental burst from the gun, I took it slow and easy on the desert tracks. At military headquarters in Ramadi, an English-speaking army captain told us we had been trespassing in a prohibited area, and therefore he would have to confiscate our film. "Do you mind?" he politely added. Now that I understood what the agitation was all about and a gun was no longer poking at my back, I was brave enough to retort, "Yes, I do mind. All our pictures from Bagdad are on that film and none are from that military area." He thought for a moment and said, "Okay, you may go." And off we went again, film and all.

This time, we took the track that skirted the nuclear station or whatever the ruined facility was. Inside the car, the thermometer cracked when the temperature reached 130°F (55°C). Our lifesaver was the "desert cooler," a brilliant contraption desert dwellers used for supplying cool drinking water. This was a tightly woven jute sack with a one-gallon capacity. It was almost watertight but always wet to the touch. Hung on the front grill of the car, the contents of the cooler slowly evaporated in the dry heat, replicating the cooling function of an air-conditioning unit, and thereby chilling the water for drinking. The dry, hot air caused painful cracks on my lips. It also left white salt streaks on the creases of my pants where the sweat evaporated as soon as it appeared. Despite drinking copious amounts of water, our urinary system seemed to be on holiday. Our body fluids vaporized through the skin at an astonishing rate.

Pushing on toward Amman, we came to an area where the track had been pulverized into fine powder by passing vehicles. This dust literally moved like liquid when disturbed. Traction was minimal, and my Peugeot fishtailed all over the place. I passed several cars trapped in this dust sea, their owners furiously sweating to dig them out. I resisted the urge to stop and help, for if I had done so, my car would have ended in the same morass. White-knuckling my steering wheel, I ran the windshield wipers at full blast to see through the puffs of dust clouds. We, car and people, emerged from the ordeal looking like sand sculptures. During the rest of my ownership of this vehicle, which was three more years, I would keep discovering this desert powder in the most obscure nooks and crannies.

On the Jordanian side of the border, the desert turned into an equally inhospitable rocky wasteland, but there was at least the semblance of a road and the ground was firm. I remember the pleasure of washing away the dust at the first rest stop, and ah, the beer that fizzed down our throats as we rested and counted our blessings.

We left the car at Amman airport and took the first available flight to Beirut. After landing, I approached an information desk to look for accommodation. A mob descended on me, dozens of hands grabbing at me and yanking me to select a different hotel. I settled on a downtown suite that turned out to be excellent and cost only US$7 per night. There was definitely something wrong with this picture, I thought. Beirut was dubbed "Paris of the East." A former French colony, the city was as indulgent as its namesake. Residents of the oil-rich Gulf States flocked there every summer to sample the hedonistic pleasures and cooler weather. My visit was at the peak of the tourist season, yet the usual visitors from the Gulf States were staying away.

My instincts were correct. In the aftermath of the Six-Day War, the influx of PLO militants and other Palestinian refugees into Lebanon had upset the delicate balance between Christians and Muslims. What I witnessed at the airport was a sign of the sectarian tensions that kept tourists away and would blow up into all-out civil war.

I presented myself to the UNESCO regional representative. This international civil servant of unspecified nationality asked me politely, "What can I do for you?" His question took me by surprise. I patiently explained to him the purpose of my visit, thinking he hadn't put two and two together. He still had no inkling of what I was talking about. I whipped out the urgent cable from UNESCO and pointed to his name, designated in black and white as my interviewer. By then, heat was rising up my collar. I had scrapped my grand tour, dragged my family through grueling terrain, and spent precious time and money to get here. This could be a life-altering event for me, but for this bureaucrat, I was just a piece of paper lost in the shuffle.

As I suspected, UNESCO Headquarters in Paris had forgotten to inform the interviewer about the interview. The representative promised to check with headquarters and suggested that I take a day or two off to view the sights of Lebanon. He hoped to have news for me when I returned.

The letdown didn't dampen our appetite for sightseeing. We rented a car and drove to the Roman ruins of Baalbek. These were magnificent temples made of giant stone columns brought across the mountains from Aswan, Egypt. What intrigued me most was the "Pregnant Woman" at the nearby quarry. She was an impeccably cut stone slab, one of the biggest in the world, at a size comparable to that of an eighteen-wheeler. For some reason, she only got partway out of the quarry. Using the dimensions of the slab and the specific gravity of rock, I estimated that this pregnant woman weighed 1,200 tons! It blew my mind how such a precise cut and transfer were possible before the invention of laser measurements and hydraulic power tools, at a time when Jesus was walking around in nearby Jerusalem.

When I called on the UNESCO representative again, he was no more enlightened than before. I left him my résumé and other information. He promised to report back to headquarters. I said goodbye, too fed up to care. If I never heard from him again, so be it.

From Beirut we flew back to Amman, picked up our car, and launched straight into our greatly reduced grand tour. Instead of six weeks, we would cut it to three, and instead of aiming for India, we would go only as far as Iran. Our first destination on the revised route was Nineveh in northern Iraq. As it turned out, we couldn't even get that far. Shortly after Baghdad, a military roadblock forbade us to travel further north. We were about to enter Kurdistan, which already was in a low-level conflict with Saddam Hussain's Sunni regime.

Unfazed, we turned east toward the Iranian border to complete the rest of our tour. We arrived in the late afternoon at the small border post of Khosrovi. Perhaps to make up for the smallness of the one-room station, the paperwork was enormous. By then, I had grown used to filling lengthy forms for customs and immigration. I thought I had seen them all, but this little border post proved me wrong. In addition to the standard paperwork, it also kept a set of ledgers to record the nationalities and particulars of the visitors. As each nationality had its own volume, the officer searched the bookshelf for the binder marked "Iceland."

But Iceland was nowhere to be found. This caused quite a commotion among the men. The commander took over, grilling me about the geographic whereabouts of my country. I have to say his geography wasn't bad. His eyes lit up when I said this place was an island, about 500 km northwest of England. "Aha!" he said. "That country isn't called Iceland. It is called Ireland. There is a one letter difference." I quickly said he was right, and there must be a misprint in my passport. Sloppy Irelanders. So I carefully filled in all my particulars in the Irish ledger. After all I had plenty of Irish ancestors from my family's Viking days.

Once across the border, the country became mountainous. We were driving through the Alborz mountain range, which traverses northern Iran from east to west. Its highest peak is the breathtaking Mt. Damavand. At 5,600 meters (18,400 ft.) above sea level, this snow-capped volcano is the highest mountain in the Middle East.

After leaving the highlands, the ecosystem changed drastically on our descent to the Caspian Sea. The dry, pleasant mountain air gave way to heat and humidity, and barren rocks exploded into luxuriant vegetation, including rice terraces more commonly associated with tropical Asia. We found a nice beach on the shores of the Caspian and took a dip in the warm brine. It wasn't particularly refreshing, but we had to do our tourist duty. The Caspian Sea, despite its name, is a lake, in fact, the world's largest lake. The water, however, is salty because the Caspian has no outlet to flush out the salts that have leached into the water.

We turned south toward Teheran. Upon exiting a tunnel near the top of the mountains, the scenery abruptly changed back from tropical green to desert brown. Tehran turned out to be a big, ugly city of concrete and cinder blocks, with plenty of white-clad men and a few women in black chador bustling about. We pushed on to the city we really wanted to see—Isfahan, the aborted goal of our botched shortcut a few months earlier.

Passing a small but prosperous-looking town, we decided to spend the night there. At an outdoor restaurant, we asked the waiter about hotels in the town. He gave us a name and directions. As we were finishing our meal, a well-groomed Iranian couple who had been sitting at an adjacent table approached us. They informed us that the hotel the waiter mentioned was a fleabag unfit for travelers like us. They would be honored to host us in their home for the night. Monika and I looked at each other with disbelief, which quickly brightened into delight. And so we spent a very pleasant night at the home of total strangers. I have long since lost contact with the Iranian couple, but this is yet another example of the endearing hospitality of Iranians.

Isfahan wall details.

Isfahan, like Tehran, was a large and bustling city, but unlike Tehran, it was an architectural wonder, not so much because of individual buildings as the sum of them all. The palatial mosques with their divinely tiled domes, the plazas surrounded by buildings each a feast for the eyes, the manicured gardens and even gas stations covered in ornamental inlays, all wove together into a glorious fabric. An overview of the street scene gave one an impression of uniformity. A close-up look, however, revealed diverse, intricate details embroidered on tiled facades. Some were in blue ceramics, others in earth tones, and the variety of patterns was infinite. Isfahan is proof that harmony doesn't mean conformity. Rather, it is a fellowship of creativity within the bounds of prevailing aesthetics.

We arrived back in Kuwait after a few more days on the road. And thus concluded our tour of the Middle East, spanning from Beirut in the west to Isfahan in the east, from the Caspian Sea in the North to the Persian Gulf in the South. We had one week to service our well-used car, pack up and drive home to Scandinavia.

We loaded our meager possessions into the Peugeot one day in August 1968, said goodbye to our coworkers, and set off for the long journey. We got as far as downtown. I braked for stopped traffic, whereas the truck behind didn't. Having no brakes, it used the rear end of our Peugeot as a stopping device. Luckily nobody was hurt, but the trunk of my car was crushed and the rear doors couldn't close properly. To add insult to injury, the truck driver didn't have insurance.

We moved back into the empty apartment. The Peugeot dealership assured us our car was reparable, but it would take at least a week. My heart sank. Our exit visa was expiring in seven days, and applying for another one would take weeks. I hung around the garage, watching the mechanics roll my poor truncated Peugeot onto a giant rack and literally stretch the car back to its original shape. Painting, however, took longer. I went in and out of the shop several times, only to be met by *"Bukrah, Insh'Allah,"* or "Tomorrow, God willing." Finally, just before close of business on the seventh day, my golden Peugeot, as beautiful as when I first set eyes on it, was ready to come home. We threw in our belongings, dashed to the Iraqi border, and exited the country two hours before our visas expired and our coach turned into a pumpkin.

We retraced our route through Iraq and into Jordan. From there we headed north toward Syria, this time armed with long-awaited transit visas. "This is not a visa," the border guard said, pointing disdainfully at the Syrian embassy's stamp. "It just means now I can give you a visa, or not," he added. When I protested, he called his colleagues over to back him up. Monika and I stood our ground, arguing heatedly that the officials at the Syrian embassy had approved our crossing and he had no right to override them. If we had known at the time the guard was just trying to squeeze a small bribe out of us, we would have gladly complied. But the idea didn't enter our minds. My only thought was the outrageous detour we would have to make if we couldn't cut through Syria. Finally the guard must have realized we were too clueless to pay up. He flicked his hand at us as if he were shooing flies. Of course, we were most happy to get out of his sight.

Driving through Syria was like traveling in a time warp. The villages looked as if they had been built in biblical times—probably because they were. The few vehicles on the road were donkey carts, and electrical and telephone lines were noticeable by their absence. In the late afternoon, we stopped at a gas station to inquire about accommodations for the night. Somebody pointed at what he claimed was a youth hostel in the distance. I looked and saw a structure standing head and shoulders above the village. It appeared more like a castle to me, but the man insisted it was a youth hostel. We went back on the road and soon came to a drawbridge over a moat. *If this isn't a castle, I don't know what is*, I thought. We drove over it and arrived at a spacious courtyard.

I could immediately see this wasn't just a castle but a roman amphitheater as well. The arena was built into the bowl of a hillside, and the tiers of seats were still visible. Atop the structure stood the castle, a massive block of stone guarded by archers watching us through slits, or so I imagined. Stepping into the lobby, I was half expecting to see Kirk Douglas dressed up as Spartacus, brandishing his sword at me. But no one was home. After hollering "hello" several times, a young man ambled out. He checked us in, and we signed a guestbook that hadn't been used for a week. He took us through a hall with arched ceilings and up a narrow winding staircase to our room. The furnishing was Spartan—twin beds, a desk and chair—but it was clean.

We dined in the main room at an enormous table capable of seating some two-dozen guests. My imagination was really going wild now. The hotel staff had told us this was once a crusader's castle. I could see myself dining with a ragtag bunch of warriors, swapping stories of escapades and conquests. As it was, my family and I sat there for much of the evening, waiting for dinner to be served. I ordered two beers for a start. They took a *long* time to appear, and when I ordered a second round of beers, the waiting period was equally long. I later discovered there was no kitchen in the castle. Food and drinks were transported by runners from some distant caterer in the village. If I had known, I would have ordered four beers at one go.

Our journey through Syria took us to Damascus, Homs, Hama, and Aleppo, all well-known names in the devastating civil war that started with the 2011 Arab Spring protests. It is with sadness that I look back at my Middle East travels in 1967 and 1968. Since then, Middle Eastern history has been a litany of war: the Lebanese civil war 1975-1990, the Iran-Iraq war 1980-1988, the Iraqi invasion of Kuwait in 1990, the first Persian Gulf War involving the U.S. and its allies in 1991, the second Persian Gulf War in 2003 that deposed Saddam Hussein's regime, the ongoing Syrian civil war that opened parts of the country to the terrorist group ISIS, and on and on with no end in sight.

With a mix of fondness and relief, we took leave of this ancient land. In his travelogue, *Travels with Charley*, John Steinbeck notes that after a certain length of homebound journey, the mind refuses to absorb new stimuli, and the overriding imperative is to get to the end of the trip.

My experience matched his. The remainder of our journey is like a plate of scrambled eggs in my mind. A few scenes stand out of this mush: sitting on the terrace of a Hilton Hotel in Istanbul while watching a surfaced Soviet submarine propel through the Straits of Bosporus; people lined up on a dreary roadside in Bulgaria, waiting to purchase corn from a government store; and the three of us taking turns in the bathroom of an Austrian restaurant in Vienna—of all places!—where we had consumed something that disagreed with our stomachs.

We sped through Germany on their high-speed autobahns, crossed on a ferry into Denmark, and drove straight to the harbor in Copenhagen. An Icelandic freighter happened to be docked at the quay. The captain asked us to purchase the necessary freight documents from the shipping company, and our Peugeot was on its way to Iceland. The three of us arrived by air in Reykjavík the following day. We were home.

CHAPTER 18

ICELANDIC INTERLUDE

My homecoming in the fall of 1968 couldn't have happened at a worse time. Ten years earlier, I had left Iceland an upbeat country that had nothing but growth and prosperity on its horizon. Now I was returning to an Iceland reeling in economic depression. For two years in a row, the country's fish exports fell well below average due to low international demand. The Gross National Product plunged by a whopping 15 percent between mid-1966 and mid-1968. Nature further exacerbated matters by whipping up gales that sank trawlers off the coast. Helpless in the face of these destructive powers, the Icelandic government resorted to the only remedy at its disposal. It cut the value of the króna in half through two devaluations. While this boosted exports, it also raised the price of imported goods. For an island country that depended on imports for everything, this had a dire impact on everyday life. Prices skyrocketed while wages stagnated. The mood at my reunion with friends and relatives was as gray as the rain that poured during those bleak fall months.

Monika and I rolled up our sleeves. Recession or not, we seriously wanted to make a go of it. We were also lucky to find a very affordable apartment. This was the Tjarnargata 43 of my childhood. While Erlingur had long since sold his share in the triplex because its apartments were too small for his family of four boys, my parents had stayed put. At the time of my return, they were occupying the first floor apartment, while the second was owned by a cantankerous middle-aged couple. My parents still owned the third floor apartment, which they rented to me at a discount. This was the unit where I had spent my early years peering down at the British military barracks in the nearby field. It was a strange feeling to start my new life in my old home and be the grownup sleeping in my parents' bedroom. I was half expecting my siblings to be darting in and out. But of course I knew it couldn't happen, for Gústa was a language professor at the University of Montpellier in France, and Kristján was studying in Sweden.

Well-paying jobs were hard to come by during a recession. As always, Mom pulled strings. In a tiny nation where the degrees of separation are one or two rather than the customary six, networking is in our blood. In this case, the string Mom tugged was her close friend whose son-in-law happened to be the resident architect at the aluminum smelter at Straumsvík, some 12 km south of Reykjavík. I considered myself very lucky when he agreed to hire me. The Swiss-owned smelter was the first large-scale industrial enterprise in Iceland. When I joined, the construction of its first phase was nearing completion.

And that was how I became a bit player in the economic revolution of Iceland. Fishing and agriculture had been the country's traditional bread and butter. Suddenly both sectors were collapsing. Fishing was prey to the vagaries of international forces beyond our control, while agriculture had never been profitable because of the long winters, cool summers, and shortage of arable land. Government subsidies had sustained the family farms, but with the flight of the younger generation to greener pastures, the kind of farming that had molded my youth was a dying occupation.

What other resources did Iceland have? It didn't take an expert to notice the water everywhere, pouring down as rain, gushing in rivers and waterfalls, frozen in glaciers, and boiling in hot springs. Water in and of itself is a precious commodity, but water in the form of energy is a tremendous source of wealth. Harnessing the vast potential of hydrological and geothermal energy became a matter of urgency for Iceland. Today, we call it green energy because it is from renewable sources and doesn't create harmful greenhouse gases. Iceland started using hydroelectric power in 1904 when a private entrepreneur installed a small hydroelectric power plant not far from Reykjavík. Since then, massive engineering feats have propelled this modest beginning into a giant state enterprise capable of harnessing much of the country's hydroelectric potential. Serious geothermal development began in the 1930s, when the city of Reykjavík built a network of pipelines that brought hot water for indoor heating. The first electrical power plant to run on geothermal energy was built in 1969. Nowadays these two sources provide over 85 percent of all energy consumption in Iceland. On a per capita basis, Iceland's electricity production was the largest in the world in 2016, more than twice that of Norway, the runner-up.

Exporting this green energy, however, is difficult. At the time of writing, plans to build an underwater cable to transmit electricity across the Atlantic have been shelved. There is a better way to spread Icelandic power—by attracting foreign companies to come to Iceland to set up factories that consume monstrous amounts of energy. Few, if any, other industrial processes are as energy-intensive as aluminum production. I was happy to be a part of this project.

The principles of aluminum production are simple. The main ingredient is alumina or aluminum oxide $(Al_2 O_3)$, a common chemical element found in rocks. At the smelter, it is mixed with two other compounds in a string of pots. Enormous amounts of energy are required to melt the mix and release the oxygen from the alumina. The final product is pure liquid aluminum. To satisfy the power-hungry smelter, a hydroelectric power plant was built in the highlands in tandem with the factory.

My main job at the smelter was to design lab facilities that monitored the production processes. When operations commenced a couple of years later, the event was hailed as Iceland's grand entry into the world of industrial mass manufacturing. The output was 33,000 tons per year, modest by international standards but huge for Iceland. Today, the fully-built smelter and a couple of additional ones in other parts of Iceland produce about twenty-five times that amount, accounting for almost 40 percent of the value of all goods produced in Iceland.

Shortly after I began work at the smelter, I got an unsolicited job offer. This was from the small architecture firm of Þorvaldur S. Þorvaldsson and Manfreð Vilhjálmsson. They were a creative duo best known for their masterpiece, the National and University Library in Reykjavík. They were also particularly enamored of Finnish architecture, hence their overtures to me. I also suspected that a thread from Mom's sewing club could have linked me to Þorvaldur. His aunt was a member of this club. In any case, my skills were commensurate with their needs. Although I would have preferred working with them, I couldn't very well walk away from the smelter, a job that I had just started. We settled on an arrangement whereby I worked evenings and weekends at their design office, which meant virtually all my waking hours were devoted to work.

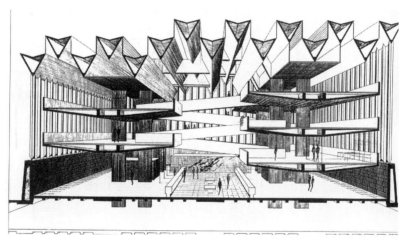

My interior-perspective sketch of a Central Bank building.

I recently found a lead pencil drawing of mine in an Icelandic Literary Society monograph on the life and work of my employer, Manfreð. The draft is an interior perspective of the new headquarters of the Central Bank of Iceland, part of an architectural competition the firm was engaged in.

We didn't win, but I was happy for the opportunity to show off my artistic flair to my new bosses.

Although the job was part-time and lasted only a few months, it became the beginning of a beautiful decades-long friendship. Whenever I go to Iceland, I make it a point to visit Þorvaldur, Manfreð, and their families.

Life on the home front, unfortunately, wasn't as amicable. I was at work most of the time and Steinn was in school, which left Monika fretting and brooding at home. Given the slow economy and her inability to speak Icelandic, she couldn't find a job. She attended Icelandic language classes at the university, but aside from that, she had no other diversion than housework, which she detested. She particularly hated polishing the brass edges of the hallway steps. My mother, the guardian of the common areas in the building, kept her brass edges shiny, and she expected the same of the other residents. My wife and my mother never had an outright confrontation, but their ringing silence in each other's presence seemed louder than a barroom brawl. Joining this fracas was the belligerent couple who lived on the floor between my parents and us. They banged on the floors and walls at every perceived noise and bad-mouthed Mom to Monika, using divide-and-conquer tactics to get at my parents.

In the past, whenever the home atmosphere started to smell of gunpowder, I would defuse it by taking Monika on a trip. Such appeasement wasn't possible when I had two jobs to juggle. As the tension mounted, Monika and I drifted farther apart. She slept in one bed and I in the other. We both knew we were at breaking point, and yet we weren't ready to admit matrimonial defeat. Grasping at straws, I proposed going back to Helsinki, where we owned a flat. We could move back once the rental lease with our tenant expired. Monika, on the other hand, hadn't given up her dream of settling in Sweden. We had another egg in our nest, but since it hadn't hatched yet, it couldn't be counted as a chick. Since my "interview," UNESCO had written to say that I had been recommended for the Malawi job, but first they had to screen two other candidates. The letter had reignited my hope, but I also recognized the need to shield myself from disappointment.

With no easy solution in sight, I could only put one foot in front of the other and plod through "suicide month." November bears this nickname because of the gloom it brings. Situated at sixty-four degrees north, just below the Arctic Circle, Iceland enjoys summer days of near perpetual light and winter days of near perpetual darkness. In the height of summer, the sun never really sets, as it creeps up again moments after it dips below the horizon. The opposite is true during the depth of winter. The sun rises reluctantly around 11 am, hovers barely above the horizon like a heavy lead ball, and calls it a day around 3 pm. Late fall, however, is the worst. In winter, at least there's snow to brighten the landscape. In November, there's nothing but rain, gale, and gloom. No sensible Icelander carries an umbrella, because it's totally useless against the gust-driven horizontal rain. We prefer to suit up in raincoats, rain pants and boots, and we charge in a slant into the howling downpour. While other Scandinavians share the experience of short days and long nights this time of year, stormy fall weather is unique to my beloved country.

November passed, and I faced December with equal dread. Christmas was a time for family get-togethers and exchanging presents and hugs and kisses. The thought of my mother and wife performing these rituals together, icy smiles frozen on their faces, churned my stomach. About a week before this torment, a letter bearing the UNESCO logo arrived. I tore open the envelope. My eyes swam over the pages and latched on to the most beautiful words in the English language: "pleased to inform you …" I got the job! My title was to be Associate Quantity Surveyor, and I was to show up as soon as possible in Zomba, then the capital of Malawi. Monika was just as thrilled. When I broke the news to my parents, Dad congratulated me with his customary stoicism. Mom didn't utter a word, but her downcast eyes said it all. She had thought I was home for good, and now I was leaving again after only three months. Perhaps I should have muffled my exuberance, but I was young, two months shy of thirty, and didn't understand the longings of the elderly. A new adventure lay ahead, this time in the jungles of Africa, and my Viking heart throbbed with anticipation.

The plan was for me to travel to UNESCO in Paris for a week of briefings in January. Monika and Steinn would visit her family in Finland and join me in Malawi a few weeks later. "Malawi" soon rolled off our tongues as though it was a popular vacation spot, but we had little idea where we were going. When I first heard of the job, I had tried and failed to locate Malawi in the atlas. Further research showed that the place I should be looking for was Nyasaland. Malawi had been established as an independent country only a few years earlier, and most atlases didn't show it yet. This wasn't just any adventure but an expedition to discover a new land.

CHAPTER 19

MALAWI

alawi lies like a small squiggly worm in the heart of East Africa. It is slightly larger than Iceland and is hemmed in by three much meatier neighbors: Mozambique, Tanzania, and Zambia. In spite of being landlocked, the country claims a 600 km coastline along Lake Malawi, which makes up a fifth of the country's total area. It is no surprise that the country is named after the lake. "Malawi" is derived from Maravi, the old name of the tribe that lived there. A few years before my arrival, the country was called Nyasaland, meaning "land of the lake." There is no escaping it—the lake defines the country.

When I arrived in Malawi in January 1969, it had been independent for only five years. Before then, it had been part of the British Empire in Africa. As my plane was about to land, I saw a terrain as lush as I had imagined—rolling green hills and bushland immediately below and verdant mountains in the distance. What caught my eye were the ubiquitous "rondavels" that dotted the landscape.

Map of Africa with Malawi in black

These were round, mud and wattle dwellings with conical straw roofs that housed most of the rural residents.

Malawi's population at the time was four million, the majority impoverished subsistence farmers. Today, the country's population has exploded to sixteen million, in spite of a major AIDS epidemic, making it one of the most densely populated countries in the world, and also one of the poorest.

Beginning in 1850, David Livingstone's exploration of the region had paved the way for Europeans to reach the East African Highlands. Some of the geographic names are the legacy of those days. For example, Blantyre, the largest town in Malawi when I lived there, was named after Livingstone's birthplace in Scotland. When Livingstone failed to return to Britain on schedule, a Welsh American journalist, Henry Morton Stanley, launched an expedition to look for him. When he finally found the Scotsman a short distance north of Malawi's current border with Tanzania, he uttered the legendary greeting, "Dr. Livingstone, I presume?"

As in other parts of the world, British involvement in Africa began as trade, which soon turned into a land grab. From the late nineteenth century and well into the twentieth, European settlers took over large acreage to establish coffee and tea plantations in the highlands. The locals pushed back, and thus began the bloody cycle of rebellion and suppression that lasted for almost a century. In the new world order after the Second World War, the era of European colonialism was clearly coming to an end. Pressure from the colonies, buoyed by the United Nations' principle of self-determination for all peoples, gathered momentum, and colonies fell like dominos. In 1964, the British relinquished their colonial hold on Nyasaland, and the Republic of Malawi was born. Dr. Hastings Banda, a rebel leader and a European-trained physician, became the first president of the new republic. He was soon infected by the disease that plagued many freedom fighters turned ruling class, namely, amnesia. Memories of his struggle against oppression were erased, and all that mattered was his desire to hang on to power forever. He declared himself President for Life.

Zomba, then the capital, was a pleasant, sleepy town during my stay there. (I called the residents "Zombies," which aptly reflected their unhurried disposition.) The town was really one big golf course surrounded by well-appointed red brick bungalows. These were spacious residences replete with separate servants' quarters. Occupying these houses were senior government officials, most of whom were still British. Because of the shortage of qualified personnel during the transition, the Malawi civil service employed a large number of British technocrats, paid for by the British government. The Malawians who lived in Zomba belonged to the highest echelons of government, such as the president and his ministers. Other locals lived outside the town in the traditional rondavels. The exception was the domestic servants, who had their own quarters on their masters' properties.

As the country's colonial past began to fade, new types of expatriates, such as myself, began to arrive. The old colonial hands often lamented the influx of "foreigners" to Zomba. Once, on overhearing such a remark from a Brit, I couldn't help ribbing, "Aren't you a foreigner, too?" The reply was a huffy: "No, we're not foreigners, we're British."

On my first day of work, I walked into a building located between the golf course and the clubhouse. It was a whitewashed, one-story brick structure shared by my project unit and the U.S. Agency for International Development (USAID). Because my recruitment had been seriously delayed by bureaucratic snags, I expected to find a beehive of activity and a pile of documents on my desk demanding immediate attention. Nothing could have been further from the truth. The project manager, a Scottish architect whom everyone called Sandy, welcomed me. His appearance was the ultimate stereotype of the British colonialist in Africa: handlebar mustache, khaki shorts, and white knee-highs. A wizened man in his fifties, he walked with a bowlegged shuffle. He took me around and introduced me to the group of ten or so staff. They were stratified into expats in the senior positions and locals performing menial tasks. After making the rounds,

Sandy declared it was teatime. He sat me down and we chitchatted about my trip and the weather over endless cups of tea brought by the office boy.

The project I worked on was Malawi's first World Bank-financed education project. It would expand and renovate twelve existing secondary schools and construct a new teacher-training college. The objective was to develop the manpower needed to grow the economy. To be fair to all the regions, the schools were spread along the length of the entire country. The total cost would be US$7 million, out of which US$6.3 million would be a loan from the rich member nations of the World Bank. The terms of the loan were most generous, like those from parents or a wealthy uncle. This type of loan, with zero interest and a repayment period of fifty years, is called a "credit" in World Bank parlance.

So, what did UNESCO have to do with a World Bank-financed project? The world of international aid is as complex as a spider's web. It all started when the designers of the project envisioned the need to establish a project implementation unit comprised of educators, architects, and accountants. The Malawi government lacked the professionals and, at the same time, didn't want to borrow money to recruit experts from overseas. It turned to other organizations for grant funds. One source was the Associate Experts Program, administered by the United Nations Development Program (UNDP), an umbrella UN organization established to assist poor countries. Much of the actual work was carried out by the specialized agencies under it, such as UNESCO for education, FAO for food and agriculture and so on. Since the Malawi project was in education, UNESCO became the administrator.

The Associate Experts Program is like an internship. Its goal is to expose young professionals to developing nations. "Associate" refers to their junior status. A number of wealthy nations contribute to this fund, with the condition that each donor will only pay for the recruitment of its own citizen. This means the Swedish government will only pay for a Swedish citizen, the U.S. a U.S. citizen, and so on. As an Icelander, I didn't have a prayer of getting in, as Iceland wasn't a donor at that time. Had I known that when I applied, I wouldn't have bothered.

As luck would have it, the Swedish government decided to hire me as an honorary Swede. Its international development arm, called SIDA, wanted to contribute to the Malawi project. The Dutch had already snatched the architect opening, so the only one left was the quantity surveyor. However, the job title "quantity surveyor" doesn't exist in Sweden. It is a specialized profession unique to the UK and its former territories. The main job of a quantity surveyor, or QS, is to itemize the quantities of materials needed for a construction project, based on its detailed designs. In other countries, this breakdown is carried out by the building contractor.

UNESCO looked at my résumé and informed SIDA that my experience in Kuwait, a former British protectorate, made me close enough to being a quantity surveyor. SIDA decided that since I was a Scandinavian who had worked in Sweden, I was close enough to being a Swedish citizen. A flurry of memos must have flown around the two agencies. Finally SIDA waived its citizenship rule and gave my application the green light.

During my first few weeks in Zomba in January, I lived in a government guesthouse, but when Monika and Steinn arrived the next month, we moved into one of the government-owned bungalows. Shortly thereafter we decided it was too expensive relative to my salary. The grapevine had it that a Dutch associate expert was leaving the country, so Monika and I went to check out the flat he was vacating. The location was good, my office only a five-minute walk away, and the next-door neighbor was none other than President Banda. Although all I could see was the massive red brick walls of the palace compound, I figured what was good enough for the president was good enough for me. When I got there, I realized why Banda chose this spot. The sloped front yard was literally the foot of the Zomba Plateau, a majestic fortress-like mountain that watched over the town. The back of the apartment looked out into a luxuriant valley and another mountain. The view all around was so grand it made the little two-bedroom apartment feel big. Monika and I decided to take it on the spot.

It was a cozy, simple place built of red brick and, like most buildings in the area, had red-polished concrete floors. The verandah doubled as my workshop, although I could only work there during the dry season. There was no air-conditioning, and none was needed, for although Malawi is located in the tropics, the climate is temperate because of the altitude. None of the windows had insect screens, and we had to sleep under mosquito nets. The house was a veritable zoo of flying and crawling bugs of all sorts and sizes far greater than their European cousins. The hairy spiders were as large as my hand, and the monster cockroaches devoured the tasty, delicate parts of my tape recorder. Our favorite was the insect-eating geckos, which we named and played with like pets. Occasionally, a snake slithered in to see what was happening. We would greet it with a barrage of flying objects to let it know it wasn't welcome.

Once, I heard Sally, the neighbor's dachshund, creating a ruckus in my backyard. I looked out and saw her prancing around a large silvery snake wielding a hood. A cobra! I ran out and picked up a hefty broomstick, part of the chair I was making. It crossed my mind that it could be a spitting cobra, which meant I should keep my distance from its venomous projectile. I whacked it on the head a number of times while Sally goaded me on, yipping excitedly. After a few more whacks to make sure it was truly dead, I picked it up with the stick and went over to the British woman who lived next door. I told her to check Sally for snakebites. As I dropped the dead snake on the ground, it twitched and zigzagged away as if its tail was on fire! Sally and I looked on with disbelief.

Monika's mood was lighter than at any time in our marriage. First of all, she was overjoyed to have escaped her "prison" in Iceland. Secondly, she found a job at the government-run Statistics Institute of Malawi. Her boss was British, and she was his trusted assistant supervising a crew of local staff. She settled down into a comfortable work routine, and her dark, heavy moods grew farther apart. Like other expats, we hired a couple of servants to take care of the housework. The ice between Monika and me softened, although I still had to watch for weather changes. Adapting to a new country is harder for some than others.

Steinn was the true internationalist in the family. By the ripe age of seven, he had already lived in five countries on three continents and visited a dozen more. In his early years in Finland, he spoke Swedish with his parents and their friends. At daycare, he babbled in Finnish with the other tots, leading him to make the astute observation, "Children speak Finnish, and when they grow up, they speak Swedish." When he was four, we took him to visit his Aunt Gústa in France. He picked up a game of soccer with some children at a park. In a matter of minutes, he was yelling in French to his teammates, "*À moi, à moi!*" In Kuwait, he spoke English with an American twang, as well as street Arabic. In Iceland, he came home mouthing Icelandic, and in Malawi, his English took on the crisp edge of a British schoolmarm. He was enrolled in second grade at the British-run Harry Johnston Primary School. As always, he blended right in like a chameleon. The only time he had a problem with British curriculum was when a textbook portrayed Vikings as villains. Having learned the opposite in Iceland a few months ago, he didn't like that at all.

With everyone in the family happily settled, I could devote my attention to work. The problem was, I didn't know what my work was supposed to be. Well before my arrival, my boss Sandy had decided to delegate most of the responsibilities of his unit to various government ministries. The Ministry of Works and Supplies took over construction-related activities, the Ministry of Education managed equipment procurement and fellowships, and the Ministry of Finance handled the transfer of donor funds to Malawi. I must say Sandy was right—these were the appropriate agencies to carry out these functions. However, what duties were left for the project implementation unit? Sandy left it up to me. After studying the situation for some days, I decided I could perform three useful functions without duplicating what others were doing: clean up the project accounts, create periodic progress reports for UNESCO and the World Bank, and travel to the field to supervise project construction.

Sandy neither approved nor objected. He was too busy to care. He had been elected chairman of the Gymkhana Club, and the volunteer job consumed all his time and energy. Gymkhana, an Indian term coined during British rule, started as a sports club and had broadened into a gentleman's club. The Gymkhana in Zomba was a relic of the colonial era, and its membership was British and white except for a few Malawian government ministers.

The club hosted a variety of sports activities, such as golf, tennis and cricket, but the most important sport was played out at the bar. After working hours, you would find most of the expat community congregated in the club in various stages of inebriation. Gin and tonic was the drink of choice. After all, that drink had been credited with saving the lives of countless colonialists over the centuries, although it was the medicinal properties of the tonic, rather than the gin, that prevented malaria.

This club became my after-work hang out too. Aside from the pleasure of socializing over drinks, I also needed to network and keep abreast of the goings on in town. The place was a cauldron of information, some pure gossip, other essential dos and don'ts in local custom. For instance, the dress code for women is a skirt long enough to cover the knees. Malawian men have a fetish for the soft, dimpled flesh behind a woman's knees. To walk around the streets of Malawi exposing that part of the body was asking for trouble. I eagerly passed that information to Monika. Fortunately, this was the pre-miniskirt era, and all her dresses were decent by Malawi standards.

For Sandy, the club was all-consuming. He came into the office every morning, greeted his staff, and disappeared to the club for the rest of the day. For such dedication to public service, Queen Elizabeth II awarded him the title of Most Excellent Order of the British Empire (MBE). When he went back to London to receive his medal, I assumed the mantle of acting project director. I took a deep breath and dived into the dusty pile of unanswered correspondence sitting on Sandy's desk.

The project accounts typified the general mess in the unit. While trying to decipher the status of the project, I discovered on page two of the accounts that we had already run out of money. The accountant was a young, pleasant Malawian whose highest degree was an elementary school diploma. Despite the lack of training and guidance, he did a valiant job of keeping track of expenditures. First, he translated the credit amount of US$6.3 million into Malawian pounds, which was £2,600,000. Next he meticulously subtracted the expenses down to every shilling and pence and to each pencil purchased. This intense focus on detail must have taken his eyes off the pounds, for he never noticed when several zeroes ran away right under his nose.

I persuaded Sandy of two things: First, our project accountant needed serious hand-holding; second, we needed a machine that could deal with the maddening complexity of calculating in Malawian pounds, shillings and pence. He agreed on both counts, and I became a de facto accountant for the first and last time in my life.

I remember the calculator well. It was an Olivetti the size of a toaster oven and weighed at least ten pounds. It could only perform the four basic mathematical functions, which it did very slowly, loudly and ponderously, especially when clonking out multiplications or divisions. The cost of the machine was the princely sum of £800. In today's terms, that would be more than US$10,000.

Supervision of construction was the most satisfying part of my job. Once I had settled down, Sandy sent me on a tour to visit all twelve secondary schools in the project. My assignment was to assess the suitability of the overall plan for each school, taking into account the topography and the conditions of the existing buildings. Normally, this was an architect's function, not the quantity surveyor's. The reason for the anomaly was that Sandy had no faith in the competence of the Dutch architect who had got the job I wanted. Leo was a handsome fellow, passionate about tennis and courting an attractive Irish expat, whom he later married. However, work-wise, he wasn't one to take initiative. During our tenure together, I wasn't aware of any contribution he made.

The office Land Rover took me to the project sites up and down the country. I would have preferred to drive myself, but government regulations stipulated I had to use a driver. It was just as well, since I was usually very sleepy on these trips, most likely due to the weekly dose of chloroquine as a malarial prophylaxis. The potential side effects include sleepiness and damage to one's eyesight. I was lucky to have suffered only the former.

The moment I left Zomba, I would be reminded of where I was: *not* a British country club but a poor African country. Vehicular traffic on the highway was sparse, but the entire road teemed with carless, often shoe-less Malawians. They were men, women, and children walking to work, school, the fields, markets, wherever they needed to go, sometimes long distances. The women were dressed in colorful *chitenje*, a sarong-like garment wrapped around the waist, and of course, draping over the back of their knees. On their heads they carried baskets laden with goods, bundles of firewood, and anything and everything that needed to be transported. I once saw a woman carrying a baby on her back and balancing an axe on her head.

The trips south of Zomba were usually one-day affairs, at most two. The road between the capital and Blantyre was two-lane wide and paved with asphalt. It was truly a "highway" by African standards. But south of that, the road dwindled to a narrow gravel track surfaced with two asphalt strips. When two vehicles passed from opposite directions, the common practice was for both to drive off to the side to make room. But not all drivers were sensible. Some liked to play a game of chicken, at times with disastrous results. Fortunately my driver was a cautious fellow who always gave oncoming vehicles a wide berth.

At the southern tip of the country, a spectacular scene scrolled past me. A uniform carpet of bushes rippled across the plains all the way to the foothills of the towering Mulanje Massif. Here and there, majestic acacia trees shaded this carpet like gargantuan parasols. I had never seen such a green before; it was vibrant and oily, like jade. Recalling what my buddies at the club had told me, I realized these were tea plantations. The elevation and climate of this region were perfect for tea growing, which was why the British introduced the plant from India. It was also why the British Empire in Africa ended not far from here. Where the mountains tapered into lowlands, the British had deemed the heat and humidity unsuitable for humans. They left these disease-ridden parts to their rivals, the Portuguese, who colonized the unwanted lands and called them Mozambique.

My first stop was the town of Cholo, now called Thyolo. It was the center for tea processing and trade. Indians dominated the commerce here, as evidenced by the signs on the low whitewashed buildings that read A. Patel, L. Patel, K. Patel, etc.

The secondary school there was a clutch of small buildings: a classroom block, an administrative office and an assembly hall. The World Bank project was to renovate the buildings and add new ones, namely laboratories, home economics workshops, and wood and metal workshops. The walls were made of brick, but anything wooden, such as the doors and window frames, and even roof trusses, had been badly chewed up by termites. I had reviewed the designs before the trip and thus had an idea what to expect. The consultants who did the design were headquartered in Salisbury, Southern Rhodesia (now called Harare, Zimbabwe). Strictly speaking, this firm shouldn't have qualified because it was located in a pariah state. When a white colonialist called Ian Smith declared independence from Britain and formed an all-white government in Southern Rhodesia, the international community refused to recognize it and imposed a trade and travel boycott on the territory. The Rhodesian firm should, therefore, have been excluded from World Bank financing. But somehow, this problem had slipped through the cracks, perhaps because the principals of the Salisbury firms had declared themselves to be British nationals.

I knocked on the door of the headmaster and obtained permission to inspect the buildings. Notebook in hand, I wandered around. School was in session. About three hundred teenagers, ranging in age from twelve to eighteen, sat in the classrooms. A knot started to twist in my stomach. Before then, I had been reading documents at my desk. But this was real—the school, the teachers and students. The future of these youngsters depended on how well I did my job. What credentials did I have to qualify me for this task? US$7 million may not sound like a lot now, but back then it was a huge sum for a small country. *How can I make sure the money is well spent? Am I competent? Do I know what I'm doing?*

My self-doubts were making me dizzy. I grabbed myself by the scruff of the neck and shook the US$7 million out of my mind. I told myself to focus on this one particular school and this one particular assignment, which was to critique the consultant's design. I hadn't been impressed during my desk review, and now the site inspection confirmed my observations. In the consultant's plan, the new buildings would be located haphazardly across the school site. Only a blind man throwing darts at the map could have come up with a layout like this. A competent architect would have taken into consideration the rudiments of his trade. Esthetically, the external space between buildings has to feel right, and practically, buildings too close together can be a fire hazard, while those too far apart means longer electrical, water and sewer lines, and thus higher costs. The blind man who drew up this plan also had no regard for orientation. In the tropics, the amount of sun exposure can make a huge difference to one's comfort level. In these parts, windows should never face east or west because they will let in the sun's low rays. Facing north or south is good, because the tropical sun is on top of the building from late morning till mid-afternoon. The plan had other failings, such as the non-modular fashion of the classrooms, which meant future changes would be difficult to accommodate. By the time I finished writing down my comments, I was feeling more confident I could make a difference. This school would be a better place of learning because of my suggestions. Since construction hadn't started yet, there was still time for revisions. Or so I thought.

The trips to northern Malawi were much more extended affairs because of the distance and condition of the dirt tracks claiming to be roads. These one-lane trails were made of clay, which meant that they became as slippery as wet ice during rains. In one tropical downpour, my driver lost control of our Land Rover, and we found ourselves in the ditch. The driver tried to restart the engine, but it was as dead as a doornail. Not even a click or whir. "Oh my God," said the driver, throwing up his hands to indicate there was nothing else to do except wait for help. I had heard many tales at the club about hapless travelers who had to wait long periods for help when their vehicles broke down. In one account, Monika's boss and his wife were traveling from Zomba to the Indian Ocean coast when they came across a stranded truck on a lonely stretch of road. They stopped, found the truck driver at a nearby hut, and offered assistance. He explained the gearbox of his lorry had given out a year ago; he had sent a message to his company to send a replacement and was still waiting for it to arrive. In the meantime he had built the hut, found a local girl, and they were getting married.

Unlike the truck driver from Mozambique, I wasn't willing to go with the flow. My experience in the BP repair workshop had taught me that the absence of a click or whir meant that the problem was probably in the connection between the starter button and the starter motor. If that deduction was correct, jamming a piece of metal between the two electrical terminals of the motor would send a current from the battery straight into the motor, bypassing the starter button. I found a tire lever in the trunk and got to work. By then it was pitch dark and still bucketing. I must concede I was very nervous as images of lions and snakes flashed through my mind. Working entirely by touch, I located the starter motor and its pair of terminals. I grit my teeth and jammed the lever between them. A burst of sparks showered on me. The motor whirred, and in seconds the engine was purring.

The driver readily agreed to let me take over the vehicle. Getting the Land Rover out of the ditch was easy, but once the car was on the camber of the slippery road, I could feel irresistible forces pulling us back into the ditch. It was like balancing on a tightrope. Gripping the wheel with every sinew in my anatomy, we made it to Hotel Lilongwe, our destination for the night. I cleaned up in my room the best I could, changed into dry clothes, and got to the restaurant before the kitchen closed. "Sir!" said the head waiter when I asked for a table. "Our policy is that there is no admission to the dining room without a tie." So I ended this memorable day eating a steak and kidney pie, dressed in a T-shirt and shorts with a colorful restaurant-owned tie knotted around my neck.

As the rainy season progressed, the roads north of Zomba became impassable muddy quagmires. Sandy, therefore, decided to change our mode of travel. Traveling by small planes in the African bush was a common way of getting to remote places. For much of our travels we used a Cessna 172, single engine, four-seat plane, one of the most popular and successful small planes in history.

It was exhilarating to fly in these planes, especially when there were only the pilot and me. I would be sitting in the copilot seat, eyeing the control yoke, my fingers itching to wrap around it. After a couple of flights with the same pilot, a white Rhodesian, I felt we had warmed up enough for me to broach the question. "What are these instruments for?" I started and gradually worked up to, "Can I try?" The pilot humored me. Finally, I was holding the control yoke and my feet were pressing the rudder pedals. The plane tilted and turned, swooping up and down at my beck and call. I was as exhilarated as a little boy in an amusement park. The highlight was when the pilot granted me my wish to land the plane. Following his instructions, I downed the flaps, shifted the throttle lever to reduce power, kept it just above a stalling speed, and gently let the plane down the grass strip. My only regret was that the wheel brakes were located by the pilot seat, so the satisfaction of grinding the plane to a halt wasn't mine. On another flight, I asked the pilot if I could handle the takeoff. His answer was a flat no.

Most of our trips were uneventful, but there were also nail-biting moments. During the thunderstorms that we frequently encountered, the turbulence would cause the needles on the navigational aids to oscillate like windshield wipers. Sometimes the pilot resorted to using the highway to find his way to the airstrip, which meant descending below the clouds to a few hundred feet above ground. I had never experienced such a rush as the earth zoomed past under my nose. Those on the ground could hear and feel us too. I remember watching a team of frightened pigs tear across the village square when our plane roared over their heads.

Then there was the time when our Cessna slid off the runway on the grass airstrip in Zomba. A downpour had turned the grass into a slippery skating rink. When the pilot jammed on the wheel brakes, the plane went on gliding toward the maize field at the end of the runway. "We're not going to stop in time," I noted with a strange feeling of detachment. The pilot came to the same conclusion and tried to turn the plane 180 degrees. But he only managed 90 degrees before we slid sideways into the cornfield. The right wing plunged into the wet soil and stopped the plane dead. Nobody was hurt, but that plane didn't fly again for a long while.

Working in developing nations is full of perils. In my thirty-year career in international development, several of my colleagues have died or been severely injured in accidents. In one car crash, a British woman simply bled to death in the backcountry of Sudan because no medical care was available. Catching exotic diseases is another risk. One would think returning to the developed world for medical treatment would be the best course of action. However, that isn't necessarily true because most doctors in advanced countries have no experience in tropical diseases. A long time ago in medical school, they may have read about illnesses such as malaria, dengue fever, and schistosomiasis, but they would have a hard time diagnosing them in real life. I was lucky throughout my career that no major mishap befell me, especially given my exploits. My philosophy is: As long as I survive, there's nothing to worry about. And if I don't survive, then all my worries are over.

Monika was eager to see more of Africa, too. We vacationed near and far, beginning with a weekend trip to Lake Malawi. For a landlocked country, the white sandy beaches were some of the finest in the world. The water stretched endlessly, and during storms the waves were the size of ocean rollers. It was also crystal clear and as fresh as Icelandic spring water.

Monkeys mobbed the trees close by, chattering, swinging from branch to branch, and observing us as we observed them. We swam in the lake, all the while watching out for crocodiles, hippos, and the giant monitor lizards sunning on the rocky island nearby. All wild animals should be treated with awe, no matter how harmless they look. Even a roly-poly hippo can bite when annoyed and leave huge teeth marks on a person's body.

Our greatest excitement in Africa was seeing the wildlife. Although we weren't so naïve as to think wild animals roamed the streets, we were on the lookout for them everywhere we went. One of our favorite haunts was the Zomba Plateau, which was right on the doorstep of our home. The climate up there was cool and pleasant, and the vast tracts of cedar and pine, as well as crisscrossing streams and waterfalls, made it a prime tourist attraction. The place was full of treasures, and I had learned to drive slowly so as not to miss anything. Once, stopping by the roadside, we found trees bearing large red berries. I picked one and recognized it as lychee. We feasted on the sweet, delicious fruits. With juice still dripping on my chin, I spotted another kind of red berries further up the road. We went to explore and discovered a bed of wild strawberries, plump and ripe. Needless to say, they didn't go to waste. The most exciting drive-by encounter happened while coasting down the mountain late one night. Rounding a hairpin bend on the narrow dirt road, I stared straight into the yellow eyes of a leopard hypnotized by our headlights. It leaped back out into the night, but not before I had a good look at the rosettes on its handsome pelt.

On our annual vacations, we ventured farther afield. In August 1969, we drove across neighboring Zambia to Victoria Falls. Columns of water thundered down a steep gorge. The earth trembled, and I could feel my heart bumping against my chest. The sight and sound shook me out of every thought. I could only stand in the mist and soak it in. I saw a family of elephants wading across the Zambezi River, dangerously close to the edge of the cliff where the curtain of water thundered into the void below. I was a little concerned that the calves might be swept over the precipice but reminded myself they had been bathing in the Zambezi well before I came along.

On the way back to Malawi, we went on several detours. The first took us to the Kafue game reserve, one of the largest in Africa, which at 22,400 square km was easily the size of a small country. Kafue was best known for its walking tours. Instead of watching game from the safety of a car, visitors could trek from camp to camp under the guidance of a ranger. However, having heard a story about a lion attacking tourists, we decided trekking on foot was too hazardous.

We hired a guide to drive around with us. He was a muscular African dressed in khaki uniform, who possessed the quiet, alert air of a hunter. While I drove, he sat in the passenger side. Suddenly he told me to stop. "There's a lion around here," he said and got out of the car. After walking in the scrubland for a bit, he came back. Without a word, he picked up his rifle and went out again, and this time he took a roundabout path into the bush. To our utter disbelief, a lioness walked into the open, followed by a pair of cubs. Right in front of our car, they crossed the road. It was quite a sight—mommy lion sashaying like a model showing off her magnificent figure, while two frisky fur balls toddled alongside. I have no idea how the guide sensed the lions' presence, and how he could so confidently shepherd them toward us.

Our second moment of excitement in Kafue came the following day when we entered elephant country. We were traveling without a guide on rutted dirt tracks, which allowed us to travel no faster than about 25 mph without shaking our car and bones to pieces. In a clearing we came upon a herd of a dozen elephants, including several cows, calves, and a huge bull. Steinn opened the window and yelled "Hello, elephant!" It must have been perceived as a serious insult in elephantese, because the bull came charging at us, bellowing furiously and flapping his ears. I drove away as fast as I dared, which was about the speed at which the bull was galloping. Gradually the gap between us widened, and we were lucky there were no obstacles on the track such as another elephant. This was the only time during our safaris that I felt concerned for our safety. Elephants had been known to sit on cars—legend had it they were particularly fond of Volkswagen beetles—and I was glad we didn't become one of these stories.

Map of central Africa. My travels are shown in broken lines.

We went on to Lake Kariba and the Kariba dam on the Zambezi River. One wouldn't expect such an engineering marvel in the middle of Africa. Lake Kariba is the world's largest artificial lake and reservoir in volume, four times larger than the Three Gorges Dam in China, which was built much later. The Kariba Dam was built by the electrical power authority of Rhodesia and Nyasaland in the late 1950s, when these territories were British colonies, and continues to supply electricity to these areas today. At the time, it was one of the largest development projects that the World Bank had ever financed. The scale of the dam is stunning. The weight of the water (approximately 200 billion tons) is so enormous that it reactivated faults in the earth's crust and triggered earthquakes as large as five on the Richter scale.

After Kariba, we headed upcountry with the intent of reaching Lake Tanganyika in North Zambia. We gradually realized this goal wasn't feasible. "NO GAS" signs decorated the deserted gas stations along the road. We decided it was time to head east toward home. But as the gas gauge needle sank lower and lower, we were still a long way from the border. We weren't going to make it no matter how gingerly I stepped on the gas pedal and how much I coasted downhill with the engine turned off. Passing a modest-size town, desperation spurred me to action. I followed the main road into the town center, marched into the town hall and rapped on the mayor's door. Desperation also gave me the eloquence I normally lacked. I convinced the chief constable to sell me gas from government-owned pumps. The alternative I painted for him wasn't appetizing: a family of stranded foreigners, destitute as their money had run out, and illegal as their visas had expired. The constable wrote me an authorization, which I took to the station that serviced official vehicles. To watch my Peugeot guzzle the gas felt as satisfying as quenching my own thirst after weeks in the desert.

By the end of our first year in Africa, we had checked off the list of standard safari animals: antelopes, zebras, cape buffaloes, giraffes, elephants, rhinos, hippos, warthogs, jackals, hyenas, wild dogs, leopards, cheetahs and, of course, the most prized king of the jungle. On one long weekend, we drove to Gorongosa National Park in Mozambique to see the Lion House, the landmark of this game reserve. This structure was originally a tourist lodge, but it was built on a plain that flooded every year (the architect should be drawn and quartered!) and had to be abandoned. The lions soon discovered the vacant building and claimed squatter's rights. During our visit, about eight lions lazed around at the lodge, inside the rooms and atop the roofs and walls. They yawned, scratched, stretched, and gazed dreamily at the world. But we weren't fooled. These aren't house cats, but powerful, aggressive animals that can tear you to shreds in seconds. Visits in a personal vehicle such as ours are no longer allowed. Nowadays, tourists to Gorongosa view wildlife in a special vehicle operated by park rangers.

Our African adventures came to a halt at the start of 1970, our second year in Malawi. January to April was the rainy season, rendering many roads impassable. The unreliable supply of gasoline also made extended road trips dubious. Worse yet, there were reports of FRELIMO, the Mozambican freedom fighters, planting land mines on the roads. Our long-weekend trips to the beaches of Mozambique became too risky. This destination had been the escape of many expats in Zomba, and now we were confined to spending the weekends at Lake Malawi, or at the golf club.

It was just as well, though. Monika was pregnant and in no condition to go on another one of our crazy excursions. Our major travel that year was a tame "home leave" paid for by UNESCO. This was one of the perks of an international civil servant—he and his family enjoyed a trip back to his home country every two years. For us, the trip was a few weeks each in Iceland and Finland.

My daughter Tora made her entrance into the world in December. The nearest hospital was in Blantyre, an hour's drive from home. While I fretted about the distance, Monika was unruffled. She was still unruffled when the birth pangs started, saying it had taken Steinn a long time to make his debut. Finally she consented to go in the late evening of December 16, and I floored the gas all the way to Blantyre.

During the drive, the contractions were coming fast and furious. This baby wasn't dawdling. We rushed into the emergency room and were immediately ushered to the delivery room. A nurse handed me an admission form. While holding Monika's hand and filling out the form with the free one, I heard a baby bawl. I looked down and there was Tora protesting the rude interruption to her snug existence. My first thought was, "Wow, it's a girl!" We hadn't had a girl in our family since my sister's birth in 1934.

After Tora was born, our family trips were limited to places nearby. For work, however, I continued to travel extensively to all the project schools, as well as the site for the new teaching training college. This was my childhood dream, the "What I want to be when I grow up" kind of job. Playing in the muddy field near my childhood home had inspired in me an image of Valhalla as one huge construction site where the work was never done and the air was thick with smells of dirt and sweat. The construction sites at the schools came close. Everything was done by hand and with the simplest tools—shovels, picks, axes, handsaws, hammers, and trowels. The work was on the scale of a do-it-yourself home project and thus a great lesson in basic construction. From setting out the building to pouring concrete and plastering walls, I took in every step of the process. These lessons would prove most useful several decades later when I was building a house with my own hands. That was when I fully appreciated the skills of the Malawian workers. On my first attempt to lay a brick wall, I realized it wasn't as easy as they had made it look. One has to have the right touch, which can only be acquired by practice. Laying down a brick has to be as gentle as putting a baby to bed. Too much pressure will squish the mortar, and from then on nothing will be straight.

I acquired another valuable skill in Malawi. In fulfilling my title of "quantity surveyor," I learned to be one. I picked up the art of breaking a job into tasks and quantifying the materials required for each task. I also learned to estimate the amount of money due to the contractors at every stage, and check the contractor's work against the legal agreement. Toward the end, the craft of quantity surveying was no longer a mystery to me. Most importantly, I became familiar with the ins and outs of bidding documents, from detailed design documents to the bill of quantities and legal agreements. This special knowledge would later be my "open sesame" for many doors.

My assignment in Malawi was most rewarding for me personally. The people I supervised contributed to my professional growth, and I contributed to the project by nudging it forward while keeping costs within budget. However, the project implementation unit, as a whole, was redundant and a waste of money. My critique of the building plans at each site fell by the wayside, because my boss was too busy running the country club to crack the whip on the consultants, and I didn't have the authority to carry out my own recommendations. Helping these flawed designs materialize into flawed buildings grated on me. I knew that some of these classrooms would turn into ovens by noon, a hardship to teachers and students that could have been prevented by sensible orientation. The saving grace of the project was the teacher training college, which had been designed by a competent architect. When I left the country, the construction was close to completion.

Despite the imperfections, the Malawi undertaking was my baptism into the religion of international aid. Cooperation, not dominance, became the new creed of the postwar order. Lessons of the First World War had taught us that punishing the vanquished was the worst way to keep the peace. Pushed to a corner after the Versailles Peace Treaty of 1919, Germany had nowhere to go but to lash out with ever-greater vengeance. Rising out of these toxic ashes wasn't a phoenix but a fiend named Hitler. Thus after the Second World War, the victors adopted the more humane policy of helping their enemies rebuild. U.N. initiatives such as the World Bank and International Monetary Fund, together with the U.S. Marshall Plan, were created to deal with the financial chaos and reconstruction challenges in the aftermath of war. Billions of dollars of investment poured into the devastated countries of Western Europe and Asia, friends and foes alike, and resurrected ruined cities to some semblance of their past glory.

The two world wars also jolted the world into realizing how intertwined we had become, like parts of the same body. An ailment in one spot, something as minor as a sore toe, can slow down the whole body. After reconstruction was complete, the world community turned its attention to helping the plethora of newly independent countries that were once European colonies. In Africa alone, almost fifty new states were born. Aid organizations proliferated, some multilateral under U.N. aegis and others bilateral under individual governments. Of course, foreign aid wasn't completely altruistic. During the Cold War, the two superpowers jockeyed for influence in the "Third World." Aid became another weapon in the battle for supremacy. Be that as it may, the prevailing philosophy of the postwar days was to give soft power a try—anything to avoid the all-out carnage of the first half of the twentieth century.

My family and I packed up and left for Iceland shortly before Christmas 1971. My UNESCO supervisor in Paris had broached the possibility of a new and interesting assignment in Africa. However, experience had taught me that before a contract was signed and sealed, I had to be prepared for other scenarios. To me, the worst case was having to resume the battle with Monika over where to settle: my preference was Iceland or Finland, hers Sweden. Our marriage, which had started off on the wrong foot, had limped along for ten years. Tora's birth gave us hope for a new beginning, but whether it would lead to a better place would depend on our next move.

CHAPTER 20

SWAZILAND

My Associate Expert position in Malawi was supposed to be a dead-end job. If I wanted to pursue a long-term career in international development, I would have to hone my skills through work experience, advanced studies, or both. As far as I knew, this was the only way to drop the "associate" hat and become an unconditional "expert." Thus in 1971, my last year in Malawi, I was most pleasantly surprised when my UNESCO project officer, John Beynon, contacted me about a new appointment. He invited me to apply for a UNESCO P3-level job in Swaziland. At the time, I had moved up from P1 to P2 on the UN professional scale, both junior grades reserved for "associates." P3 was a genuine expert and usually a headquarter job, but it appeared Beynon had bypassed convention to create this position for me. I was flattered, of course, and expressed my enthusiasm.

I would like to think my stellar performance in Malawi was the reason for the offer. But to be honest, luck should take most of the credit. In the early 1970s, the Swedish Government was pouring funds into the states bordering South Africa as a diplomatic way of giving the finger to the apartheid government. One of these investments sought to rehabilitate Swaziland's National High School, a venerable old institution that had fallen into decay. The school catered to the political elite in Swaziland, and many of its students bore the royal family's Dlamini name. The project was organized by UNESCO, but it was funded exclusively by SIDA.

Thus, all personnel had to be Swedish citizens, including an honorary Swede like myself. As in Malawi, I became the chosen one because of my knowledge of the British bills of quantities system.

In February 1972, after a two-month break in Iceland, the whole family traveled from Reykjavík to Mbabane, capital of Swaziland. We stopped for a few days in Paris for a briefing at UNESCO headquarters and another few days in Khartoum, Sudan, where I attended a short orientation on educational buildings in Africa. While in Sudan, we noticed fourteen-month-old Tora had loose bowel movements. We thought

Swaziland as a tiny blip in southern Africa

nothing of it, assuming it would pass. But the problem quickly worsened. By the time we got to Mbabane, the loose stool had turned watery, and she was delirious with fever, refusing to eat, and more alarmingly, drink. The small hotel room we stayed at became a mess of foul smelling diapers and towels. We took her to a clinic, where the doctor diagnosed her illness as amoebic dysentery, a disease that she had probably picked up in Sudan.

The doctor, a white South African, prescribed antibiotics and of all things, Marmite, a salty, tar-like paste the British spread on their breakfast toast. He said smearing Marmite on Tora's lips from time to time would encourage her to drink. It would also replenish her lost salts. Monika hovered over the sick child day and night, doing what the doctor told her to. When the tide started to turn, the poor baby was little more than a pair of large sunken eyes that reminded me of pictures of children at Auschwitz. With admirable patience and fortitude, Monika continued to coax the child to eat and drink. Gradually Tora recovered.

With Tora on the mend, we began appreciating our new host country. Wedged between the Republic of South Africa and Mozambique, the Kingdom of Swaziland is one of the smallest countries in Africa. On the map, the mini state looks like a ladylike bite out of the side of South Africa. It had been an independent kingdom until Europeans discovered Africa and scrambled for pieces of the "dark continent." Among the contenders for Swaziland were the British and the Boers, settlers of Dutch descent. The British won this battle and Swaziland became a British protectorate for sixty years. When I arrived, it was a fledgling country like Malawi and many other African states.

Despite its small size, Swaziland has a diverse topography and climate: cool in the highlands, hot and dry in the lowlands, and comfortably temperate in between. Dense pine forests grow on the higher elevations, corn, pineapple and citrus on the middle plateau, and sugar cane at lower elevations. Cattle, important both as an economic asset and a status symbol, roamed everywhere. A man chose a wife not by her looks or brains but by the number of cattle her father could afford as dowry. Several weeks into my new job, I was bantering with a gorgeous-looking secretary in the Ministry of Education. She proudly told me that her father was offering a herd of fifty cattle as her dowry. I never had the chance to follow up on the outcome of that bid.

The climate in Mbabane was pleasant. We never missed the air conditioners, but we certainly appreciated the coal-burning fireplace in our living room. In July, winter in the southern hemisphere, we often woke up to see frost glistening on our lawn.

During my time in Swaziland, the country was ruled by King Sobhuza II. He was the supreme ruler; his decisions were absolute. Fulfilling his duty of continuing the line, he produced a prolific pool of successors—more than two hundred children from seventy plus wives. Each year the king would add a queen or two by summoning eligible women to dance for him. In the spirit of learning about local cultures, I accepted a government invitation to one of these events at the stadium. Monika and I couldn't believe our eyes. Tens of thousands of young women, virgins no doubt, swayed and stepped to drumbeats. They were clad in the same costume—a belt of tiny beads covering their private parts—and not a thread more! The variety of shapes in such a large sample of female forms was mind-boggling. The king was somewhere in a secluded booth in the stadium, probably keeping a scorecard. At the end of the day, he would pick his next bride(s). I had seen pictures of some of the queens, and to my untutored eye, they looked curiously similar—light-skinned and well-endowed.

Sobhuza II was a beloved ruler. He was a man of the people, often appearing in traditional leopard loincloth and feather headdress. During my stay there, he disbanded parliament, claiming democracy was "un-Swazi." However, he routinely consulted with a community of elders. Under his leadership, the country exploited its rich natural resources and the economy thrived. Another asset was the king's liberal social mores, which made the country a hot attraction for their straitlaced neighbors. South Africans flocked across the border to carouse with Swazi women, try their fortunes at the casinos, and watch Stanley Kubrick's sexually explicit film, *A Clockwork Orange*. The movie showed for well over a year in an Mbabane movie theater.

My first task was to find myself an office. Unlike in Malawi, where an established unit awaited me, I had to fly solo in Swaziland. By then, I was seasoned enough to wing it. First of all, I had to decide on the location. My terms of reference stated that my duty station would be the industrial town of Manzini, close to the high school and about an hour's drive from Mbabane. At the same time, I was expected to liaise with officials based in the capital. With no one to consult, I took it upon myself to change my duty station to Mbabane. The search for housing followed, and within two weeks of our arrival, we moved into a three-bedroom row house, close to the center of town and reasonably priced.

Finding an office was more complicated. On my first visit to the Ministry of Works and Supplies, the Chief Architect told me in as many words to get lost. He was a shrunken, shrewd, and gruff European hired under some U.N. program to advise the ministry. He said he couldn't spare any of his precious office space for a dubious operator like me.

Like a homeless orphan, I approached with trepidation my next potential foster home. This was the Ministry of Education, the beneficiary of the project, since Swazi National High belonged to it. The chief adviser to the Permanent Secretary gave me quite a fright when he received me. Ingvar Anzén was a burly, fierce-looking Swede with folds of wrinkled skin covering one eye. Once we started talking, however, I began to relax. He was amiable, listened attentively, and showed genuine concern about my plight. I later learned that Ingvar was a retired director of a school district in Northern Sweden and had been an ice hockey player in his youth, which explained his disfigurement. At the end of our meeting, Ingvar was raring to adopt me. A couple of days later, he informed me that the Permanent Secretary had concurred, and I could move into my new office.

Ingvar and I established a project steering committee. It met every three months to review progress, set directions, and establish priorities. The committee of six was my sounding board, pointing out holes in my proposals but mostly rubber-stamping them.

Swazi National High School from the air. The three parallel classroom/laboratory blocks at the center were the ones I worked on in 1972, Phase One of the project. Courtesy of Ludo Kuipers, a coworker in the Ministry of Education.

Construction began in earnest in mid-1972. By the end of the year, the contractor had completed the first phase—three blocks of classrooms and laboratories. The consultant architect, a Portuguese Mozambican named José Forjaz, did an exemplary design. As shown in the picture, the layout is a lesson in good taste as well as functionality. The buildings are comfortably couched among stands of trees, and the spaces between the structures are proportioned in such a way that they feel like rooms with the sky for ceiling. A covered walkway connects all the buildings—a blessing on rainy days. The classrooms are modular and their orientation pays attention to the trajectory of the sun. This design was everything the secondary schools in the Malawi project weren't.

It was a joy to work with the congenial and competent José. Sometime during my last year in the country, he disappeared. Nobody in his office knew where he was. Alarmed, I went to see his Irish wife, Moira. She received me with equanimity but refused to tell me anything except José was all right. Much later, I learned he had returned to Mozambique to join the liberation movement. This news was all the more astonishing because José was a white settler, supposedly an enemy of the people. But the native Mozambicans embraced him, and when they declared independence in 1975, José became one of the stars in the new government.

With the construction program well underway, I turned my attention to furnishing the school. A Swedish furniture designer had prepared blueprints for a student desk-and-chair set. I hired two shops to produce the necessary prototypes. If the results were good, they would be used as models for all schools in Swaziland. The desk turned out fine, but the chair was prohibitively costly. After reviewing the numbers with José, I scuttled the idea of these custom-made chairs. I settled on a plastic bucket seat that was available on the market at an affordable price. The law of "you get what you pay for" bit me sooner than I expected. After a year of abuse by rambunctious teenagers, the store-bought chairs began to fall apart.

For the desk prototype, the government's Tender Board put two packages out to bid, one for the desktops, and the other for the tubular frames.

The winner of the desktop contract took me by surprise. It was the Prisons Department, which had submitted the lowest bid, and all things considered, was the best candidate for the job. In some countries, employing workers at below-market wages constitutes unfair competition and thus illegal. Swaziland, however, had no such laws.

This gave rise to a new problem. I had stipulated in the bidding documents that the desktop manufacturer would assemble the frames and tops at the school. But this procedure became impossible because the workers couldn't leave their prison. The pickup truck I had purchased with project funds came to the rescue. I drove to the frame maker in Manzini, stacked as many frames as possible on the truck, and delivered them to the prison for assembly. I also transported the finished desks from the prison to the school. Because of the bulk of my cargo, I could only take a few at a time. I ended up making more than a dozen trips and got to know some of the inmates quite well.

The prison was in the Ezulweni Valley, not far from the school. It was a maximum-security prison for people convicted of serious crimes, some punishable by death. I was, therefore, a bit nervous on my first trip. After driving through the front gates, I ran into another pair of gates, trapping me in a holding pen. The guard asked for my papers. He disappeared and after several long minutes, returned with a pass for me. The second pair of gates opened, and I drove into a large, rectangular yard. Following the guard's instructions, I steered into a gravel trail flanked by well-maintained lawns. What met me on the other end was totally unexpected. It was so ordinary! The concrete floors and corrugated iron roofs of the workshops looked a lot like my BP garage in Reykjavík. About a dozen men dressed in shorts and T-shirts went about their chores. These could be workshops anywhere in the world. But as I got out of the truck and looked around, I realized this was a prison all right. Barbed-wired walls surrounded the compound, and armed guards surveilled from the watchtowers at each corner.

On one visit, I detected a somber mood around the shops. It was as if somebody had died. I was told somebody indeed had—executed by hanging that morning. I took a quick count and was relieved to find none of my workers missing. My best mate was the man in charge of varnishing, a convicted murderer who had served half of his thirty-year sentence. He was an excellent craftsman, and I respected him for not only maintaining his sanity under the circumstances, but also his skills. We often took breaks together, sitting on a workshop bench, chatting, and sharing a smoke.

As my confidence grew, I took on a responsibility that wasn't in my job description. This was supplying the schools with education equipment, which nobody seemed to be doing anything about. I kick-started the process by approaching the staff in the Ministry of Education. From then on, experts from the Ministry and UNESCO teamed up and carried the ball forward. They prepared the lists of equipment commensurate with the curriculum and put them out for international bidding. A few months later, boxes of microscopes, scales, beakers and test tubes for the science labs, pots and pans for the home economics lab, and cameras for the photography class arrived at the port in Mozambique and were transported by rail to Manzini. I drove my truck to the railway station several times to pick them up and deliver them to the school.

Monika and me at the U.N. Day party in Mbabane in 1972.
Courtesy of Ludo Kuipers.

I was executive, supervisor, architect, secretary, and deliveryman all in one. My extreme hands-on involvement flew in the face of the notion that U.N. staff were supposed to be advisors. I was expected to guide and train local staff, so they could carry out future projects on their own. However, since nobody in government cared to appoint a counterpart to work with me, I had no one to transfer my skills to. I operated as if running my own business, and neither the government nor UNESCO raised an eyebrow. Compared to the Malawi project, where I had to put up with incompetent and indifferent colleagues, my experience in Swaziland was much more gratifying. The school was completed on time and within budget. However, I didn't contribute an iota to my primary duty—building up the government's capacity to implement its programs. This is a failing of many donor interventions and has cultivated an unhealthy dependence in some developing countries.

On the home front, the children flourished on Swazi soil. Monika and I had been ambivalent about staying on in Africa because of Steinn's education. At the end of our stay in Malawi, he was ten and would soon attend secondary school. During those days, few African countries offered good options beyond the elementary level. Most British expats sent their children to boarding schools in their home country. During school holidays, planes between Britain and Malawi were filled with youngsters visiting their parents.

Although we disagreed on many things, Monika and I agreed wholeheartedly that this wasn't acceptable for our family. We were thus relieved to discover that Swaziland offered an alternative. The Waterford Kamhlaba School, located in Mbabane, was part of a global education movement called United World College. At the time it had thirteen schools and colleges spread all over the world, and its stated objective was to unite nations and cultures to build a peaceful future. The first such school opened in Wales in 1962. One year later, a young British teacher, Michael Stern, came to Mbabane to open a multiracial school called Waterford Kamhlaba. A former schoolteacher in Johannesburg, he was poking South Africa's apartheid in the eye. Waterford's rigorous academic program, delivered in an enriching, multicultural environment, was everything a parent could hope for. We jumped at the chance to enroll Steinn. If he ever went back for a class reunion, he would find among his alumni people bearing historic last names such as Mandela (after their daddy, Nelson) and Tutu (after their daddy, the Archbishop).

Tora sprang back from near death to a healthy, happy toddlerhood. Her nanny was named Patience, and she certainly had plenty of it. During our first year in Swaziland, Tora spent much of her time bouncing on Patience's hip, a wrap tying her to her nanny's waist. In the beginning, I worried that her dangling head might fall off as Patience's hips swayed and bucked while she carried out household chores. I kept wanting to reach out and prop up the lolling head. Noticing that all local children were raised in this fashion, I soon relaxed. Tora quickly outgrew Patience's hip and was running merrily around the house.

While the word "thriving" sums up my children's growth, its antonym must be used for my marriage. We had been incompatible from day one. The occasional pockets of marital bliss had fooled us into believing that happiness was attainable if only the circumstances were right, such as a satisfying job for Monika, a better job for me, another child, another trip, another home, another country and so on. Swaziland put an end to the self-deception, for now our incompatibility had fully bloomed. Every individual has his own peculiarities. A compatible couple complement each other's quirks and bring out the best in each other. An incompatible couple pour fuel on each other's fire and burn the house to cinders. My marriage was a classic case of the latter. For instance, when Monika nagged me, I would retreat into my cave, which could be a physical place such as my room, or a mental wall of silence. This would enrage Monika. She would raise her voice, which would push me deeper into my cave, which would enrage her more. When the scene became unbearable, I would run into my truck and drive around until the fire had burned out. The only way to change our incompatibility was to change our behavior. But neither of us was self-aware enough to initiate that.

Alcohol didn't help, and we were both guilty on that score. The drinking started in Malawi, where gin and tonic flowed like water in expat gatherings. I see it as the toll of a nomadic lifestyle. Lacking the stability that allowed the cultivation of hobbies and deep friendships, partying and drinking filled the vacuum. Alcohol washed away whatever self-control we had. Monika shrieked louder than ever, while I clammed up tighter than ever.

Alcohol inflames other vices as well. At expat parties, where wives were bored, husbands restless, and both inebriated, the temptations were plenty. All that the devil had to do was sit back and cackle every time the frailest among us fell into sin. Both Monika and I began to explore other relationships. It was rather awkward, given the smallness of our circle.

But in spite of our loveless marriage, we still enjoyed traveling together as a family. In our second year in Swaziland, we took a three-week road tour of South Africa. The moment I crossed the border, a battery of public toilets affronted my sensibilities and became a symbol of the country in my mind. Instead of the usual separation of the two sexes, this segregation multiplied fourfold into toilets for whites, blacks, Asians, and those of a mixed race, called colored. Up till then, apartheid had been an abstraction to me, and now it hit me in the gut, at the level of the most basic human needs. I felt embarrassed and ashamed of my skin color. The moral stench of apartheid would follow me throughout the trip.

Our first stop was Johannesburg, the financial hub and largest city in South Africa. This was the Klondike of Africa, the site of large deposits of gold. A bizarre sight unfolded as we approached the city. Gargantuan mountains streaked with sickly gray and yellow tints rose up around the mines. These were tailings, the unwanted and often poisonous heaps of mining dirt. Once inside Johannesburg, we found a sprawling metropolis with sleek high-rises and modern malls similar to major cities in the U.S. But there was something sinister about this picture of prosperity. The people walking on the streets and riding in cars, the shopkeepers and shoppers, the hotel managers and receptionists, were all white. The handful of blacks we saw were hotel maids, construction workers, and street cleaners. We soon learned that Johannesburg was a whites-only city. Blacks, who made up 90 percent of the country's population, had to leave when their work was done.

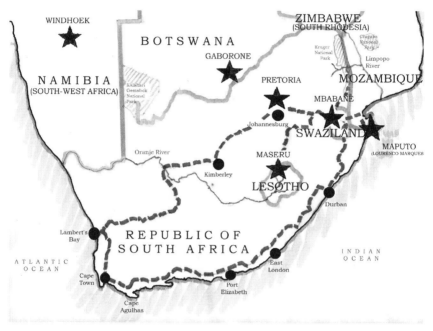

Map of southern Africa. My family trips are marked in broken lines.

A couple of days later, on the way out of the city, we saw where the 90 percent lived. They huddled in segregated towns such as the notorious SOWETO (South Western Townships) on the outskirts of Johannesburg. It was a ghetto of corrugated iron hovels and pot-holed streets. Blood would spill several years after I drove on these streets, when South African police would open fire at protestors, and scores would die.

The diamond mine of Kimberley was the second place that made a lasting impression on me. Open-air mining had long since ceased and all that remained was the Big Hole, a deep crater filled with water. From 1871 to 1914, some 50,000 miners dug the hole with picks and shovels, yielding

2,720 kilograms of diamonds. The museum there showed remarkable pictures of the mining operations. Each miner (whites only) bought a claim that was a few square meters in area and a depth of as far as he could dig with picks and shovels. A photo shows a vast web of ropes covering the vertical walls of a large pit. These block and tackle-operated hoists were the only means of getting men and matériel in and out. The term "undermining" probably originates from this place. As miners descended at different speeds into the bowels of the earth, those at greater depth transgressed into the claim areas of their competitors. Eventually this type of excavation became impossible to sustain, and all the claims were consolidated under the ownership of one company: De Beers. The days of surface mining were over, and the company switched to underground mining.

Of course, Monika couldn't leave without a souvenir. To her chagrin, not a speck of diamond was on display in the shops at Kimberley. It turned out that although this place was one of the largest sources of the world's diamonds, they were all shipped overseas. She finally bought a tiny diamond in Cape Town and had it set into a ring.

We continued southwest toward the Karoo, a semi-desert that was once daunting to explorers because of its extreme swings from scorching to freezing, and drought to flood. Midway through the Karoo, I began to notice a change in the weather. The wind that whipped our faces was becoming unpleasantly hot, close to searing. I looked forward to the Atlantic coast, which wasn't far away, and fantasized about frolicking in the cool ocean. Then I noticed a strange phenomenon in the distance. A low, dark cloud filled the entire horizon and was spinning toward me like a gigantic tumbleweed. The world suddenly turned dark, the wind howled, and the desert temperature plummeted to arctic level. We closed the car windows and turned on the heater.

What we had just witnessed was the effect of the Benguela current. This current is the fastest-flowing part of the South Atlantic Gyre, which churns up the icy waters of Antarctica and hauls them up to the vicinity of the Cape of Good Hope, causing sensational shifts in the weather.

When we reached the coast a short while later, we witnessed a beneficial effect of the current. Where cold water collided with the warm, the resultant upwelling brought with it a rich menu of plankton, which in turn attracted large schools of fish. The fishing town of Lambert's Bay looked like a replica of an Icelandic fishing town. The blustery weather, the churning ocean beyond the harbor, the shabby jetties, and rusting fishing vessels and gear were strangely similar. The only difference was the skin color of the fishermen.

Cape Town was the jewel of South Africa. Tucked under the majestic Table Mountain, surrounded by vineyards and flanked by two oceans, Indian and South Atlantic, it was an unforgettable place. After a week of immersion in the black and white rigidity of South Africa, I immediately noticed a nice change in Cape Town's color scheme. People of black, brown, yellow, and white skins mingled with ease. The atmosphere was much more relaxed and livelier than in dour Johannesburg, where the division was so strict that even the air breathed by different races was different. We did, of course, what tourists do. We took the gondola to the top of Table Mountain for a panoramic view of the town and ocean.

We also drove the long, winding road to the Cape of Good Hope. Standing on the bluff at the tip of the peninsula, I couldn't help feeling, "Is that it?" I had expected monster waves and roiling turbulence where the two oceans met, where the hopes of generations of European seafarers had been dashed, but all I saw on that day was calm blue waters.

In the minds of most people, the Cape of Good Hope is the southern tip of Africa. But that is actually Cape Agulhas, which juts a bit further south into the ocean. We visited it on the way out of Cape Town and saw the wreck of a freighter sticking out of the water. Though sorry for the freighter, I was happy to see the tales of sailing hazards in these parts were more than just legends.

Next came Port Elizabeth, where Monika's cousin lived. He was the son of the uncle and aunt with whom Monika stayed in her first year in Helsinki. In search of economic opportunities, he had moved to South

Africa, lived out the dream, and become a staunch supporter of apartheid. He was the one who had imbued his parents and Monika with ridiculous ideas about the innate inferiority of blacks. Monika was excited about reuniting with the cousin her uncle had bragged so much about. We found a modest bungalow at his address and knocked unannounced on the door. A middle-aged woman greeted us. She told us brusquely she and her husband had divorced, and he no longer lived there. When Monika asked for his new address, the ex-wife dismissed us with a shrug. Obviously the divorce had been bitter.

Monika swallowed her disappointment, and we moved on. Further east along the Indian Ocean coast, we drove through some "Bantustans." These were supposedly black autonomous areas, but they were more like concentration camps. "Self-government" and "independence" are noble words, but the motives of the white government were pure evil. The government's strategy was to corral black Africans into racially homogenous enclaves, allow the inhabitants to do whatever they wanted within their territories, but strip them of South African citizenship and voting rights. This vile machination was born out of fear that the black majority would seize power and chase white settlers out of Africa. The villages I passed were utterly depressing. Identical tin-roofed, cinder-block cubes lined the streets, creating a prison-like atmosphere.

The inhumane policy of apartheid cast a dark pall over the sunniest spots in the country. At Durban, the busiest port in Africa as well as a tourist destination known for its beautiful beaches, people of different colors couldn't swim at the same shore. One joke goes like this. An American tourist asks a waiter at his hotel, "Is this the Indian Ocean?" The shocked waiter says, "No, sir, this is the European ocean. The Indian ocean is a couple of kilometers further south."

We got home shortly after Durban, our minds overloaded with impressions. For me, the misery of apartheid left a sour taste in my mouth, despite the spectacular scenery. I was convinced that South Africa was a powder keg that was going to blow up sooner or later. For Monika, however, South Africa was a sweet spot for whites to succeed and prosper. Although she never got to meet her cousin, the trip confirmed her belief that South Africa was a great land of opportunities. She thought apartheid worked well—witness the law and order everywhere we went—and she believed that was the way it was going to be forever. I was aghast when she said she wanted to emigrate to South Africa. I added one more item to our list of incompatibilities.

During my last year of working on Swaziland's National High, a team of World Bank staff contacted me and sought my advice. They were preparing an education project in the country, the first of its kind to be financed by the Bank, and wanted to pick my brain. Grant Sinclair was my principal contact with the Bank team. He and I are both architects and speak a common professional language, and we have remained friends ever since.

The Bank team visited several times, and I became more and more enmeshed in their activities. The project they were designing was about three times larger than my high school undertaking, and much more complex. It involved the development of an industrial training institute, a teacher training college, a curriculum development center and a number of rural education centers. It came as no surprise when both Bank and government officials probed my interest in becoming the director for the project. While I greatly appreciated this confidence, I was of two minds about accepting. This assignment could become a capstone of my exploits in developing countries, after which I would return to Scandinavia with my trophies and settle down. Or it could lead to a lifetime of short-term assignments and wandering from one poor country to another. Monika and I discussed this at length and came to a partial agreement. We agreed the new job in Swaziland would be my last before settling down for good. As to which country to call home afterwards, we left our preferences on the table for future consideration.

By mid-1974, I was the director designate of the World Bank-financed project. I would remain a staff of UNESCO, the administrator of my contract. My new job would carry a P5 level position, which meant I would have traversed the entire U.N. professional pay scale of P1-5 in six years. It felt surreal and, I cannot lie, good for my ego. At thirty-five, I thought I was on top of the world. I had conquered strange lands and reaped the reward of a golden paycheck. But my exhilaration had a bittersweet tang. This job marked the beginning of the end of my Viking days. I was definitely going home afterwards.

CHAPTER 21

VÍNLAND

Vínland, which means land of wine, is the ancient Norse name for North America. Vikings discovered America around the year 1,000 AD, five hundred years before Christopher Columbus. This isn't just a myth or wishful hubris. Two Icelandic sagas have recorded the event, and most importantly, evidence dug up at an archeological site in Newfoundland proves the presence of a Viking longhouse. Both sagas tell about the accidental discovery of North America by Icelandic seafarers. Blown off course, they came upon an icy and barren land. But while the accounts differ in details about who did what, they agree on the key character in this drama. He was Leif Eriksson, son of Erik the Red. Artifacts from L'Anse aux Meadows, situated at the tip of Newfoundland, indicate the Vikings had set up camp there. There is also indication, from both the unearthed objects and the saga accounts, that they had gone much farther south. According to the sagas, the Vikings found wild grapes on their expeditions and thus named the place Vínland. Judging by the growth range of wild grapes, archeologists believe that these explorers might have visited the territory now known as the United States of America.

The U.S. had always held a fascination for me. It was a superpower and a high-tech mecca. It was also the home of Frank Lloyd Wright, one of my architect heroes. My dream of spending a year there hadn't yet materialized, but I did visit it in September 1974. As the director designate for the World Bank-financed project in Swaziland, I traveled to the U.S.

as part of the negotiating team. The World Bank headquarters is located in Washington, D.C., and all its project agreements were finalized there. I was awe-struck as my Swazi colleagues and I sat on one side of the massive negotiating table, while the Bank team sat poker-faced on the other. But after the first day of arguing about inconsequential details, I realized the pomp and circumstance was mainly for show. The real work had already been done in the field, and the rest was mostly posturing. The schedule was leisurely, and thanks to Grant Sinclair, who took me around, I saw many of Washington's official edifices along both sides of the National Mall. The promenade was a New World replica of the Champs-Élysées in Paris, which was no surprise since a Frenchman, Pierre L'Enfant, had designed it. A collage of other scenes formed during my weeklong stay: oversized American cars with snouts as long as a barracuda, a row of dilapidated boarded-up buildings close to my hotel in downtown D.C., and jungles along Rock Creek Parkway wilder than anything I had seen in Africa.

Shortly after my return to Swaziland, I received a letter from the World Bank. It invited me to Washington, D.C. to interview for a position in the education division of its East Asia and Pacific department. I was dumbfounded. I had never applied for such a job, and what on earth did I know about East Asia and the Pacific? It took me a while to figure out a probable explanation. Some time back, I had sent my credentials to the World Bank for their approval of my appointment as the Swazi project director. Apparently, my résumé had found its way to the personnel department. My first reaction was to write them back and tell them they had made a mistake. On second thought, though, I realized this opened up a whole new frontier for my career. I discussed it with Monika, who agreed it was a good opportunity as long as it was another *temporary* assignment. On the understanding that everything in life is temporary, I wrote back to the Bank to express my interest. However, since I already had a firm job offer in Swaziland, I concluded by saying I would only agree to come to Washington if they would give me a definite yes or no at the end of the interviews. I didn't want to travel the long distance just to wind up on a roster of potential recruits for the Bank.

Two months later, I landed at Dulles Airport again. At the Bank, a personnel officer handed me a two-day schedule. I was to arrive at each interviewer's office at the designated time. Trudging from one room to another, I soon became acquainted with the solemn twelve-floor office block. It was nothing fancy; in fact the green plastic upholstered chairs were on the tacky side. Nonetheless, there was a weightiness about the place. This was truly a "world" bank, providing financing to governments to fight poverty in every corner of the globe. It embodied the postwar movement to right the wrongs of the past and strive toward the utopia of prosperity for every nation. Securing a job here would be the pinnacle of my career.

I was nervous, of course, but not to a nail-biting extent. I had worked on Bank-financed projects in Malawi and Swaziland, so I was confident I could do the job. Each interview lasted half an hour to one hour, and ranged from friendly chitchat to serious technical discussions and a condescending lecture about the Bank's lofty mission. I had no idea who those people were, but I knew there were two (whose positions were displayed in plaques in front of their offices) I had to impress.

One was Richard Johanson, chief of the education division of the East Asia and Pacific region. In other words, my boss if I was hired. Richard, a pleasant and thoughtful American about my age, presented me with a set of architectural drawings. "These designs were prepared for a trade school in South Korea," he said. "If you were to review them, would you approve?" I took a deep breath and flipped through the sheets. My heart lightened. The blueprints were such a blatant disaster that their creator would flunk first-year architectural school. I told Richard so and went on to point out the flaws with great pleasure.

The other man I had to particularly impress was Syed Kirmani, the department director; in other words, my prospective boss's boss. Kirmani was an older Pakistani, and after the initial pleasantries, he began a monologue that droned on and on, punctuated with plenty of "I mean" and "you see." I struggled to follow his meandering arguments through the fog of his soft voice and my jetlag. Slowly, words strung into sentences. I realized he was giving me his credentials—something about being in charge of constructing a large dam in the Pakistani boondocks, and the government had to build a village and schools for the workers' families. He was telling me he knew something about building schools … and much more. By the end of his rambling, I realized who he was: the chief engineer in charge of building the Tarbela Dam, the largest earth-filled dam in the world and a mammoth engineering feat that turned the Indus River into a source of electricity and irrigation. The World Bank, a major financier, touted the project as a great achievement of international cooperation.

I was still wondering where this was leading when Kirmani unleashed his make-or-break question. "We have both worked on the government's side—I mean, the other side of the World Bank. We had to do things according to Bank rules, you see. Tell me, what do you think of the Bank's procurement procedures?"

I debated with myself for a split second. Shall I tell the truth or what he wants to hear? And do I know what he wants to hear? I finally stuck to the adage we teach our children: "Honesty is the best policy."

"I think the Bank's procurement procedures are overly rigid," I ventured and went on to suggest a scenario. For instance, if the government needs to buy several bottles of olive oil, according to Bank rules, it would have to go through international tendering. In hindsight, this was a ridiculously simplistic example, but that was what came off the top of my head. I carried on, telling him that international tendering is a lengthy and expensive process when the government can easily buy the olive oil on the local market at a reasonable price. My conclusion was: "International competitive bidding is very effective for large items, but a lot of small stuff can be purchased locally, quickly and cheaply. I think there should be more flexibility in the Bank's rules."

Without giving me any clue about what he thought of my critique, Kirmani went on another longwinded soliloquy. I didn't know much about his experience at the time, but eventually I would learn he had wrestled with Bank authorities over many aspects of the Tarbela construction. And the contention wasn't over olive oil but enormous items, such as turbines, generators and tons of earthwork. Many years later, I would also learn that my critique of the Bank had scratched Kirmani's back where it itched.

I boarded the plane at Dulles airport with a job offer safely tucked away in my briefcase. The outcome had felt preordained at the time, but several years later, Richard told me the interview panel had been split down the middle. The naysayers thought I was unsuitable because of my language limitation. Of the three languages most used in Bank work—English, French and Spanish—I was fluent in only one. Another down vote came from a senior Swedish educator, Mats Hultin. Mats, who later became a friend, was turned off by my ignorance of a Swedish architect well known in Sweden for his school designs. But the votes that mattered the most were those of my future boss and boss's boss, Richard and Kirmani. Both gave me the thumbs up.

On returning to Swaziland, I had only a month to wind down my business before departing. On the professional level, I found a well-qualified substitute to replace me as project director. On the personal level, however, matters were much stickier. I tossed and turned over it many nights and finally came to a conclusion: this marriage can't go on. The children had been the glue that kept us together, but the relationship had crumbled beyond repair. I understood full well what separation meant. Monika would take the children back to Sweden while I took up my post in Washington. But my job would take me to Asia several times a year. I could finagle transits in Europe and take days off to spend time with Tora and Steinn. This wasn't an ideal family life, but anything was better than the current situation. For my children, growing up with a part-time dad would trump watching their parents tear at each other's throats full time.

I braced myself for the discussion with Monika. I would allay her concerns about abandonment. I would assure her that she wouldn't suffer financially. I would provide for her and the children's every need. She would be free to settle down in her beloved Sweden, get a job if she wanted to, and raise the children in the excellent Swedish schools. Since we were moving anyway, this was the perfect time to go our separate ways.

Finally, I delivered my proposal. Monika looked at me with shock and hurt. Her lips twitched, and I got ready to beat a hasty retreat into my cave. I was fully expecting her to lash out at me, which, though unpleasant, would only strengthen my resolve. But instead of barking, she spoke in a sad but controlled voice. For the first time, she admitted that the pitiful state of our marriage wasn't entirely my fault, at least not a hundred percent. She was conciliatory and willing to make amends. I was stunned. Her uncharacteristic niceness sent my compass spinning in confusion. She went on talking about my "temporary" assignment at the World Bank, after which we would move back to Sweden and live happily ever after. She felt our marriage was salvageable and begged me to give it another try. I sat staring at her, too bewildered to argue.

CHAPTER 22

MY EARLY YEARS AT THE WORLD BANK

If my Viking forefathers could see me, they would hustle out of Valhalla and fight their way into the World Bank. During the seven years I spent in the Asia and Pacific region, I traveled on business to China, Indonesia, Korea, Malaysia, Papua New Guinea, Pakistan, Philippines, Singapore, and the Solomon Islands. Within those countries, I visited not just the capitals and big cities but also the most isolated corners, where people stopped to gawk at the first white man they'd ever seen—me.

On average, I made four trips a year, ranging from two to six weeks each. I had the time of my life on these travels. Much of the work was familiar, a variation of what I did in Malawi and Swaziland, but the worlds they opened up were beyond my wildest fantasy. I could never have imagined these scenes: in Papua New Guinea a woman suckling a piglet while sitting in the copilot seat of a small plane; in Lahore, Pakistan, two cyclists each shouldering one end of a stack of eighteen-foot planks on a teeming street, weaving between cars, donkeys, camels and elephants; and in Indonesia, the corpse of a long-dead, mummified grandmother sitting at the dinner table with her family. The kaleidoscope of human behavior filled me with wonder.

The gray offices at the Bank's headquarters, however, filled me with dread. Soon after my first day in April 1975, I learned that nothing cuts a person down to size as quickly as a bureaucracy. For the past several years I had been my own boss, making decisions on the fly and informing my distant supervisors in Paris when the desire moved me. Nobody queried my decisions, and I felt like a lord in my fiefdom. The moment I entered the Bank, hammers descended from every direction, banging me down to a cog in its giant machinery. When I drafted a letter to a borrower, something as measly as acknowledging receipt of their letter, half a dozen bureaucrats would scribble on it until I could no longer recognize it as my handiwork. And if I forgot to send it to a concerned party for clearance, a memo copied to my boss would land with an angry thump in my in-tray. Every decision I made had to be vetted for compliance with Bank rules and regulations. I bowed to the rule-keepers the first year, careful not to incur their wrath. I was also lucky to have a supportive chief like Richard Johanson to guide me. Without his help and that of several senior colleagues, I wouldn't have lasted the year.

The Bank´s official name is The International Bank for Reconstruction and Development. It had started as a financier for the reconstruction of countries torn apart by the Second World War. After that was over, it switched its attention to the development of poor countries. At first, the Bank continued to do what it knew best—financing investments in infrastructure—but it soon discovered that *reconstruction* and *development* were totally different beasts that shouldn't be handled in the same manner.

For a country like France, all it wanted from the Bank was heavy equipment for *reconstruction*. Once these physical resources were in place, the country had all the knowhow to rebuild its damaged roads, bridges, railways and so on. However, for countries such as Chile and India, recipients of the first Bank *development* loans, hardware wasn't enough. Developing nations lacked the educated manpower to plan, implement, and later to operate and maintain the brand-new systems. This was when the Bank realized it had to consider a country's manpower needs too. It began to invest in skills training associated with its infrastructure projects, or what was called "project-related training." Thus began the Bank's involvement in education. From a narrow initial focus on technical training, its interventions gradually cascaded down to the fundamental building blocks—primary and secondary education. The idea was to give the population a solid ABC education, after which industries and specialized training institutes could provide relevant skills.

When I joined in 1975, the Bank was at the zenith of expansion. The president was Robert S. McNamara, the former U.S. Defense Secretary who had left the Pentagon because of his misgivings about the Vietnam War. He became the longest-serving World Bank president from 1968 to 1981. His plans for the institution were ambitious—quadruple lending and extend into every field to meet the essential needs of the developing world. He felt that building only big dams, power plants, and railway systems wouldn't necessarily improve ordinary people's lives. The Bank needed to invest in agriculture, education, and healthcare, too. His speeches brimmed with idealism, but of course, realpolitik was also at play. The Cold War was at its peak, and if the West didn't show largesse, poor nations threatened to turn to the East for patronage. Putting his big ideas into action, McNamara reorganized the Bank in 1972, quadrupled the number of staff, and fulfilled his lending goals.

By then, people could see that this institution with the audacity to call itself the "World Bank" was living up to its name. In the postwar years when money was scarce, the Bank provided financing for much-needed construction works. But its intellectual contribution was equally important, for money spent unwisely can do more harm than good. Borrowers often cringed at the endless sermons of Bank technocrats on the importance of economic analysis, long-term planning, strategy and so on, but this nagging had produced good results. Take my native Iceland as an example. In 1973, a volcanic eruption in the Vestmann Islands off the Icelandic south coast threatened to destroy the only harbor in the area. Such an eventuality would be disastrous, as these rich fishing grounds were the only lifeline of the community. While Iceland agonized over whether to wait and see or build a new harbor immediately, the Bank took the long view. It reviewed the proposal for three new harbors on the south coast of the mainland and deemed that they made economic sense regardless of the outcome of the eruption. The worst-case scenario didn't happen—the old harbor was saved through heroic human efforts. At the same time, the new harbors were put to good use, contributing to the prosperity of the small towns in the region.

The Bank's push in the power and transport sectors also launched a new economic era in Iceland. Not only did the Bank help to build the structures—a string of hydroelectric and geothermal facilities and a network of roads—it also introduced sound business practices to ensure the operations' longevity. If left to their own devices (knowing my countrymen), the Icelandic agencies would probably have undercharged their customers, leading to financial distress down the road. The Bank was guilty of some misguided ventures too, but in my homeland, the successes far outweighed the failures.

While studying in Finland, I had read about the World Bank's river-taming feats—the Tarbela Dam in Pakistan, Kariba in Rhodesia, and Furnas in Brazil—and salivated at the idea of joining the esteemed institution one day. But I thought it was a pipe dream, since I was an architect, not a dam engineer. Somehow, though, the star I followed must have pointed straight at the Bank's gates. Just when I was professionally ready for the Bank, the Bank was ready for me.

My first "mission" for the Bank was to Pakistan. In Bank parlance, staff visits to client countries are called "missions," a reflection of the military culture McNamara brought with him from the Pentagon. I was the rookie on a four-member team, eager to learn from my seasoned coworkers. I had seen schools in the boondocks of Africa, but they didn't prepare me for the primitive conditions of those in Pakistan. Some of the primary schools I visited didn't have a single piece of furniture, not to mention blackboards, textbooks, water, or sanitation. Children sat on concrete floors in jam-packed classrooms (when they were lucky enough to have classrooms). In some schools, the children sat in the sun, or in the shade of a tree if there was one. Schools for boys and girls were segregated.

Families tended to keep their girls home, partly for socioeconomic reasons and partly for practicality because girls had a harder time coping with the lack of toilets in the schools.

Íslenzkur arki- tekt í Pakistan

— sviptur ferðafrelsi vegna herlaga og útgöngubanns, sem þar eru í gildi

HV-Reykjavík — Ég hef engar fréttir fengið beint frá eiginmanni mínum, en eitthvað hefur greinilega orðið til þess að hann er tepptur á ferð sinni um Pakistan. Síðastliðinn fimmtudag gat hann hringt í Alþjóðabankann, sem hann starfar hjá, og látið vita af sér. Ég fékk þá skilaboð um að hann sæti fastur inni á hótelinu sem hann dvaldist á í Karachi en þegar ég reyndi að hringja þangað, náðist ekki til hans. Á laugardagsmorgun fékk ég aftur skilaboð um að hann væri heill á húfi, þá kominn til Islamabad, og sömu sögu er að segja í dag, því það var hringt frá bankanum og okkur sagt frá því að hann væri í Islamabad, heill á húfi, en greinilega sviptur ferðafrelsi, sagði frú Monica Sigurðsson, eiginkona Sverris Sigurðssonar, arkitekts, sem starfar á vegum Alþjóðabank-

ans, en Sverrir er staddur í Pakistan og hefur, að því er virðist verið sviptur ferðafrelsi.

Sverrir var að sinna störfum í tengslum við efnahagsaðstoð sem Alþjóðabankinn veitir Pakistönum, og átti hann að fara til nokkurra staða í landinu. Sem kunnugt er af fréttum, hafa óeirðir og stjórnmálaórói í Pakistan leitt til þess að herlög hafa verið sett á þar og útgöngubann lagt á. Þegar þetta skeði var Sverrir staddur í Karachi, sem er syðst í Pakistan, á ströndinni við Arabíska hafið. Nú hefur hann verið fluttur til Islamabad, sem er nyrst í landinu, af orsökum sem ekki eru kunnar, en sá staður var ekki meðal þeirra sem Sverrir átti að fara til þar.

Sverrir hefur starfað hjá Alþjóðabankanum um nokkurra

ára skeið, en hann vinnur þar í deild sem nefnist Suðaustur Asíudeild. Þegar Tíminn leitaði eftir upplýsingum þar í gær, í aðalstöðvum bankans í Washington, reyndist engar upplýsingar þar að fá. Sverrir og fjölskylda hans eru búsett í Washington.

Í gærdag bárust litlar fréttir

Sverrir Sigurðsson, arkitekt.

af ástandinu í Pakistan aðrar en þær að þar virtist allt rólegra en í síðustu viku en útgöngubann og herlög þó enn í gildi.

10 ára drengur náði jafntefli við Spassky

ÞJ-Húsavík. — Boris Spassky og kona hans Marina, komu til Húsavíkur sl. föstudag í boði Taflfélags Húsavíkur. Á laugardaginn tefldi Spassky fjöltefli við 36 menn í Félagsheimilinu á Húsavík. Tíkar fóru svo, að stórmeistarinn vann 29 skák-

ir og sjö skákum lauk með jafntefli.

Meðal þeirra sem náðu jafntefli við Spassky, var 10 ára gamall drengur, Haraldur Sigurjónsson, og sömdu þeir um stórmeistarajafntefli.

An article in an Icelandic newspaper in 1977 notes my adventures in Pakistan during martial law.

While I was visiting Karachi in 1977, the military staged a coup. General Zia arrested Prime Minister Bhutto, dissolved parliament, and declared martial law and a travel ban. I was stuck in the hotel for a few days, sparking concerns over my safety. The headline of an article in the Icelandic paper *Tíminn* read, "Icelandic architect in Pakistan—deprived of his freedom of movement because of the imposition of martial law." The paper made this modest inconvenience of mine seem like a life-threatening ordeal. Once the travel ban was lifted, I went on to Islamabad and continued my mission. The only riots I knew about were from reading the papers. Nonetheless, for the people of Pakistan the consequences were major. In addition to the abrupt turn from democracy to dictatorship, President

General Zia injected elements of *sharia* into Pakistani law and steered the country toward Islamic fundamentalism.

Throughout my travels in Asia, I witnessed a common thread among the people I met. Be it the swamps of Borneo and Sumatra, the jungles of Papua New Guinea and the Solomon Islands, the rebel territory in the Philippines, or the lawless Kalashnikov-toting areas on the Pakistan-Afghan border, the thirst for education was universal. When parents refused to send their children to school, it was usually for a good reason. In one remote Indonesian village that could only be reached by motorboat through flooded jungle (I had to close my eyes while whizzing past gigantic trees), the villagers got into an angry argument with the ministry officials escorting me. The locals, on overhearing remarks that they were too primitive to understand the value of education, hotly retorted that they were very familiar with the value of education, but it wasn't worth their while to send their children to schools of such low quality that they didn't learn anything!

The Bank's objectives in its education investment were to increase enrollment in schools and improve their quality. Its success rate in Asia varied widely. The country I visited the most, frustratingly, was one of the low achievers. After all the missions, the hundreds of millions of dollars poured into its education system, Pakistan's progress was flat at best. Reasons for failure included civil unrest, lack of government commitment to education, and a high level of corruption. One school I visited had been commandeered by a local politician and used for his grain storage. In many places, "ghost" teachers were on the payroll and receiving salaries despite either never setting foot in the schools or being dead. I thought the ultimate nonsense was when university students rioted against a new government regulation that forbade cheating. This kind of ethos was hardly the atmosphere for academic excellence.

On the other end of the spectrum, I'm most proud to have participated in the growth of several Asian powerhouses. In my opinion, a country's economic progress depends on the education of its people. I don't say that because education is my field, but because the facts bear out my observation. South Korea, one of the "Asian Tigers," is a good example. When I visited South Korea in the early 1980s, it wasn't roaring yet. It was still at the stage of producing tennis shoes and other low-tech items. Since the end of the Korean War, Seoul had seen its share of coups, assassinations, and riots. But regardless of the political scene, the drumbeat toward education advancement was strong and steady. The government's investment in education was as substantial as any advanced country's. The mission of my team was to help the country build up its science and engineering education. The Koreans were eager to send a large number of students overseas for training. Fearing brain drain, my team questioned the wisdom of this program. To which our Korean counterpart smiled and said, "We don't want them to come back after graduation. We want them to stay in their countries of study and work to become mid-level scientists, engineers, and managers. At that stage we will make them an irresistible offer to return home." True to its word, South Korea carried out this policy. The impact was astounding. From a maker of T-shirts and pajamas, the country bounded up the manufacturing ladder and became one of cars, computers, smartphones, and high-definition TV screens.

In November 1980, I was honored to be on one of the Bank's pioneer missions to Beijing. One notable point: China's first loan application to the Bank wasn't for some large infrastructure construction, as most had expected. It was to modernize its higher education system, starting with twenty-seven of its most prestigious universities. I thus arrived in Beijing to a land of blue and green Mao suits.

The late Chairman Mao Zedong was a god-like figure, and everyone had to emulate him, including dressing like him. The unisex jacket was adapted from a traditional Chinese costume and was a kind of nationalistic comeback to the Western business suit. I have to say the men looked rather handsome in the tunic with four roomy pockets, but the shapeless garment didn't flatter the women. I also have to say I had never seen such masses before. Peeking out of the Red Flag limousines that transported me around,

I watched in amazement the never-ending phalanx of bicycles, seven or eight deep, streaming by.

Communications with Chinese officials were full of surprises. Sequestered in the Soviet camp for thirty years, China had an ample supply of Russian translators. English translators were rare, and training a new cadre took time. Many of the English interpreters assigned to the Bank team could hardly speak the language, and some confessed to really being Russian translators. After the decades of separation between East and West, thought processes were different too. These two factors were a formula for hilarious misunderstandings. At one meeting, my colleagues pointed out to the Chinese that the bloated staffing of the universities was a drain on the budget. These extraneous personnel were farmers and street sweepers who had been recruited during the Cultural Revolution to enhance the "redness" of the institutions. "Keep the real teachers and administrators and fire the rest," one of my colleagues advised. After the interpreter relayed the message, a shockwave swept the Chinese faces. The reply we got was: "We don't do that in China. We are not a dictatorship!" Fortunately, we had a fluent Chinese speaker on our side, and she noticed a translation error. Our recommendation to "fire" the unqualified staff had been translated as: "Line them up and shoot them all!"

The task of our team was twofold. Since we knew nothing about China's education system, the first step was fact-finding. How did the system work, what were its strengths and weaknesses, and what were the areas that needed support? The second job was more immediate. It was to flesh out the details of the forthcoming lending operation. The twenty-seven universities were spread out all over China. We couldn't visit them all but could, at least, get to a representative sample. The team leader, an American named Frank Farner, divided the visits among the six of us. Without hesitation he sent me to the northern borderlands abutting Siberia. This was December, clearly the perfect assignment for an Icelandic polar bear! Little did my colleagues know what they were in for. While Chinese authorities considered central heating a necessity north of the Yellow River, they thought it was an unnecessary luxury south of it. Thus, when I was basking in comfortably heated hotels and government offices in the boreal city of Harbin, my colleagues were shivering in unheated meeting rooms in the "southern capital" of Nanjing, where temperatures could dip well below freezing. Their only source of warmth was the cups of hot tea around which they desperately wrapped their hands.

My visit to an engineering university in Northern China.

Everywhere I went, the reception was befitting of royalty. Never mind I was just a grunt back in Washington; in China I was an ambassador from the Western World. In fact, many of our Chinese counterparts considered our mission to be a follow-up to President Richard Nixon's visit to China in 1972. In Yanbian, the autonomous Korean-speaking region that borders North Korea, 2,000 primary school children welcomed me one morning. They sang and danced in colorful ethnic costumes while I stood clad in a homemade Icelandic woolen sweater, waving and trying my best to look regal. In the afternoon, another 3,000 secondary school children overwhelmed me with their theatrical talents. Frankly speaking, the excessive attention was downright embarrassing and made me feel like an impostor.

Back in Beijing and later in Washington, negotiations for a loan for the twenty-seven universities ground on in earnest. As eager as both sides were to close the deal, there were many gaps to bridge. Where compromise was impossible, the Bank simply put the component aside, as in the case of construction. Our procedures called for international competitive bidding, while the Chinese way was to hand a fixed-price contract to a state-owned company. As neither side would budge, the Bank decided not to finance this part.

Some differences, however, couldn't be resolved so easily. The thorniest question was how to treat Taiwan. Unwilling to throw its former member under the bus, the Bank insisted that Taiwan should be eligible to bid on contracts for the China project. China agreed in principle but adamantly objected to the mention of "Taiwan" in the legal documents, since it would imply Taiwan was an independent country. The protracted debate was heading toward a stalemate when a clever Bank staff came up with a suggestion. What about "Taiwan, China?" We anxiously watched the opposition huddle over the comma. An older Chinese official who had studied in the U.S. in his youth explained to the others the significance of ",": it places Taiwan as a subordinate of China. The team leader straightened up and faced us. "We agree!" he said. The room let out a collective sigh of relief. This saved-by-the comma episode would go down as a pivotal moment in Bank history.

My job was to figure out the overall management arrangements and project costs. The Bank's lending for this operation would amount to US$200 million, an exceptionally large sum at the time for a soft-sector operation. It would cover equipment and technical assistance, which the Chinese agreed to procure in accordance with Bank rules. One of the components, the formation of a foreign advisory panel, would have lasting effect. Our team leader, Frank, persuaded the government that after decades of international isolation, Chinese universities would benefit from periodic reviews by top-level academics from all corners of the world. This panel functioned long after the project ended.

The Chinese were fast learners, and they knew they had much to catch up on. Once, when a Chinese delegation came to Washington on Bank business, a few of us took them to the cafeteria for refreshments. A Chinese official picked up a tea bag and was about to tear it open when one of us stopped him and showed him the proper usage of a tea bag. The man nodded gratefully and dunked his tea bag into his cup of hot water. Next he picked up a packet of sugar. Applying his newfound knowledge, he put the whole thing, bag and all, into the cup. In the same spirit, the Chinese promptly became so well versed in Bank jargon that they could manipulate it to their own advantage.

Malaysia holds many memories for me too. On my first visit in 1975, Kuala Lumpur, the capital, was a small town dispersed around a cluster of ornate three-story British colonial buildings. It was a drowsy place of tropical lushness, siesta, and teatime. This impression of mine changed quickly on subsequent trips. Malaysia wasn't sleepy at all. The federation of nine sultanates, newly freed from British domination, was in a hurry to go places. I would witness a long period of economic growth spurred by business-friendly policies, rich natural resources, and the emphasis on education for all. Malaysia's achievements soon earned it the title of "Tiger Cub." The fast-paced development, however, had its disadvantages, such as the slashing and burning of natural forests to make way for palm oil plantations, and tearing down of historic buildings for boxy high-rises. Most egregious of all was the government's policy of discrimination against the ethnic Chinese population, who were seen as too powerful. Once in a while, mobs rampaged against Chinese communities, causing terrible loss of life and property. The Malays are normally a gentle people, but when provoked, they're notorious for running "amok," a Malay word.

I regret to say that the memory of Malaysia that stands out most in my mind is a tragedy—the loss of two colleagues and my narrow escape from the same fate.

I arrived in Kuala Lumpur in November 1977 to review the results of the recently completed first education project in Malaysia. It was a skills development operation and included assistance to the University of Science in Penang. As this was a relatively simple task, I was alone on this assignment. Penang is an island north of Kuala Lumpur, a tourist destination with lavish beach resorts and glittering casinos. The flight there was less than an hour, and my plan was to make it a day trip toward the end of my mission. Meanwhile three colleagues arrived in Malaysia to assess the merits of a proposed new project: Olof (Olle) Bergman, a Swedish educator who led the mission; Zia Naimi, an Afghani architect; and Don Hoerr, an American economist. We were all staying in the same hotel. Having spent more than a week by myself, I was happy for the company. Zia had been particularly helpful during my breaking in at the Bank. A fellow architect several years my senior, he had taken it upon himself to teach me the ropes. Don was a consultant slated for recruitment as permanent staff. At dinner one night, Zia and Don mentioned they were going to Penang to check out a teacher training institute. Since I had business on the island too, they suggested we travel together. However, the timing of their trip wasn't right for me, and I declined.

Late Sunday night, Olle called me, saying that Don and Zia hadn't returned from Penang as scheduled. He also told me there were unconfirmed rumors about a Malaysian airliner hijacking. Olle called the airline, the airport, and every authority he could think of, but got nowhere. Thoroughly alarmed, the two of us sat glued to the TV until late into the night. The news was confusing. Most reports agreed that the aircraft had originated from Penang, but the destination varied between Kuala Lumpur and Singapore. Some reports stated that the aircraft had crashed in Vietnam, or in the Andaman Sea, while others said it was still airborne over the South China Sea. We dozed off for a few hours. In the morning we checked again with the hotel. Once again, they confirmed our colleagues hadn't returned. We notified Washington and waited.

The emerging story was grim and central parts of it have never been satisfactorily explained. What is known is that shortly after 7 pm, MAS 653 took off as scheduled from Penang. The final destination was Singapore, with a short stopover in Kuala Lumpur. When the plane was on its final approach to Kuala Lumpur, the pilot reported to the tower that the plane had been hijacked. Air controllers cleared him for emergency landing, but moments before touchdown the plane took off again. The pilot radioed, "We're now proceeding to Singapore. Good night." That was the last communication.

The plane crashed in a swamp near the southern tip of the Malay Peninsula. All ninety-three passengers and seven crew members perished. No official conclusion has ever been reached about the identity of the hijacker(s). A confidential briefing for the World Bank's management confirmed reports that the two pilots had been shot. One of them was recorded as saying, "Please don't shoot." The unmanned aircraft continued flying until it crashed.

In Kuala Lumpur, Olle and I continued our vigil. I had been scheduled to depart in a few days, but Washington asked me to stay on. We were expecting to be called on to identify our colleagues' remains. Olle talked about Zia's ring, a large distinct red stone he was sure to recognize. I shivered at the thought of viewing my friends' bodies. In a daze, Olle and I packed up the dead men's belongings. Olle, trained as a nuclear physicist, was a deeply spiritual man who had grown up in Africa as the son of a missionary. His presence calmed me. I couldn't think of a better person to go through this nightmare with.

Days went by, but the dreaded call to identify the dead never came. The plane had plunged deep into the swamp, burying everyone and everything with it. There was nothing left to identify. During this waiting period, I took over Zia's task. With a heavy heart, I pored over the scribblings in his notepad. I would finish his work on the teacher training institutes in Malaysia. That was the least I could do for my mentor and friend.

CHAPTER 23

POINT OF NO RETURN

After three years in Vínland, this Viking had reached the point of no return. Although he didn't know it yet, he was destined to settle in the New World.

To appease Monika's plea to move back to Sweden, we had bought a summer cottage near Stockholm. It was supposed to be a home base for exploring the Scandinavian job market. Who was I fooling? I loved my job at the World Bank and had every intention of staying until retirement. I had bought a house in the northern Virginia suburb of McLean. It was a fixer-upper and became my hobby when I wasn't traveling.

Monika tried to find a job in the U.S., but her opportunities were limited because of our visa status. I had a G-4 visa, a work permit for employees of international organizations. Being my dependent, Monika was also on a G-4, which meant she could only work at international institutions like the World Bank, IMF, or embassies. This limited job market was virtually impenetrable, as it was inundated by applications from other G-4 spouses, many highly qualified. At home alone while I traveled, Monika became extremely unhappy, and her disdain for the New World grew into an intense loathing for all things American (the crassness, ignorance, and low quality of everything from schools to supermarket tomatoes). She drowned her misery in drinking and became increasingly volatile. She yelled at the children and threw at me glasses, dishes, bottles, whatever was available. Steinn and Tora locked themselves in their respective rooms. Since I couldn't lock Monika out of the bedroom we shared, I took refuge in the basement.

Her paranoid streak, which had flashed now and then in our marriage, came into full view. She took to hoarding nonperishables, such as rice, which she kept in large metal canisters, and tins and jars of preserved food. She made me turn a basement room into a grocery store with shelves extending from floor to ceiling. The purpose of this hoarding, she said, was to prepare for nuclear war. The Cold War was raging during these years, and the specter of nuclear war was real. But her hoarding was totally irrational. We were living in a Washington, D.C. suburb, within a few miles of such obvious nuclear targets as the Pentagon, the CIA, the White House and Congress. A nuclear holocaust would simply incinerate our home, all its inhabitants, and all the stored food in the basement.

This hopeless state of marital affairs had gone on far too long. At work, I was the funny Icelander who bantered with colleagues and told silly jokes. At home, I was a miserable hostage tiptoeing around his captor. Leaving was impossible, for any mention of a separation would bring on an onslaught of flying objects. I was like a caged animal, and if it weren't for the periodic escape of the business travels, I might have killed myself. Then one day in 1982, Monika made a move that would save my life. Shortly after Tora graduated from grade school, Monika packed up and took her to Sweden, not on vacation but for good. Steinn had finished high school the year before and was attending George Mason University close to home. On his mother's insistence, he applied to the Royal Technical University in Stockholm and got in. He, too, left for Sweden. Here I was at the age of forty-three, abandoned, alone, and staring at an uncertain future. But if truth be told, the strongest emotion I felt was *relief*. Monika had miscalculated. She thought I would follow her to Sweden, my tail tucked between my legs. She didn't realize this was my long-awaited chance to flee. Although I dearly loved my children, I knew the toxic air at home couldn't be good for them either. Given my globetrotting job, swinging by Europe to see them could be part of my commute. They could also visit me during vacations. At long last, we could all breathe again.

I was more married to my job in Washington than ever. The position of deputy chief in my division was vacant, and I was high on the shortlist for it. Normally, after seven years in the same unit, the custom at the Bank was to rotate to a different region. But this deputy vacancy was an opportunity not to be missed. It would be a small step in terms of grade and salary but a giant leap into the rarefied realm of "management." To my disappointment, I wasn't selected, but in retrospect this was a blessing-in-disguise. Management wasn't my thing. I later had a taste of it when I became a team leader with personnel responsibilities, and I hated it. Having authority over a coworker and juggling personalities under my command rubbed against the grain of my personality. I would much rather mind my own business and concentrate on the technical work that was my strength.

I no longer had any reason to stay in East Asia. The region I wanted to transfer to was called Europe, Middle East and North Africa, EMENA for short. My trips to East Asia required flying over the Pacific, but traveling to EMENA would be across the Atlantic with a layover in Europe. This meant I could see my children in Sweden three or four times a year.

The transfer took place smoothly. My adjustment, however, was anything but. I soon discovered that my new division was like a totally different institution. Although it was a unit of the same Bank, it bore no resemblance to the style of my former office. The manager made all the difference. Compared to Richard, who was encouraging and progressive, my new boss, a British educator named Roy, was a dinosaur and an ill-tempered one at that. My first brush with him was over the introduction of a computer to the division. I told him about the fabulous Apple II sitting in a corner of my old East Asia division. Though a bit expensive at US$8,000, it operated a spreadsheet called Lotus 123 that could greatly reduce the time for estimating project costs. Roy shut me up before I could finish. According to him, the office technology in EMENA was "perfect." Staff submitted drafts in longhand to a typing pool that used a centralized word processing system. The document's author got it back the next day, but if an edit were made, even a comma, he had to resubmit it to the typing pool. Back and forth, a draft could take days or weeks to finalize. Then there were the cost tables, which were complex and interlinked. Calculating them by hand was a cumbersome and error-prone tedium. But Roy believed in old-fashioned writing and arithmetic. In his view, anyone trying to use newfangled machinery to streamline his job was simply lazy and ripe for a dressing-down.

Nonetheless, he couldn't stop me from buying my own computer. Revolution was in the air, and although I had no idea how big it was going to be, I couldn't stand crawling at snail's pace when I could complete the same work at lightning speed. The personal computer market was burgeoning. In response to Apple II, IBM launched its own personal computer, and a third company, Compaq, produced the world's first portable PC. It was a sewing-machine-size contraption with a tiny screen but a full-size keyboard. Of course, I had to have one.

Thus I invested $3,000 of my own money on a Compaq, and another $400 on a book-size printer. My first mission with these machines was to Turkey. The computer weighed twenty-eight pounds, and although the printer was dainty, the reams of tractor paper easily weighed ten pounds. Once I got to Ankara, I asked around for a transformer, since the voltage there was 220, as opposed to 110 in the U.S. In those days computers weren't capable of switching voltages automatically. After being told that UNDP had one, I went to their office to borrow it. Without thinking, I picked up the black box by the handle. My back muscle twisted with a wrenching pain. That transformer must have weighed more than a sixty-pound bag of mortar! I was used to hefting heavy loads of construction material, and yet I had never hurt my back before. The rest of my trip was torture, as every action I used to take for granted—walking, sitting, standing, even lying down—became cause for teeth-gritting.

Learning from this lesson, I purchased a lighter-weight transformer and brought it along with my computer, printer, and reams of paper on my next mission. One night in my hotel room in Lahore, I woke up with a coughing fit. I turned on the light and saw smoke spewing out of the transformer. I grabbed it and threw the smoldering device into the bathtub. This episode taught me another lesson—not every transformer had the capacity to handle the load. Mine got overheated and caught fire. Thankfully, the only casualties were my scalded hands. The hotel room smelled of acrid electrical smoke for days after.

The change to a new way of operating was rocky, but totally worth it. I became so attached to my Compaq that I brought it to the office and tethered it to my desk with a bicycle lock. I bypassed the typing pool and began producing my own reports on a primitive word processor I had found on the market. The word processor couldn't handle the cost tables that needed to be embedded in the text, so I printed them out and cut and taped them into the report. A few days later, a colleague ran into my office to proclaim calamitous news. Our boss, Roy, and his boss, Jack, had taken offense to my "rounding errors," which I had footnoted in my report. I laughed, believing they would understand once I enlightened them on the workings of a computer. Jack, the American assistant department director, summoned me to his office. I explained that a rounding error wasn't really an error, but testimony to the infinite computing capability of the machine. His bulldoggish face turning red and puffy, he snapped, "We do *not* tolerate rounding errors in EMENA! We are a quality outfit here!" I continued to argue, but it was like explaining the wheel to a Neanderthal. He ordered me back to my office to redo the tables manually.

To punish me for my recalcitrance, my two bosses banished me to the least desirable country in the EMENA region: South Yemen. The communist regime in South Yemen wanted little to do with the World Bank. An assignment to that country meant that my career was put on a shelf to collect dust. The full name of the country was the People's Democratic

Republic of Yemen, a Soviet ally. Its northern counterpart was a U.S. ally named Yemen Arab Republic.

In January 1986, a violent power struggle erupted between two tribal factions in South Yemen. I had departed just in time, but a colleague wasn't as lucky. She cowered in her hotel bathtub as canon projectiles pierced the building. The warring factions were fighting for control over the twelve-story hotel, the tallest prize in Aden, the capital. She, together with other foreigners, was evacuated by the Queen of England's personal yacht, which happened to be in the vicinity. When I visited again three months later, my favorite hotel was so riddled with bullet holes that it looked like a wedge of Swiss cheese.

North and South Yemen united uneasily in 1990 following the collapse of the Soviet Union, but the merger never cemented. The conflicts over religious and tribal matters continue to rankle. Since 2011, a calamitous civil war fueled by Saudi Arabia and Iran has killed thousands of civilians and threatened millions more with starvation and disease. The U.N. has declared Yemen "the world's worst humanitarian crisis."

The country was quieter when my managers exiled me there, and I found South Yemen and its people enchanting. Yemenis place great value on friendship and would adopt you as a brother if you let them. However, I would never want to cross one of them. The national costume for men was a long skirt and vest, a curved dagger displayed front and center over the belly, and a bandolier for AK47 ammunition slung across the chest.

Aden is a port located near the entrance to the Red Sea. It once served as a bustling way station for British ships sailing to and from India through the Suez Canal. After Israel captured the Sinai Peninsula from Egypt during the 1967 Six-Day War, Egypt closed the canal to keep the Israelis from using it. Aden became a ghost town, and although the canal reopened in 1975, the city has never recovered. Nevertheless, the dilapidated down-town buildings, with their extravagant wood carvings on the facades, bore witness to a glorious past. The coastal cliffs around Aden were stunning, and from my hotel room (before it was shot to pieces), I could see vast flocks of pink flamingos wading in the tidal pools at the beaches below.

I had come to South Yemen expecting an empty desert and the horrible food my colleagues had warned me about, but instead I found a place of unsurpassed visual delights. Wadi Hadhramaut, a long, broad and deep valley, was one of them. Fenced in on both sides by impressive mountain walls, the valley is completely cut off from the surrounding areas. It had virtually no rainfall, but what little there was in the surrounding desert seeped as groundwater into the valley. Even the shallowest of wells produced ample water for drinking and irrigation. Green fields and coconut trees crisscrossed the desert. A major town in the valley, Shibam is a caramel brown tableau of high-rises built of mud bricks more than a thousand years old. It is known as the first skyscraper city in the world, earning it a place on UNESCO's world cultural heritage list. During my time in EMENA, I would also witness the magnificent cultures of Jordan, Turkey, Tunisia and Portugal, but no place fascinated me as much as Wadi Hadhramaut. If only my bosses knew what kind of "punishment" I was suffering!

Another benefit of working on South Yemen was the light workload. It was a backwater fit for rounding error slobs like me, but it also gave me plenty of time to hone my computer skills. For the remainder of my time in EMENA, I would use the magic of computers to produce reports in a fraction of the time that others needed. I kept abreast of the fast-developing industry and taught myself to do simple programming. I adapted a mainframe program to my PC, so I could enter data right there in the field. These skills doubled my efficiency and saved the institution many hours of redundant work.

While my colleagues slaved away nights and weekends, my enhanced productivity allowed me to stick to a forty-hour workweek. The free time allowed me to pursue my private life. My romance with Veronica Li was blossoming into a stable relationship. Veronica had joined the East Asia Education division shortly before I left. She was a former journalist and graduate of the Bank's Young Professional Program, the conduit for recruiting the world's best and brightest. After a year of training in various parts of the Bank, she entered my division as long-term staff. Our professional paths met only briefly, but our friendship continued to develop. She was also in the process of divorce and single mom to a nine-year-old son. Her background can't be more different from mine—born in Thailand to Chinese parents, raised in Hong Kong and Taiwan, and immigrated to the U.S. at fifteen.

Veronica and me.

Her upbringing was a mix of Confucianism, Catholicism (hence the baptismal name Veronica), and American individualism, which she learned very well during her studies at Berkeley in the sixties. Perhaps it was this hodgepodge of cultures that made her so adventurous. She took up skiing, even bravely following me down black diamond slopes, and we learned to windsurf together. She didn't flinch at trying out rotten shark and other Icelandic delicacies—neither did I when she served up chicken feet and thousand-year-old eggs. I, too, had been around and was open to the diverse flavors of life. We commuted together to work by bicycle and frequented classical music concerts.

Both our divorces were finalized a year later. Wary of the rebound effect, we took our time to tie the knot. I was like a man recovering from a long illness: shaky on my feet and cautious of the next step. But since neither of us minded living in sin, I moved into Veronica's house so that her son, Ho-Yin, could stay in his school district. We had no plans to start a family, and instead worked on melding the two families. Tora spent the summer in the U.S. throughout her teenage years and became good friends with Ho-Yin, who is two years younger. Steinn, by then a grown man, visited too, though less regularly because of school and work obligations. This was a period of change and growth for all of us. We were like soft-shell crabs, free from the hard skins of our previous lives, preparing for a bigger and better existence, and yet feeling vulnerable in our nakedness. The first time Veronica and I had a serious argument, I took to my old habit of clamming up. She waited me out, and when I emerged after three days, we carried on as if nothing had happened. Although my mollusk behavior didn't spark fireworks from Veronica as it had Monika, it hurt our relationship in ways I couldn't have fathomed. She had thought my withdrawal was a precursor to breaking up. At a dinner at our home, Veronica mentioned my silent treatment to our guest, Robert Castadot, an older and wiser colleague and a close friend. He looked me in the eye and told me how disturbing my conduct was for the other party. He should know, he said, because he was once on the receiving end of such treatment from his ex-wife. Since then, I have tried my best to avoid shutting down in my shell.

Veronica and I got married without fanfare in 1990. By then we had ironed out most of the kinks in our relationship. Our marriage has been the best period of my life. We respect each other and give each other plenty of space to pursue our different passions: she the piano and writing, and I my woodwork and various construction projects around the house. Whenever friends envy her for having a live-in handyman, she would say cheekily, "You like living on a construction site?" She is a people person, I a "thing" person, and together we are both. Without her, we wouldn't be enjoying the wonderful get-togethers at our home, and without me, she would let the home fall apart and not even notice it. Finally I learned the meaning of compatibility: to be happy in separate pursuits and twice as happy in joint ventures.

In 1987, the entire World Bank underwent a dramatic upheaval. The U.S. Congress, as a representative of the Bank's largest shareholder, demanded radical changes to the bureaucracy. President Ronald Reagan appointed a former Congressman, Barber Conable, as the head of the Bank with the instructions to make the Bank a leaner and meaner organization. The process was chaotic, starting with the firing of every staff member. Most of us were rehired a short while later into a new and different organizational structure. Others were retired early. For me, personally, the upheaval was a godsend. Gone were the medieval lords who believed computers were the tools of the devil. Both Roy and Jack were out. Their replacements couldn't be a greater contrast. The new department head was a friendly Tunisian engineer named Abderraouf Bouhaouala. The first time he called me to his office, I quaked a little in my boots, still smarting from my run-in with Jack. But the new director put me at ease immediately. He told me he was once the Bank's point person for the Búrfell hydroelectric scheme in Iceland. Chuckling, he related a story of Icelandic hospitality. Toward the end of his work in the country, his Icelandic counterparts decided to give him a treat: salmon fishing. Like a good sport, he went along and found himself in waist-high rubber waders standing precariously in a fast-flowing ice-cold river. Shivering and trying hard not to fall in, he waved his fishing pole around. After a decent show of effort, he waded back to shore and, teeth still chattering, thanked his hosts for the most rewarding experience of his life.

My immediate boss was Ralph Harbison, a forward-looking American economist in his mid-forties. He took over the EMENA division for social sectors, which now included not only education, but also health and social protection. One of his first actions was to insist that everyone learn to use word processing. He brought me in from the cold, giving me the most exciting assignments anyone could hope for.

Two years after the Bank's internal upheaval, the Berlin Wall fell, creating a tsunami of pro-Western forces in the former Soviet satellite states. Communist regimes gave way to democratically elected governments. Overnight, the list of countries that wanted support from the World Bank increased drastically. I soon found myself shuttling between Hungary, Poland, Romania and Bulgaria. Other colleagues worked in Yugoslavia, Albania, the Czech Republic, and Slovakia. Then in 1991, the Soviet Union disintegrated into fifteen independent states, all clambering onto the World Bank bandwagon. These were heady times. These countries had suffered under Soviet domination, their economies strangled by the central planning imposed on them. They wanted to return to the free market, but after decades of mind-stunting communism, they needed plenty of assistance. The World Bank was in a good position to help, since it had the resources and accumulated experience from all over the world. Thus, while parts of the Bank worked with governments to privatize their economies, the task of my division was to reform the education and health systems to fit the new reality. My division also had responsibility for creating a social safety net for workers privatized out of their jobs, retirees deprived of pensions, patients denied care because national health services had gone bankrupt, and so on. In any upheaval, there are winners and losers. In this case, those who had depended on the state from cradle to grave found themselves in free fall. The measures the Bank introduced were aimed at helping the losers get back on their feet.

The Hungarians, all fired up to return to the illustrious past of the Austro-Hungarian Empire, named their higher education project, "The Catching up with Europe Project." Key to this effort was a novel concept called "competition." Under communism, Hungarian universities were used to receiving guaranteed budgets from the government regardless of performance. In the new approach, they would have to submit competitive budget proposals and receive funding based on merit. Most universities embraced the innovation with enthusiasm, and when word got around, Bulgaria decided to adopt the same budgeting mechanism. However, disgruntled stakeholders of the old system assassinated the officer in charge, killing the reform as well.

In Poland, we faced a situation that couldn't be described in any way other than "revolution." Without mincing words, the Bank told the government that the entire Polish economy, in fact the whole society, had to be revamped if the country were to grow. One of our first interventions was labor market privatization. Under the communist regime, the Ministry of Labor assigned school graduates to lifelong jobs in state-run companies. The new system of private enterprises would take away this security and replace it with opportunity, with all its risks and uncertainties. To smooth the bumps in the transition, the ministry would provide employment counseling, training for new workers, and retraining for redundant workers. The jobless would receive unemployment benefits to tide them over, and when all else failed, welfare to safeguard them from destitution. Our Polish counterparts were polarized over this agenda. Our meetings often broke out into shouting debates between the capitalist and communist camps. As none on our team understood Polish, we could only guess from the body language that passions were high on both sides. In the end, the capitalists won out and the Bank agreed to finance the project. This revolution took place in an orderly, civilized way, with no bloodshed, only plenty of meetings. If Chairman Mao were around, he would have to eat his words, "Revolution is not a dinner party … A revolution is an insurrection, an act of violence by which one class overthrows another." Poland and several other ex-communist states proved it doesn't have to be that way.

In Romania, we parachuted in with an emergency healthcare program. The Romanian health system was in dire straits. Life expectancy was declining, infant mortality rising, and AIDS spreading. The worst crime of the Ceaucescu regime, in my view, was his brutal assault on women's health. Believing that strength lay in numbers, he thought increasing the Romanian population would make his country great. He therefore banned contraception. Women died during illegal abortions, and those who carried their pregnancy to term often abandoned their babies to orphanages. A Bank colleague who visited one such institution came away horrified by the conditions. Newborns were left alone for long periods without human contact, and soiled toddlers sat vacant-eyed in their cribs, some tied to their beds to prevent escape. Groups of foreigners staying at our hotel were trying to adopt children, but few wanted the mentally scarred ones—which included just about every child in the orphanages. After a week of fact-finding, our team realized something had to be done immediately. We rushed the first operation through the Bank's board of directors and started to plug the largest holes to keep the ship from sinking.

Generally speaking, the Bank's interventions met with greater success in countries that are considered "Central European." Hungary and Poland took to the market economy like newly hatched sea turtles racing to the ocean. On the other hand, the countries that are squarely in Eastern Europe and geographically closer to Moscow had a harder time breaking away from the communist orbit. The progress of Romania and Bulgaria didn't proceed as swimmingly, but they eventually reached the ocean at their own pace.

For some, Yugoslavia in particular, the transition came at a high cost. Although the Bank had prepared a lending program for the country, it fell apart before any projects could be approved. Yugoslavia was a union of half a dozen republics with diverse religions and a history fraught with hostility. The iron grip of Josip Broz Tito had held them together, but the moment the dictator died, the bad blood came gushing out. The republics agitated for independence and hurtled into a series of tribal wars. The world watched in horror as the conflict in Kosovo degenerated into ethnic cleansing of the Muslim population.

Helping to reconstruct the post-Cold War world took up much of my time. The responsibility also came at a point when my computer investment was paying large dividends. The ability to complete the tasks much faster meant I had time to spare. Under the previous benighted management, I would have kept it a secret. But with an informed boss like Ralph, I was confident he would make good use of me. Ralph asked me to mentor newcomers and encouraged me to take an active role in shaping policies.

I welcomed the challenge. By then I could do the nuts and bolts of Bank work in my worst jetlagged state. I was itching to expand my horizon. I was fifty years old. The thought of doing the same grind for another decade was depressing. I had already decided management wasn't my bag. What else could an architect do in the World Bank? Already certain leaders on the top floor had labeled people like me "narrow technical specialists." I felt if I didn't branch out now, I would be stuck with this belittling epithet the rest of my career.

With Ralph needling me on, I wrote about issues that affected the Bank across all sectors and regions. One of them concerned the question of measuring the success or failure of a project. In the social sectors especially, our documents were filled with statements of good intentions, but at the end of each operation there was no attempt to measure what had been achieved. I became a champion of introducing concrete yardsticks into human development projects. In education, these indicators would be changes in enrollment rates, graduation rates, number of textbooks supplied, number of qualified teachers and their attendance rates, and so on. Around that time and not of my doing, Bank President Lewis Preston issued a report critical of the Bank's failure to measure the impact of its operations. He was saying exactly what I had been saying! This was pure serendipity, but my senior managers must have thought I knew something they didn't. EMENA's director—a tall, dashing, bearded, and turbaned Sikh named Harinder Kohli—appointed me to coordinate the annual review of the region's entire investment portfolio. This exercise covered not only the social sector but also industry, energy, agriculture, transport, urban, water and finance. Ralph cautioned me this might be way over my head, but I plunged in anyway and managed to dog paddle to shore.

Ralph left the division shortly after, and an American educator named Stephen Heyneman took over. Intelligent and good-natured, Steve was as pleasant to work with as Ralph. Unbeknownst to us at the time, we later discovered that he and I had worked at the same school in Malawi in the early 1970s. His son and my daughter were born in the same hospital.

Our paths never crossed then because I was a construction supervisor and he a Peace Corps English teacher. But the missed connection has been amply made up for. Today, Steve and I are neighbors on the Eastern Shore of Maryland. My work experience with Steve was excellent. He continued Ralph's personnel policies and set in motion my final promotion in the Bank.

CHAPTER 24

FINDING MY WINGS

Thanks to the nurturing of my bosses Ralph and Steve, I found my wings. Like a full-fledged eagle, I was ready to leave my nesting territory and set up my own roost. My sight was no longer confined to one school at a time. I was aching to exert some influence at the policy level, now that the rigid Bank regulations that had instilled me with the fear of God were no longer intimidating. Rules were made by humans, and if others could do it, so could I. However, the question remained—where should I go? This was 1993. I had spent an exciting decade in EMENA, well over the average term in one office. A transfer was way overdue, and this time my destination would be my last. I was fifty-four years old, eligible for retirement in a few years. Factoring in my stint at UNESCO, I could retire with full pension at fifty-seven.

I got a tempting offer while naked in the Bank's locker room. The proposition came from another bicycle commuter as we showered and changed from our sweaty outfits into business attire. He was a director in the Information Technology Department, a relatively new unit. At first glance, this seemed perfect for me. I could combine my operational skills with the rapid advances of the high-tech world. On his invitation, I went around the IT offices. A number of twenty- and thirty-somethings were clicking at their keyboards and staring at their screens as if under a spell. Although the term "computer geek" wasn't in my vocabulary at the time, I knew these people were a different breed. It became clear that I couldn't be one of them, since my computer skills were limited and self-taught, and my devotion to the electronic god was less than fervent. In the end, I turned the offer down.

Within a few weeks, another overture came my way. This was to join the policy-making arm of the Bank, often called the Center. I would be working on education projects anywhere in the world, especially those that could offer policy lessons. I would then use these avant-garde operations to affect Bank-wide policies. When I first read this job description, the word "culmination" bubbled up in my mind. It seemed that my entire international career had been grooming me for this assignment. What could be a better swan song than to wrap up my experience in twenty-six countries on five continents and pass it on? Another beauty of this position was that I would be, more or less, my own boss, cooking up my own assignments and hiring my own sous-chefs to assist me.

Around that time, an anti-globalization movement was fomenting against the World Bank and IMF. Thousands of demonstrators protested and rioted against the sister institutions during their joint annual meetings. Some accused the organizations of conspiring to impoverish poor nations, a broad-brush conspiracy theory that was impossible to address. Other criticisms, however, were reasonable and prompted Bank management to look into them. One was the issue of accountability. Protestors complained that the Bank was interested only in pushing money down governments' throats. After the millions of borrowed money had been spent, what was the impact on the poor countries? Were people better off or just choking in debt? This criticism hit its mark. Every Bank staff knew the way up the institutional ladder was to deliver new projects for Bank financing. The emphasis was always to lend, lend, and lend, with much less concern for the results of investments. Spurred by the stone-throwing crowd, Bank management did what bureaucracies do—they set up a taskforce to study the issue and come up with an action plan.

When I started at the Center, an internal movement to measure results was in full swing. The million-dollar question was: How should outcomes be measured? One way was to quantify the tangible products of the Bank's projects, precisely the indicators I had been advocating when I was in EMENA. For example, in a vocational training project, we could easily count things like the number of schools built, the staffing of each school, and enrollment. Evaluating the impact on people's lives, however, wasn't as straightforward and required the patience of Buddha. We would need to conduct a tracer study to track the students for five, ten, or more years. The study would answer questions such as: What was the graduation rate? How many graduates found employment, and did they get jobs that could be attributed to their training? Were their salaries comparable with those from general schools? Did industries prefer hiring vocational school graduates over those from general schools? A well-crafted survey could provide the relevant information.

My contribution to this endeavor was my "Indicators Paper," which Veronica liked to tease me about because of my obsession with it. Well, of course, this was my brainchild. While my colleagues in agriculture, transport and other sectors bemoaned the task as another bureaucratic chore, I was happy to lavish attention on my baby. Management appreciated that and held up my Indicators Paper as a model for others to emulate. My head became rather inflated, but fortunately I had a sensible wife to keep it from bursting.

Ironically, I struck the highest note of my career a few months after my retirement, when I was retained as a consultant to complete ongoing work. The assignment showed up in my office in the form of a buck that everybody had been passing around. His name was Marc Moingeon, a Frenchman who came knocking on the Bank's door in early 1997. A representative of Hachette, a well-known publishing house based in France, he wanted to give a seminar in the Bank, no doubt to tout the superiority of his company's textbooks. After getting the runaround from a number of stone-faced bureaucrats, he found his way to my office. I have my boss to thank for this. He had told the Frenchman I was the specialist on procurement of all education-related goods. Since textbooks fell into that category, I became the chosen one.

Monsieur sat across my desk, dark hair slicked back, elegantly dressed in a European style suit. As he hawked his wares with great élan, I racked my brains for a polite way to get rid of him.

"Thank you very much for your visit," I said as soon as he had finished. "I understand that your company's textbooks can make a big difference in the lives of children in Francophone Africa. However, an institution like the World Bank can't be seen as endorsing the product of one company over another. If we hold a presentation on *your* textbooks, we would have to invite other publishers to present theirs too."

He was silent. Just as I had thought, the suggestion turned him off. He only wanted to promote his company, not his rivals.

"A *conférence* of textbook publishers. *C'est parfait*," Monsieur Moingeon said, to my dismay.

After he left, promising to follow up from Paris, I kicked myself. What have I gotten myself into? I immediately called Philip Cohen in London. He was a long-time Bank consultant on textbooks and had become a good friend after several missions together. I told him about the soup I had jumped into.

"That is a brilliant ideeaa," Phil said in his crisp British accent. "Why haven't I thought of it myself?"

From thereon, every colleague I approached voiced the same enthusiasm. Before I knew it, this soup was bubbling thick and mouthwatering. The delicious aroma was everywhere, and I soon found myself spending every working hour on organizing this conference, which would be held in Washington. My assistant, a competent young Indian woman named Shobhana Sosale, was my right hand. Several others helped me stir the pot. Phil, with a lifetime in the textbook publishing business in the U.K. and elsewhere, contacted the publishers in his network. These publishers in turn contacted their partners in former British colonies in Africa and the West Indies. On the French side, my now-buddy Marc reached out to his associates in the former French colonies in West Africa. Aid agencies from the U.K., U.S., Canada, Sweden, and Germany heard about the conference and clamored to attend. A couple of them also pledged to cover the travel expenses of publishers in poor countries. The person in greatest need of funds, however, was me. Because this conference wasn't planned and budgeted for, I had to beg, borrow and scrounge from a variety of sources.

At this stage, I contacted the Bank's External Affairs Department to inform them of the large number of "external" people coming to the event. To my surprise, the staff transferred me straight to the top. The department head was Mark Malloch-Brown, a maverick former British journalist who would later ascend to the U.N.'s second highest position, deputy to Secretary-General Koffi Annan. At the time of my conference, he had been hired to polish up the Bank's tattered reputation. Mark immediately recognized the PR value of the conference and agreed to deliver the keynote speech.

As word spread, the trickle of responses soon cascaded into Niagara Falls. Everyone who had books to sell wanted a seat. I had to limit the number by setting criteria for attendance. At the minimum, a participating publisher should have business with the developing world. After all, the purpose of the conference was to understand the textbook industry in the Bank's client countries. Despite the importance of textbooks to education, the Bank had paid little attention to this matter. The seminar aimed to fill this gap.

When the conference opened in September 1997, sixty-five participants from twenty-one countries, nine bilateral and multilateral agencies, and several non-government groups, such as the Soros Foundation, packed the Bank's auditorium. They came from Europe, Central Asia, Africa, North America, and Latin America and the Caribbean. They included such behemoths as Oxford University Press, Macmillan, McGraw-Hill, and Heinemann Educational, as well as tiny publishing shops in various parts of the developing world. The size and gravity of the conference was too overwhelming for me to chair, so I approached James Socknat, then an Education Division Chief in the Bank's East Asia Department. He graciously agreed to be master of ceremonies. Jim and I had worked well together in EMENA. He was an American, a lawyer by training, and was soft-spoken and humble. But the moment he opened his mouth, people shut theirs to listen.

During the two-day conference, we heard a variety of presenters speak about textbook publishing for underdeveloped nations. They covered every related issue from the process of writing and publishing to the importance of local languages, copyright, curriculum, pricing, financing, storage, distribution, and teacher training. I learned more about the subject than I had ever wanted to. Until then, the Bank had treated textbooks as a procurement matter. In the education projects I had worked on, the textbook component was sometimes no more than financing the purchase of printing presses, paper, and ink for the Ministry of Education. We sort of knew this wasn't sustainable in the long run since project funds would dry up sooner or later. We also sort of knew that government monopoly wasn't the most efficient way of conducting business. And yet, as long as our bosses didn't complain, we weren't going to fix something that wasn't considered broken.

Speech after speech, the kingpins of the industry told us about the critical shortage of textbooks in developing countries. A lasting textbook supply chain was needed, and it would take the concerted effort of all the players to build it. The speakers opened our eyes to reality on the ground. We couldn't close them again and carry on as before in blissful ignorance.

I also noticed a hostile dynamic among the participants. Angry barbs flew now and then during the presentations and the ensuing Q&A. Some were aimed at the Bank, others zinged between the participants of the conference. I compared notes with my colleagues and found they were picking up the same vibes. We noticed that the participants fell into two camps. The first consisted of big publishing houses with branches all over the world; the second camp comprised boutique publishers from developing nations and catering to a domestic audience. While the former saw the latter as gnats to be brushed aside, the latter saw the former as monsters out to destroy them. And, of course, both camps attacked the Bank as an ignorant, bumbling giant. The antagonism grew more and more palpable as the seminar went on. Several times, members of the audience interrupted the speaker, short of accusing him of lying, and called out their version of the truth. Jim Socknat did an admirable job of maintaining order and civility. As the organizer, I felt I should make everyone feel at home, yet I had no idea how to call a truce. Then I noticed a most unexpected sight during a coffee break. Two people who had been shouting at each other were chatting amiably, sipping coffee and nibbling cookies together. By the end of the seminar, the tension had eased. Both sides felt better after airing their grievances, and everyone agreed to meet again to work out the differences at a future date. When I took up this task, I had no idea I would be playing the role of therapist.

At the official luncheon, I vividly remember Mark, the Head of External Affairs, rakishly leaning his left elbow on the restaurant bar and beginning his address with, "You can always count on an Englishman to deliver a good speech if he has a bar to lean on." Charming and exuberant, he hit it off with the participants, including a Ghanaian publisher named Richard Crabbe, also an outgoing man who impressed everyone with his glass-half-full outlook. I am glad I got Mark involved. Several years later, his department established the African Publishing Initiative, and the person hired to run it was none other than Richard Crabbe.

For days after the conference, I floated on air around the office, elated that the conference had gone as well as it did. At the same time, I felt I had opened a can of worms I didn't know what to do with. To wash my hands and declare my job done didn't sound right. Something more needed to happen, but what?

James Tumusiime, heralded as a pillar of indigenous publishing in Uganda, summed up my dilemma nicely. Writing about the conference for an industry newsletter a few months later, he concluded:

> Two days of intensive discussion within and outside the seminar room appear to have reinforced the thinking of the World Bank officials to start moving in the direction of ensuring sustainable

book development. It was however not clear how and when the Bank would translate the recommendations of the seminar into tangible policies and actions. Another problem was that, with no high-level representation of governments, the Bank would find it difficult to implement their change in thinking.

That notwithstanding, the seminar appears to have achieved the objective of harmonizing thinking in all those involved in the provision of books around the key issue "sustainability," a word that had all along been missing in the vocabulary of the Bank's book procurement officials.

Recognizing the importance of the endeavor, the Bank retained me for yet another year to tie up the loose ends. Shobhana volunteered to assemble the thirty-three presentations into a publication available to the public. Jim and Phil called for a policy paper, and they knew exactly the person to do it. He was Alfonso de Guzman, a congenial Filipino who was then the one and only textbook specialist in the Bank. (He had missed the conference because of mission travel.) He readily agreed to the assignment and soon produced a first draft based on the thorough working papers prepared by Phil. The Bank adopted the recommendations in our report a year later, at the end of arduous internal and external reviews. These recommendations became the Bank's official policies on providing an "affordable, sustainable supply system for textbooks" in developing countries.

The finale to my career was literally textbook-perfect. I had run the first lap of the relay race, and others had grabbed the baton and taken it to the finishing line. I believe all human achievements are the accumulation of many drops in the bucket. I can only hope that my drop had contributed to making fuller the lives of schoolchildren all over the world.

During my twenty-some-year Bank career, my time on the road amounted to seven years of living out of suitcases. This kind of nomadic life would have grown old for many—stumbling bleary-eyed out of the plane, holding back yawns at meetings, eating out every meal, catching exotic germs, and of course, missing the family. But to my own astonishment, my reservoir of wanderlust was enormous. Every trip was filled with new sights, smells, and sounds, and I enjoyed them right up to the end. My wandering also extended to the intellectual realm. I loved learning about new disciplines, such as economics and the workings of schools and universities, and the cultures of foreign countries. If I had gone back to Iceland or Sweden and earned a living as an architect, I wouldn't have flown as far and high. A truly good architect is an artist, and I know my limits in that regard. I am a fixer, a practical problem solver. I love having dirt under my fingernails, sawdust in my hair, and bloody cuts on my arms and legs. I don't have the emotional intensity to be a true artist.

I was a bureaucrat, and it suited me just fine. I got to rotate between departments, work with cutting-edge thinkers, and tinker with new toys. It was also a privilege to serve in an organization like the World Bank. Critics have attacked it for its ineffectiveness, its irrelevance to the times, the lavish travel style of its staff (all with a grain of truth), and so on. But every time somebody started singing a funeral dirge, the Bank would reinvent itself and rise out of its deathbed, ready to grab the next global crisis by the collar. In the Bank's latest reincarnation, it has emerged a champion against climate change and an advocate for war refugees. The fact is that the world has evolved into a ball of intertwining political and economic systems. Despite current movements to undo the tangle, I doubt if they will succeed, since no one has ever managed to turn back the wheels of history. As crises become more global, there will always be a need for multilateral institutions to rally nations to action. Whether one of them is called the World Bank or something else hardly matters.

The rewards of an international career are many. I can't think of a greater satisfaction than helping to improve the lives of my fellow man all over the world. In the seven decades after the war, the rates of extreme global poverty and infant mortality have decreased dramatically, while access to electricity, healthcare, and education has increased. The unequal distribution of these advances, however, remains a concern. Some of the gains made are also precarious and can be upended in a cataclysmic event.

I hope the spirit of global cooperation will continue, because the alternative, in a world armed with weapons of mass destruction, is too terrifying to contemplate.

One thing is certain about my career: Whatever I gave, I got back tenfold. I encourage young men and women to play Viking for a year or more. You'll be surprised what opportunities you may discover outside your home country. In the newfound space, you'll have the freedom to bust out of your box and reset your parameters. Surviving in a foreign country can be difficult, like learning a new language. The first one is the hardest, but it opens channels in your brain that will allow the second and third languages to flow. Embarking on my "three-year travel plan" has been the best decision of my life. The world has forced me to stretch myself to the full extent of my potential. It has also given me a trove of treasure, not to display on shelves and vitrines, nor locked in a safe, but to enrich my heart and mind, body and soul. I have, indeed, found my fortune.

CHAPTER 25

HOME

Most of my Viking forefathers returned home after their foreign travels, but some didn't. They settled permanently in places like Dublin, York, Normandy, and even as far as Istanbul. They dissolved into the local population, indistinguishable from the rest. I, too, have assimilated. I'm now a U.S. citizen, and my daughter, Tora, has chosen to leave Sweden and settle in the U.S. She, too, is an American citizen, married to an American, and raising an all-American boy. My genes have added to the melting pot of the New World.

My son, Steinn, stayed on in Sweden. Unfortunately, he dropped out of the engineering university in Stockholm, and for this I blame myself. I should have foreseen this outcome, given his language limitation and the disparities in the U.S. and Swedish education systems. But fortunately, Steinn found his calling. Having spent his childhood traveling across continents in the back of my car, he took on a career behind the wheel as the owner of a small courier company. He poured his heart and soul into this vocation. He didn't become what I wanted him to be, but what he wanted to be.

Throughout my wanderings, I have stayed in close touch with my family in Iceland, holidaying with them every other year. My parents visited me in Swaziland, where my mother was shocked to find herself shivering from the cold. Expecting Africa to be a steaming jungle, she had brought only light clothing. They also stayed at my home in the U.S. a couple of times.

Mom died at eighty-four after a long battle with diabetes and dementia. Dad took care of her at home till the end. Afterwards, he moved in with my younger brother, Kristján. My parents had always had a symbiotic relationship with Kristján and his family, living within blocks of each other. Dad was the model elder, keeping himself busy and happy by memorizing volumes of Icelandic poetry. When he opened his mouth, beautiful verses flew out. He died quickly of a massive stroke at eighty-eight.

In late 1999, I received news that my sister, Gústa, lay in a coma in a hospital in Montpellier, France. Veronica and I flew to see her, but we were a few hours too late to bid her goodbye. On a dreary winter day, we watched her carried into a crypt that belonged to the family of an older French woman who had been her long-time companion. Gústa never married. She obtained her PhD in French literature at the University of Montpellier in southern France in 1964 and a second doctorate in German literature in 1975. She became professor and dean of the Germanic language faculty at the Paul Valéry University of Montpellier. At the funeral, her friends and colleagues recounted tales of her brilliance. Once, the university was in dire need of a staff to deliver an oral exam in Romanian. The existing professor was unavailable, and Gústa was assigned the task. The exam was in two weeks. Gústa, who had spoken not a word of Romanian before, pored over the language books day and night. On the day of the exam, she conducted herself so expertly that no one was the wiser. Her success, however, was also her downfall. A perfectionist who put her siblings to shame, the only thing to help her unwind was alcohol. She died at sixty-five due to excessive drinking. I will always be grateful to my sister for prodding me to be what I am today.

Kristján became a geologist at the National Energy Authority in Iceland. He once came to the U.S. to attend a conference. The abuse he got from New York cabbies plus a week's stay at the casino town of Atlantic City, the venue of the conference, were enough to make him swear off this decadent, god-awful country. But when I organized a family reunion at my home to celebrate Dad's eighty-fifth birthday, he was forced to brave the journey again. Despite my efforts to show him the better angels of my adopted country, his first impression was too deep to erase. Nonetheless, he visited two more times to help me with my building project. Having grown up in the same woodwork shop, he was as handy as I was. Also having inherited the family's wry humor, he called himself "the cheap labor from Iceland."

Which brings me to the last major undertaking of my life. This was my childhood dream of building my own home with my own hands. The home improvement projects I had undertaken over the years—building a three-level deck that meanders around a stand of oak trees, tearing down walls, putting up new cabinets, replacing the floor and so on—had been rehearsals for my dream performance. Then one day, a friend led me to the perfect stage. Robert Castadot, the colleague who had chided me about my caveman behavior during marital disputes, invited Veronica and me to his country home for the weekend. It was located on the shores of the Chesapeake Bay, two and half hours by car from the D.C. area. Toward the end of our stay, he told us the house next door was for sale. Out of curiosity, I called the real estate agent, who showed up within half an hour.

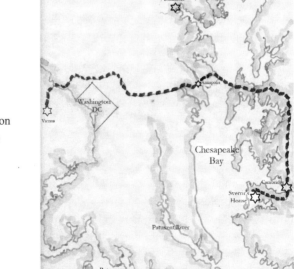

My cottage's location on
the Chesapeake Bay

The place was just a shack, a hunters' cabin for men to crash for the night and wake up at the crack of dawn to go deer or waterfowl hunting. It was also in plain sight of a crowded row of about a dozen houses. The lots were deep and narrow, each less than an acre, which meant the distance between neighbors was within eavesdropping range. Along the shore, one lawn rolled into another into one huge communal yard. The lack of privacy bothered me, but when I raised my eyes farther, I realized it had its advantage. The view from the porch swept from one end of the earth's curvature to the other. Brooks Creek, a finger of water extending from the Chesapeake, was a mere hundred feet away. Nothing, not even a tree, stood in the way of this grand vista of heaven and earth and water. My head spun with ideas of the kind of house that would justify this fantastic lot. I was as good as sold, Veronica even more so. She turned to me with bright round eyes with "yes" written all over them. "Let's sleep on it," I said, the only fiscally responsible thing to do before a major purchase. The next morning we woke up back in our own bed, looked at each other and said, yes!

We bought the place in the summer of 1992. The plan was to tear it down after I retired, which would be in four years, and replace it with an elegant cottage as a second home. Meanwhile, we camped at our shack every possible weekend. Veronica and I did what we could to make the place inhabitable, such as draining the mosquito puddles in the yard so we wouldn't be devoured the moment we stepped out. Shoring up the place, literally, was another urgent task. The water was fast eroding our lot. While I repaired the disintegrating bulkhead, Veronica constructed the riprap, a wall made by piling rocks against the shore. This job required no skills. All she had to do was drop forty-two tons of "man size" rocks, one by one, into the water. She called it her "re-education camp" to cure her of bourgeois tendencies.

In the fall of 1996, after waking up from my retirement party, the ideas that had been fomenting in my head were ready for action. I began to put together a design that embodied everything I had learned in life. First of all, the walls of my house aren't meant to separate man from nature. Rather, they are there to protect him from irritants such as heat and cold, mosquitoes and gnats, not to mention horseflies with alligator teeth, all for the purpose of enhancing his enjoyment of the outdoors in comfort. Transparency is paramount, and there would be glass everywhere to showcase the shoreline, the creek, and the gorgeous sunsets. Second, my house would look as natural as a tree in the forest, a ripple in the water. The roofs would resemble a set of cascading waves, with the final wave ready to crash into the creek. From the outside it should seem to grow out of the ground. This synchrony with the surroundings would continue inside the house, using natural materials such as stone at the entry and wood in the hearth area for contrast. Third, the structure would let sunlight in where desired and block it where not. Lastly, the outside of the building would harmonize with the neighboring buildings, which meant vinyl siding instead of brick or other sturdier materials.

We could now extend our weekend visits to four days a week. I was still working for the Bank the other three. Since much work remained on textbooks and other subjects in my bailiwick, the Bank had hired me back as a consultant for a specific number of days a year. That was perfect for me. I wasn't yet ready to give up my career completely. To be cut off from such a vital part of my life would be like sudden death. After my retirement party on Friday, I went back to my office the following Monday, Tuesday, and Wednesday. From Thursday on, I was at my shore home.

Me adjusting the roof trusses during the last phase of the project.

Another advantage of this arrangement was that the moment I got my paycheck, I could turn around and spend it on building materials. If there ever was a have-your-cake-and-eat-it-too situation, this was it.

Altogether my project took seven years to finish. Except for contracting out a few jobs that required skills or equipment I didn't have, I was the construction crew. It is a humble cottage with a master bedroom in the loft and a room for guests, and we have had many over the years. Wherever I am in the house, the outdoors is always present. Working at my computer in the loft, I see from the corner of my eye an eagle swoosh past the balcony. Reading a book in my armchair, I become aware of a flock of bufflehead ducks paddling in the water. Even in the shower, I can see the shimmering waters of

Aerial view of my house on the Chesapeake Bay. If you use your imagination, you can see the rooftops as waves chasing toward the water.

Brooks Creek framed like a painting on the window. Nighttime is as pure as before the invention of electricity. The Milky Way brushes a white arch over the house; a new moon casts a golden coin on the water, while a full moon passing over the skylight wakes me as if someone has switched on the light.

For excitement, Veronica and I like to watch the weather from the porch. A storm approaching from the Chesapeake Bay is a spectacle I would buy a ticket to watch. First it appears as a dark mass gliding across the sky, rumbling, menacing and swallowing everything that dares stand in its path. It gathers force and volume, roaring and spitting fire like a beast unleashed from hell and finally stops in front of us, glaring down with rage and pity as it gets ready to pounce on my little house. If there is anything I can congratulate myself on, it is this blurring of the boundary between inside and out.

As if to test the mettle of my handiwork, Hurricane Isabel paid the Eastern Shore a visit on September 18, 2003. Out in the Atlantic she had been a Category 5 storm, the strongest there is. When she made landfall in North Carolina, she had dwindled to Category 2; nonetheless, the winds reached 105 mph. I had been following her path for a couple of days. Worried about damage to our shore house, I decided to go there to ride it out. Veronica held the fort in Virginia.

That night, I called her to report that the worst was over. The wind had passed, and it was nothing close to the sensational warnings on the radio, rather a tempest in a teacup. Although the waters of Brooks Creek churned furiously, there was no water on the lawn and the tide seemed normal. I went to bed in the loft around midnight. Something woke me in the middle of the night. I flipped the light switch, only to find that the power was out. I couldn't see a thing, but the sound of sloshing water was unmistakable. Alarmed, I put on some clothes and groped my way down the stairs, counting each step. Finally my bare feet touched the living room floor. It was dry. I let out my breath. But where did the sloshing come from? I found the flashlight in its assigned place. Turning it on, I could see everything inside the house was as it should be, although the noise continued. At the tall living room window, I looked out and saw black water bobbing about a foot away. It slapped noisily against the underside of the porch, about four inches below the floor I was standing on. I stayed by the window for a long time, staring at the water and willing it to go back to where it came from.

Murky dawn slowly turned into daylight. My neighbors' houses stood like little islands, and all the piers had disappeared below the waves. I could make out branches, buckets, and other flotsam in the water. My gaze fastened on a big plank that had probably once been a part of somebody's dock. Then I saw its movement change. It was no longer moving up and down in place but was floating away! Our highest flood in recorded history had passed its peak.

Mother Nature had given me a reprieve. Isabel was only a warning of things to come. A plaque in the cornerstone of my cottage reads, *Rising-water,* the name I gave it to parody Frank Lloyd Wright's *Fallingwater.* The wind of a hurricane isn't the destructive force in these parts, but storm surge is.

Dorchester County, where my house stands, has been named ground zero for rising sea level caused by climate change. It is only a matter of time before the sea claims the house. For however long I can enjoy it, I will be content. I have traveled the world and made a full circle back to the dream of my youth, to build something extraordinary. My little cottage is no Frank Lloyd Wright, but it is certainly one of a kind. To me, the process of creation is more important than the end product. None of my handiworks can go to the grave with me, but the satisfaction and joy of having lived a constructive life will. My life, like all lives, has been messy. I've fumbled in the dark, stumbled, and fallen into the mud of a hellish marriage that tortured the entire family for far too long. I credit my children for their resilience, their ability to rise above their parents' problems to lead their own constructive lives. My second marriage, now approaching thirty years, was an act of divine intervention, given all the stars that needed to align for our paths to cross. Writing these memoirs has helped me sift through the dirt and discover a few gold nuggets in my life. There is gold in every life. For a person to fully appreciate his fleeting time in this world, he has to dig up this buried gold, clean off the muck, and let it shine.

ICELANDIC PRONUNCIATION GUIDE

Icelandic Letter	Pronounciation in English
A, a	the *a* in ah, bar.
Á, á	the *ou* in flounder, house.
Ð, ð	the *th* in this, that
E, e	the *e* in bed, fret
É, é	the *ye* in yet, yen
I, i	the *i* in bit, fit
Í, í	the *ee* in three, seed
O, o	the *o* in not, got
Ó, ó	the *oe* in toe, Joe
U, u	somewhere between the *u* in nut and *ew* in skew
Ú, ú	the *oo* in zoo, coo
Y, i	the *i* in bit, fit
Ý, í	the *ee* in three, seed
Þ, þ	the *th* in thunder, thorough
Æ, æ	the *i* in like, night
Ö, ö	the *u* in urgent, fur
Au, au	the *euil* in the French word *fauteuil*
LL, ll	the *tl* in bottle, atlas

The name of the volcano Eyjafjallajökull can be broken down and pronounced (approximately) as:

Ey	A (as in ate)
Ja	Yah
fjalla	fee-at-la
jökull	yu-kutl

ACKNOWLEDGMENT OF SOURCES

Chapter 1. The censuses of 1703 through 1920 are available online at www.manntal.is. Similarly, every newspaper and magazine article published in the Icelandic language, including those published in Canada in the 1800s, is available online at www.timarit.is.

Chapter 1. My uncle Óli's story about life at sea is available at ismus.is/i/person/uid-4cc86434-a0b4-4865-bf4d-0ecd2772991e.

Chapter 1. The log book of *Gyða*'s captain in 1900 was available at the online magazine, *Arnfirðingur*. It has since been removed from the Internet.

Chapter 2. Unless otherwise indicated, I have used for the account on Thorsteinsson's life: Ásgeir Jakobsson, *Bíldudalskóngurinn* (Skuggsjá, 1990).

Chapter 2. The account of polar bears in Iceland is from the Icelandic science website: visindavefur.is/svar.php?id=5506.

Chapter 2. Dates and places of family events are from picture booklets prepared by my cousin Þorkell Erlingsson.

Chapter 3. The settlement at Böðvarsdalur is mentioned in *Vopnfirðingasaga*.

Chapter 3. The information on shark meat poisoning is from: U. Anthoni, C. Christophersen, L. Gram, N. H. Nielsen and P. Nielsen, *Poisonings from flesh of the Greenland shark Somniosus microcephalus may be due to trimethylamine* (Toxicon29, 1205–1212, 1991)

Chapter 4. The history of education in Iceland is in part based on a PhD dissertation by Kristín Bjarnadóttir, *Mathematical Education in Iceland in Historical Context*, 2006.

Chapter 4. Data on the population of Iceland in 1926 is from *Hagstofa* Íslands (Iceland Statistics).

Chapter 5. Contemporaneous accounts of the British occupation rely on the books: (a) Gunnar M. Magnúss, *Árin Sem Aldrei Gleymast* (Skuggsjá 1964); (b) Gunnar M. Magnúss, *Virkið í Norðri* (Skuggsjá, 1959); and (c) Donald F. Bittner,

The Lion and the White Falcon: Britain and Iceland in the World War II Era (Archon Books, 1983).

Chapter 5. Other accounts of the war and its aftermath are from: (a) Katharina Hauptmann, article in *Wall Street International Magazine*, December 24, 2013; (b) Valur Ingimundarson, *Í Eldlínu Kalda Stríðsins* (Vaka-Helgafell, 1996).

Chapter 6. Information on Austurbæjarskólinn is from the school's website.

Chapter 9. The history of Menntaskólinn is based on (a) Heimir Þorleifsson, *Saga Reykjavíkurskóla*, (Sögusjóður Menntaskólans í Reykjavík, 1975) and (b) unpublished papers by my classmates Sverrir Ólafsson and Gylfi Ísaksson.

Chapter 11. Ásta Peltola's story is from her memoir: Sigurbjörg Árnadóttir, *Hin Hljóðu Tár* (Vaka Helgafell, 1995).

Chapter 14 and Chapter 19. Accounts of the Six-Day War and the history of British territories in Africa are from the online Encyclopedia Britannica.

Chapter 18. Accounts of the economy of Iceland in the 1960s are based on OECD reports and data from the Central Bank of Iceland.

Chapter 24. The discussion of the conference on textbooks draws information from (a) Mark Malloch-Brown, *The Unfinished Global Revolution* (Penguin Books, 2011); (b) an article in a newsletter of the Bellagio Publishing Network, November 2000; and (c) Sobhana Sosale, Editor, *Educational Publishing in Global Perspective: Capacity Building and Trends* (The World Bank, 1999).

Photos:

The photos are from the authors' collection, except otherwise specified. The authors have made every effort to obtain the permission of copyright owners to use their photos in this book. The back cover photo is of the southernmost area of Iceland with Dyrhólaey in the foreground and Pétursey and Eyjafjallajökull in the background (photo: courtesy of Haukur Snorrason).

ABOUT THE AUTHORS

Sverrir Sigurdsson and Veronica Li in Iceland

Sverrir Sigurdsson grew up in Iceland and graduated as an architect from Finland in 1966. He pursued an international career that took him to the Middle East, Africa, Asia, Eastern Europe, and the U.S. His assignments focused on school construction and improving education in developing countries. He has worked for private companies as well as UNESCO and the World Bank. He is now retired and lives in Northern Virginia with his wife and coauthor, Veronica.

Veronica Li emigrated to the U.S. from Hong Kong as a teenager. She received her Bachelor of Arts in English from the University of California, Berkeley, and her master's degree in International Affairs from Johns Hopkins University. She has worked as a journalist and for the World Bank, and is currently a writer. Her three previously published titles are: *Nightfall in Mogadishu, Journey across the Four Seas: A Chinese Woman's Search for Home,* and *Confucius Says: A Novel.*